A PRACTICAL GUIDE TO DATA
PROTECTION LAW IN IRELA

UNITED KINGDOM
Sweet & Maxwell Ltd
London

AUSTRALIA
Law Book Co.
Sydney

CANADA and USA
Carswell
Toronto

NEW ZEALAND
Brookers
Wellington

SINGAPORE AND MALAYSIA
Sweet & Maxwell
Singapore and Kuala Lumpur

A PRACTICAL GUIDE TO
DATA PROTECTION LAW
IN IRELAND

A & L Goodbody

DUBLIN
ROUND HALL LTD
2003

Published in 2003 by
Round Hall Ltd
43 Fitzwilliam Place
Dublin 2
Ireland

Typeset by Carrigboy Typesetting Services, Co. Cork
Printed by MPG Books, Cornwall

A CIP catalogue record for this book is available from the British Library

ISBN 1–85800–347–4

Forms reproduced with kind permission of the
Office of the Data Protection Commissioner.

CONTENTS

PART 1 – DATA PROTECTION LAW IN IRELAND

PART 2 – SECTORAL ISSUES

CONTRIBUTIONS

This book was written by the Data Protection Group at A & L Goodbody. The Group consists of experts from the firm and each of the sectoral chapters in Part 2 of the book have been written by lawyers specialising in those fields. These chapters reflect day to day experience of advising clients on their practical compliance needs according to their specific business requirements. The Data Protection Group comprises:

Liam Kennedy
Carol Leland
Louise Cox
Cliona Hickey
Joanne Hyde
Fiona O'Connell
Louise McNabola
Andreas Carney
Hugh Donovan
Jeanne Kelly
Laura Mulleady
Emer Moriarty Crowley
Paula Reid
Emma Martin
Patrick Quinlan
Jamie Olden

We would also like to thank Christina Bourke, Jennifer Rogers and Gráinne Sexton for their invaluable help in the typing and layout of the original manuscript and trainee solicitors Elaine Keane and Diarmuid Mawe who helped in the research for the book.

FOREWORD

Over the past decade Ireland has embraced the challenges and exploited the opportunities of the "information age". In particular, new technology has allowed Irish businesses to develop new markets and vastly expand their reach. This means increased benefits for business, consumers and the economy.

Consumer confidence is a crucial ingredient in maximising our competitive advantage in this new era. Personal information is a valuable commercial asset. It is also integral to an individual's privacy. It is vital, therefore, that we strike a balance between, on the one hand, the individual's right to control the use of their personal information and, on the other, the ability of organisations to make the most of the technological tools available. This is what data protection law aims to achieve.

This book will help businesses to comply with Irish data protection. It is a practical commercial guide aimed at business users. It makes a welcome contribution by interpreting the legislation in a non-technical way, enabling business managers to gain an understanding of their obligations. It will undoubtedly prove invaluable to business managers, helping them achieve compliance in an effective, practical and cost efficient way.

MARY HARNEY TD
Tánaiste and Minister for Enterprise,
Trade and Employment

TABLE OF LEGISLATION

ACTS

TABLE OF CASES

EUROPEAN LEGISLATION

STATUTORY INSTRUMENTS

OTHER

INTRODUCTION

This book is intended to provide a practical guide to data protection compliance from a business perspective rather than as an academic analysis of data protection law in Ireland. Your requirements will differ according to the nature of your business and the type(s) of information which you handle. For that reason we have structured the book to allow you to focus on your specific compliance needs.

Chapter 1 contains a diagrammatic guide to compliance and is accompanied by a step-by-step guide to checking your procedures and ensuring compliance. More specific detail is set out in the sectoral chapters in Part 2 of the book. All readers should consult Chapter 1 along with the chapter relevant to their own business as well as Chapter 4 which provides guidance for employers.

This practical approach has been prompted by queries from clients (over a number of years) on how to make their information management systems compliant with data protection law. Building on our experience we have aimed to distil the legislation in order to provide a practical compliance framework. We have not detailed every nook and cranny of the legislation but we hope that we have navigated a straightforward, practical and commercially effective path to dealing with the compliance issues most frequently encountered in practice. For those who need to delve deeper into the legislation we hope that the consolidated Data Protection Acts 1988 and 2003 contained at Appendix C will be of assistance.

Data protection law is evolving throughout Europe and Ireland and is only now catching up on other member states in the implementation of the 1995 Directive.[1] Experience of the Directive in the EU demonstrates the importance of businesses developing data protection procedures and the development of industry-specific codes of practice. The suggested approach to compliance outlined in this book reflects the legal principles set out in the Directive and the Data Protection Acts 1988 and 2003 as at the date of publication. Undoubtedly these principles will be refined on an ongoing basis as guidelines and codes of practice emerge in Ireland. Whilst we hope that this book will be of assistance to businesses in approaching compliance with data protection laws, it is not a substitute for legal advice which should be sought in relation to any specific issue.

---

[1] The European Directive on Data Protection (Directive 95/46/EU).

SOME KEY TERMS USED IN THIS BOOK

Commissioner	Irish Data Protection Commissioner
EEA	Countries of the EU plus Iceland, Liechtenstein and Norway
Transfer of information	Sending information from Ireland to a country outside of the EEA
The Data Protection Directive	Directive 95/46/EU
The Article 29 Working group	An EU advisory committee set up under the Directive to advise on the implementation of the Directive throughout the EU
The Act	The Data Protection Act 1988 and the Data Protection (Amendment) Act 2003

PART 1

DATA PROTECTION LAW IN IRELAND

1. A PRACTICAL GUIDE TO DATA PROTECTION LAW IN IRELAND

Introduction

Irish data protection law is governed by the Data Protection Acts, 1988 and 2003. You must comply with the legislation if you hold personal information on any individual. In a nutshell:

- The legislation protects all information on living individuals (even a name and address).

- "Processing" includes every conceivable use of information, including storing and filing.

- You must ensure that your customers, employees, etc. know what information you hold on them, why you hold it and what you do with it.

- You may need to get consent before you collect certain personal information.

- Stricter rules apply to sensitive information such as medical details.

- Sending personal information out of Ireland (even to a related company) may be prohibited (depending on the destination) unless certain safeguards are put in place.

- Individuals can insist on access to information you hold on them.

- You may need to register with the Commissioner if you handle personal information. (See page 17).

- Compliance with data protection law is mandatory and non-compliance could lead to criminal prosecution, fines, and/or imprisonment, together with serious adverse publicity for your business.

- The limited exceptions to these principles will be considered at pp. 12–14 below.

To comply with the Act the first step is to examine how information is managed in your business. You will then be able to assess your compliance needs and identify any necessary adjustments to your existing procedures.

Diagram 1 (overleaf) sets out a scheme for approaching compliance. First you need to assess whether the Act applies to your business. If it does then we suggest that you undertake an audit of your information management systems. Our guide takes you through the major questions which you will need to address in the course of your audit and we suggest procedural steps to bring about compliance. Each step of the audit process is then dealt with in further detail.

Diagram 1. Data Protection – A Guide to Compliance

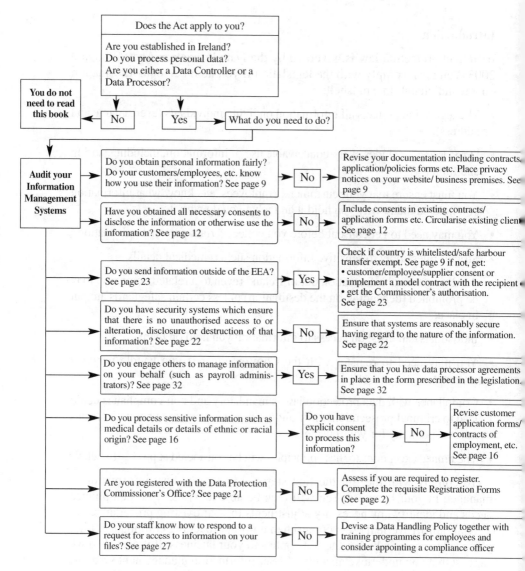

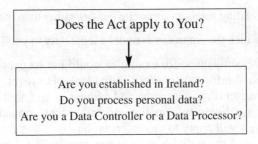

Does the Act apply to your business?

The Act will apply if:

- you process *personal* information; and

- you are a data controller or a data processor; and

- you are established in Ireland or make use of processing equipment here.

What is personal information?

Personal information is any information (even minimum information such as a name, address or email address) about a living individual held either electronically or in paper files. It includes information in the form of photographs,[1] fingerprints, audio recordings and text messages. Personal information can be stored in a number of ways such as in mobile phones, laptops, palm pilots, voicemail, fax machines and CCTV.

Paper records are only covered if they form part of a "relevant filing system". This means the file must contain a set of information relating to an individual, and the set must be structured to allow for the retrieval of information relating to that individual.

Papers located in different departments or indeed different offices or branches of a company may constitute part of the same file for the purposes of the Act.

Some personal information will not be caught, such as:

- personal information which is not recorded either electronically or in paper files (*i.e.* knowledge carried "in your head");

- personal information used for private use, *e.g.* names in a personal organiser;

- statistical information and anonymised information[2];

- information about a deceased person;

---

[1] In a recent English case a photograph of supermodel Naomi Campbell leaving a drug rehabilitation centre was regarded as sensitive personal data.

[2] Anonymised information is information which has been stripped of detail which might identify an individual. Removing a name will not always be sufficient to anonymise information, *e.g.* an address without a name may identify an individual when linked to other information such as the electoral register.

- information relating solely to corporate entities rather than individuals;
- information which the controller is under a legal duty to publish.[3]

A database of companies, for example, would not be captured by the Act unless it contained information about individuals. However, even minimum personal information is caught (name and address or an email address), and if the same database holds information on individual contacts within these companies the Act will apply to this information.

The residence of the individual does not matter. The Act will apply if a French resident places information on an Irish based/controlled website as his personal data is protected by the Act and he enjoys the rights of a data subject.

Are you "processing" information?

The legislation controls how you "process" personal information. Almost anything you might conceivably do with information would constitute "processing" including[4]:

- obtaining, recording or keeping information;
- collecting, organising, storing, altering or adapting information;
- retrieving, consulting or using information;
- disclosing information by transmission, dissemination or making it available;
- aligning, combining, blocking[5], erasing or destroying information.

Are you a data controller or a data processor?

Your data protection obligations will depend on whether you are classified as a "data controller" or a "data processor".

A data controller is "a person who controls data".[6] For example, all employers are data controllers as they hold information about their own employees. They decide the nature, content and extent of the information processed and how it is disclosed and used. Information held by a data controller may be processed by someone else on their behalf. For example, if you outsource your credit control or payroll processing you are still the data controller, as the company to whom you have outsourced is merely processing on your instructions.

---

[3] Some Irish companies are legally obliged to keep a publicly accessible register of members. The Act will not apply to such records. However, the exception will only apply where the information is made available for the statutory purpose. You will still need the individual's consent if the Register is to be used for any other purpose such as direct marketing. Equally where you provide the information to any member of the public you may wish to include a notice that the personal information can not be used without the individual's consent.
[4] Section 1(1).
[5] Blocking means ear marking information so it is not used for a particular purpose. For example where an individual indicates that his information is not to be used for direct marketing purposes, the Data Controller is obliged to block the information preventing it from being used for that purpose.
[6] Section 1(1).

Data controllers and data processors can be either individuals or legal entities (such as companies).

A data processor is a person who processes data for the data controller. Employees who merely process information in the course of their employment are neither controllers nor processors. For example, accounts staff administering a payroll are not data processors as they are carrying out the function in the course of their employment. However, an outside company would be a data processor if these functions were to be outsourced.

The primary obligation for complying with data protection law lies with the data controller. The data processor usually acts on instructions from a data controller and his duties and responsibilities will usually be prescribed by contract. However, the data processor may be required to register with the Commissioner's Office and has a statutory obligation to keep information secure and prevent any unauthorised access or disclosure.[7]

Are you established in Ireland?

The Act covers all businesses established in Ireland. You will be established here if:

- you are an individual and resident in Ireland[8];

- your company is incorporated under Irish law; or

- you are a partnership or other unincorporated entity formed under Irish law. (*e.g.* a charity); or

- you are a company with a branch, office or agency in Ireland.

The Act will also apply if you use equipment in Ireland to process information (other than for transit).[9]

Irish data protection law covers all personal Information processed in Ireland, not just data on Irish or EU citizens. It will, however only apply to information processed in Ireland. For example, a US-incorporated bank might set up a back office operation in Ireland operating a customer service function. The Irish operation might be either a related company or an unrelated agency. It is likely that the US-based corporation will only be regarded as having a branch, office or agency here where that operation is carrying out substantial business on behalf of the US parent. However where a non-EEA controller engages a processor in Ireland, that controller may be subject to the Act on the basis that he uses equipment in Ireland (via the processor). Such a US corporation would be required to nominate a representative in Ireland. This is not an onerous requirement and means that you will need to identify a point of

---

[7] Section 2C(1)(b).
[8] You are resident if you spend 183 days per year in Ireland or 280 days over 2 years with a minimum of 30 days in each year.
[9] Information will "transit" through Ireland if it merely passes through on its way to another country and no processing takes place here.

contact here. This would usually be the entity you engage to process the data in Ireland.[10]

When an Irish-based company operates throughout the EU it will be obliged to comply with local data protection law in the country in which it operates. Although all EU States were obliged to implement the Data Protection Directive, they may have their own additional national data protection requirements. Therefore, if you operate a company in another EEA state you should seek advice from local lawyers as to your compliance needs in that country.

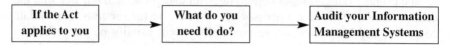

| If the Act applies to you | What do you need to do? | Audit your Information Management Systems |

If your business is subject to the Act you will need to ensure compliance. All personal data which you hold is covered, including information on customers, employees, and suppliers. In general terms you will need to ensure that you:

- obtain personal information fairly and transparently and that your employees, customers suppliers, etc. are aware of what information you hold and how you use it;

- obtain consent to disclose and use the information for all of the purposes for which you need to use the information;

- put contracts or consents in place to ensure the information is adequately protected if you send information outside of the EU or Norway, Iceland or Liechtenstein;

- register with the Commissioner for all of the purposes for which you use the information;

- ensure you have adequate security measures in place;

- put an appropriate contract in place with any company to whom you outsource processing functions (*e.g.* a payroll processor or debt collection company);

- ensure your staff are adequately trained to deal with a request for access to information which you have on file.

Why conduct an audit?

You cannot ensure compliance unless you understand precisely what information is held or used by your organisation and how it is used.

An audit will allow you to assess how information flows in and out of your business in all departments (sales, human resources, marketing, etc.) and will give you a complete picture of:

- what information you store;

- how you obtain it;

---

[10] Section 1(3)(B)(c)

- what you do with it;
- what documentation/contracts are in place;
- whether the documentation is adequate to comply with the legislation.

Armed with this information you can identify your compliance needs.

How do you conduct an audit?

One approach is as follows:

1. Devise an audit questionnaire based on the practical guide and diagram set out in this book.

2. Appoint an audit manager.

3. Send the questionnaire to relevant personnel in all departments within the business including any branch offices.

4. Require each recipient to:
   (a) complete the questionnaire;
   (b) gather sample documents such as contracts, policies, application forms, booking forms, etc.
   (c) return them to the audit manager

5. Identify any compliance deficiencies following the scheme set out below.

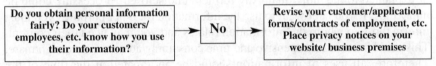

| Do you obtain personal information fairly? Do your customers/ employees, etc. know how you use their information? | → No → | Revise your customer/application forms/contracts of employment, etc. Place privacy notices on your website/ business premises |

What information do you need to provide to individuals?

You must be fair in dealing with personal information and you should be transparent about how you intend to store, disclose and use the information. In short, you must tell your customers, employees, suppliers, etc:

1. the identity of the data controller;

2. the nature of the information held;

3. the purpose(s) for which the information will be processed;

4. any other relevant information.

Identity of the data controller

This may be self-evident. However if, for example, the controller operates through an agent or if personal information is obtained via a website, the identity of the controller may not be evident and must be declared. The name of the relevant representative should also be set out where the controller is not established in Ireland but uses equipment here.

The nature of the information held

You should disclose the nature of the information to be processed. This may be evident where the person completes an application form or booking form and controls the information which is provided to you. However sometimes the information may be obtained indirectly (*e.g.* an insurer may obtain medical information from an individual's doctor or a credit reference may be obtained from a credit reference agency) or without the person's knowledge.[11] In these circumstances you must tell the individual what information you hold on them. More specific details about the nature of the information are required if sensitive information[12] is processed and this is dealt with in more detail below.

You can only process information which is relevant for the purposes for which it was obtained. Relevance depends on context. For example, in some circumstances asking a job applicant about criminal convictions could be relevant but it would be irrelevant and excessive to ask the same question in an online booking form for theatre tickets. A controller cannot obtain information on the basis that it might become relevant or useful in the future. This rule is of particular significance in obtaining information from job applicants. This is dealt with in detail in Chapter 4.

The purpose(s) for which the information will be processed

You can generally only process information for the purpose or purposes known or explained to the individual. Any further "undisclosed" processing could be unlawful.[13] If you later want to use the information for other purposes you must inform those to whom the information relates and you may need their consent. This could become an expensive and time consuming administrative nightmare. Therefore, all uses of information should be anticipated at the time of the information capture if possible.

You should specifically disclose any prospective use which is not obvious to the individual. For example, it is obvious that a car hire company will keep credit card details until a transaction is complete and payment received. Clearly, the company will send such information to the collection and return depots and use it to bill the customer. It would not be obvious to the customer that the company might use such information for direct marketing purposes or keep credit card details on file after the return of the car and payment of all sums due. Such non-obvious, or secondary, uses of information should be specifically detailed.

---

[11] *e.g.* software which tracks user information (cookies).
[12] Information relating to racial or ethnic origin, information on health or sexual life, trade union membership, religious, political or philosophical beliefs, criminal convictions or criminal proceedings: section 1(1).
[13] *e.g.* the Commissioner has held that the Department of Education breached this principle by using payroll information to identify teachers who were trade union members so as to dock their wages following strike action. The information about trade union membership had been obtained to allow for the deduction of union subscriptions from wages. The Commissioner ruled that using the information to identify union members to dock wages in the context of the strike was in breach of the Department's data protection obligations. Case 2/00.

Any other relevant information

Depending on circumstances, other information may be relevant, for example:

- Anticipated disclosure to other entities such as banks, pensions administrators, health insurance providers, credit reference agencies, etc. Where information is shared with other branches/offices of a business this should also be outlined.

- The individual should also be made aware of the consequences (if any) of their failure to provide the controller with certain information,[14] for example where failure to consent to processing will result in refusal to provide goods and services.

- If information is to be sent out of the EEA and you wish to rely on the individual's consent, then the individual should be told the country(ies) to which it will be sent and the purposes for which it will be sent. See p. 26.

- The right to access information and whether an access fee will be charged.

- The right to rectify information.

When and how should the information be communicated?

Ideally the information should be provided before you begin to process the information. The Act does not require you to use any particular means of communication. You need not specify information if it is clearly obvious or already known to the person. You can give such information orally but you need some way to demonstrate that you did so. The most convenient place to provide this information is at the point where you are actually collecting the information from the individual such as in a booking form, application form on a webpage or privacy notices which should be supplied to customers and/or displayed at the business premises.

Going forward it will be relatively straightforward to ensure that your information notices are brought into compliance. However, you may have existing customers who have not been adequately informed of the use(s) of their information. Ideally these customers should be circularised and given up-to-date information notices. The Act requires that an information notice be given to the individual where "practicable". What is "practicable" has not yet been defined and will depend on the circumstances of each case. Where existing customers are not circularised it would be advisable to include an information notice in any future correspondence (such as a bill or renewal form) and to post an information notice on your business premises where appropriate.

---

[14] *e.g* if failure to consent to processing will make it impossible to enter into a contract with a customer then this needs to be specified.

COMPLIANCE CHECKLIST

Having reviewed your existing forms and notices, if you are not satisfied that you have provided adequate information then you will need to:

- revise your documentation:

- consider whether you need to circularise existing clients to provide them with the necessary information:

- consider placing information notices in future correspondence with existing customers and posting a notice on your business premises:

- amend your business practices to prevent any collection of information which has not been disclosed.

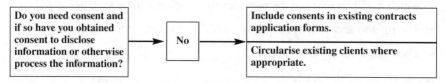

| Do you need consent and if so have you obtained consent to disclose information or otherwise process the information? | → No → | Include consents in existing contracts application forms. |
| | | Circularise existing clients where appropriate. |

Do you need consent?

Generally you will need to get consent to process personal information. The easiest way to do this is to obtain a written consent on a booking form, an application form, a contract or similar. Consent will not be necessary in certain situations.

If any of the following conditions apply you do **not** need consent:

1. The processing is necessary to carry out a contract with customer, employee, etc.

2. The processing is necessary to engage in pre-contract activities with employees/customers, etc.

3. The processing is carried out in order to comply with a legal obligation

4. The processing is necessary to prevent injury or damage to an individual or property

5. The processing is *necessary* for your legitimate business needs and there is no prejudice to the rights of the individual

If the processing is necessary for the performance of a contract to which the individual is a party

Some processing is essential in order to carry out a contract with a person. For example, if an individual books a flight to Sydney through a travel agent based in Cork, it will be necessary for both the travel agent and the airline to process the customer's personal details. The information can be processed for this purpose without obtaining his consent. If the travel agent or airline want to process the customer's details for any other purpose, for example adding them to a database for direct marketing, the customer's consent must be obtained.

If the processing is necessary in order to take steps at the request of the individual prior to entering into a contract

Consent is not required where you obtain personal information from someone in order to assess the possibility of entering into a contract with them. This is as long as the processing is restricted to that assessment. For example, a job applicant will provide a prospective employer with personal information via a CV or an application form. Clearly the candidate is providing the information in order to allow the employer to assess the possibility of employing him or her. Therefore the candidate's consent is not required. However, consent to process sensitive information may be required even at this stage unless the processing is allowed on one of the other grounds (see below).

If the processing is carried out in compliance with a legal obligation to which the controller is subject other than a duty imposed by contract

Consent is not necessary where the law requires certain action to be taken by the controller. One example is the obligation on all employers to keep records about an individual employee's working hours for the purposes of the Organisation of Working Time Act 1997. Another example would be the obligation on medical practitioners to process information on certain infectious diseases.

If the processing is necessary to prevent injury or other damage to the health of the individual or serious loss of or damage to property, or otherwise to protect the vital interests of the individual where it would be inappropriate to get their consent

Consent is not necessary where the controller can show that seeking the consent of the individual or seeking consent to be given on his behalf would cause damage to his property or interests.

This condition is only likely to arise in very rare circumstances where the life, health, property or other vital interests of the individual are at risk, it is necessary to inform a third person about the circumstances and it is inappropriate to get the individual's consent. It might arise if the individual were mentally unstable or otherwise incapacitated and where it was necessary to give personal information about them to the relevant authorities or other third party.

If the processing is necessary for the purposes of the legitimate interests pursued by the data controller or by a third party to whom the data is disclosed and the processing would not prejudice the fundamental rights and freedoms of the individual

Consent is not required for "necessary" processing which is in the legitimate interests of the controller. The availability of this ground will depend on the circumstances of each case. It will be important, however, to prove that the processing is "necessary" rather than merely "convenient" for the controller. Therefore, it may be argued that covert processing of an employee's internet usage may be necessary and legitimate where the employer has good reason to suspect the employee of improper use of the internet. However, the exemption is unlikely to apply where the employer engages in covert surveillance of all employees. This may be convenient for the employer as he can monitor all employee internet usage without alerting employees, however it may not be necessary.

If the processing is necessary for the administration of justice or for the performance of any other public function

This exemption permits processing of personal information by government bodies such as the Courts Service or County Councils in order to asses rates or other taxes or charges for example.

None of these exceptions apply? How do you get consent?

Consent is not defined in the Act. The Directive defines consent as:

> " . . . any freely given specific and informed indication of his wishes by which the data subject signifies his agreement to personal data relating to him being processed."

This definition suggests that there must be some communication from the individual to the data controller that he or she agrees to the proposed processing of their personal information. From a legal viewpoint, obtaining consent in writing is ideal because this provides concrete evidence. However, written consent is often impractical. Other methods of consent such as oral consent can suffice provided the nature and extent of the consent is clear and the individual has been given adequate information on how their information is to be processed.

There are two ways of obtaining a written consent. The customer/employee, etc. can be invited to "opt in" or "opt out". An "opt in" requires the customer to take an active step to let you know that they are agreeing to the processing (for example through a signature). An "opt out" allows the customer to let you know if they don't want you to process their information and if they do not contact you, you can presume they agree to the processing. The legislation does not make it clear whether an "opt in" or an "opt out" is required. Clearly the safest route is to request an "opt in"; however, from a commercial point of view, this may not always be practical as this would mean that you could not process information until and unless each and every customer had taken the trouble to reply and in many circumstances (particularly in dealing with non sensitive data) an "opt out" will suffice.

Consent can sometimes be implied. For example if an employee provides bank account details to allow payment by direct debit, then there is an implied consent to the employer to retain the bank details and to disclose such detail to the bank as is necessary to allow for the transfer of funds. Whilst reliance on an implied consent will be necessary and legitimate in many circumstances, it is preferable to get an express written consent where possible to avoid arguments as to context of any implied consent.

Consent to direct marketing

Generally, it will be legitimate to send your existing customers marketing information about other products or services which you provide. However, the individual must be given an opportunity to "opt out" of direct marketing[15] and this right to must be brought to the individual's attention. If you anticipate direct marketing then you should insert the necessary wording in your application forms/customer forms and provide an opt out clause along the following lines:

> "We would like to send you further information on new products available from ourselves or other companies within our group. You have a right not to receive this information. Please tick the box below if you do not wish to receive marketing material from us.
>
> I do not wish to receive marketing material from you   □   ".

If the individual initially consents to receiving marketing material he can change his mind later and require you to remove his name from your marketing database and you will be obliged to do so.[16]

How do you get consent from minors/incapacitated persons?

Consent to processing should be obtained from a parent, guardian or other relative where the person to whom the information relates is a young child or is mentally or physically incapable of giving their consent.[17]

Do you need consent to process information on a spouse or family member?

Frequently customer application forms and other forms require the individual to provide personal information about another person such as a spouse, partner or other family member. For example, an employee might be required to provide information on next of kin and an insurance policyholder may be required to give details of other lives assured. The Commissioner provides the following guidelines on the issue:

> "If you collect information about an individual from a third party (*e.g.* from a husband about his wife) you have to consider whether the individual (in this case the wife) needs to be made aware of what is being noted . . . about her. In general, the fair obtaining principle requires that every individual about whom information is collected . . . will be aware of what is happening."

One solution is to tell applicants/employees that they are obliged to inform the other members of their families that their information will be processed. If

---

[15] Section 2(8). Direct marketing refers to sending existing customers information on other products or services which you have to offer. If you pass the personal information to a third party then they will be required to get a positive "opt in" before they can send any marketing material.

[16] Section 2(7).

[17] Section 2(A)(1)(a) the section does not specifically refer to minors. Generally consent should always be sought from a relative where the child is under 14 years. From 14 years to 18 years consent could be obtained directly from the child in certain circumstances.

sensitive information or detailed information is obtained about a family member then it would be preferable to get direct consent from that individual before processing their information.

What if you use software programmes to make decisions for your business?

Any decision generated by electronic equipment without human intervention is prohibited unless[18]:

- the individual consents: or

- the software is used to assist in deciding whether or not to enter into a contract with an individual:[19] or

- the automated decision making is authorised by law: or

- the effect of the decision is to grant the request of the individual: and

- adequate steps have been taken to safeguard the legitimate interests of the individual.[20]

COMPLIANCE CHECKLIST

Review systems to ensure that you have obtained consent where required.

- If you have not obtained consent revise relevant documentation and circularise existing customers/suppliers where possible to obtain such consent to non-obvious use(s) of information.

- If you engage in direct marketing ensure that you have provided an "opt out".

- If you use automated decision making software ensure you have obtained consent where necessary.

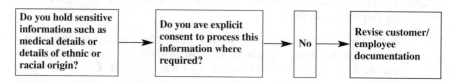

What is "sensitive personal data"?

Sensitive personal data[21] means information relating to the following:

- racial or ethnic origin[22];

---

[18] Section 6B.
[19] *e.g.* a bank deciding whether to provide a car loan might reach its decision solely on the basis of automated credit references.
[20] This will probably require you to at least inform the individual that automated means will be used in the decision-making process.
[21] Defined in section 1.
[22] Recording an individuals "nationality" (as opposed to race) is not sensitive personal data.

- political opinions, religious or philosophical beliefs;
- trade union membership;
- physical or mental health or condition or sexual life;.
- commission or alleged commission of or prosecution for an offence;
- details of any proceedings for an offence committed (or alleged to have been committed), the disposal of the proceedings or sentence handed down by any court.[23]

If you process sensitive data do you need to take extra steps?

Where the information being processed is "sensitive" you must satisfy one of the additional sensitive data conditions. This means that you must:

- comply with one of the requirements applicable to personal information generally (set out on pp. 12–14); and
- Get the explicit consent of the individual unless one of the exceptions set out below applies:

The processing is necessary for the purpose of exercising or performing any right or obligation which is conferred or imposed by law in connection with employment

For example under the Safety, Health and Welfare at Work Act 1989 there is an obligation to complete and send to the Health and Safety Authority a record of every accident in the workplace.

The processing is necessary to prevent injury or other damage to the health of the data subject or another person or otherwise to protect their vital interests where consent cannot be reasonably obtained.

Processing of sensitive data is allowed without consent where the individual is incapable of giving his consent or where it is unreasonable to expect you to obtain consent. There must also be a threat of loss, damage or injury to the individual or another person. This condition should be used in exceptional and emergency situations only.

The processing is carried out in the course of the legitimate activities of a non profit-making organisation and exists for political/philosophical/religious or trade union purposes.

Consent may not be necessary if your organisation is non profit-making and exists for political, philosophical, religious or trade union purposes. The organisation will often be a registered charity. The controller must ensure that reliance on this condition does not prejudice the rights of the individual and must obtain consent to disclose the information to a third party. This condition

---

[23] This type of information may be generated by pre-employment background checks, for example.

applies where the processing is carried out in relation to individuals who are members of the organisation or who have close contact with it. Therefore, Trocaire, for example, is entitled to process personal data on its members/ contributors for the purposes of the day-to-day operation of the organisation. It could also process information on associated individuals – for example, personnel in associated charities. However, if Trocaire wishes to disclose the data to any other party this condition will cease to apply and consent will be required.

The information has been made public.

Explicit consent is not needed where the individual has already allowed the information to become public.

This exemption will not cover a situation where sensitive information is published without explicit the individual's consent. Therefore, if sensitive information appears in a newspaper this does not mean that the information can be processed by a controller without consent. However, if an individual gives an interview to a newspaper then the exemption will apply to any further processing in so far as it relates to the information which has been put in the public domain by the individual.

The processing is required for the purposes of obtaining legal advice or for the purposes of or in connection with legal proceedings or prospective legal proceedings, or is otherwise necessary for the purposes of establishing, exercising or defending legal rights.

Processing is permitted without consent when processed for certain legal purposes including information assembled in contemplation of litigation or legal advice.

Processing for medical purposes

This exception applies where the processing is necessary for medical purposes and is undertaken by:

- a health professional;

- a person who in the circumstances owes a duty of confidentiality to the data subject that is equivalent to that which would exist if that person were a health professional.

The extent of this exemption is dealt with in Chapter 6. "Health professional" is defined as including doctors[24] and dentists.[25] The Minister can include other healthcare professionals by way of regulation. In the meantime other healthcare professionals such as nurses, physiotherapists and social workers will be included by virtue of the second limb of the definition as they owe a duty of

---

[24] Within the meaning of the Medical Practitioners Act 1978.
[25] Within the meaning of the Dentists Act 1985.

confidentiality to the patient. The definition of "medical purposes" includes processing for the purposes of preventive medicine, medical diagnosis, medical research, the provision of care and treatment, and the management of healthcare services.

The processing is necessary in order to obtain information for statistical compilation and analysis purposes.

Explicit consent is not required to process information purely for statistical analysis. This would include the compilation of data for the census or other processing function which produces an aggregate or statistical product.

The processing is carried out by political parties, candidates or other holders of elective office in the course of electoral purposes.

Political parties and election candidates can process personal data without explicit consent where the processing is done in the course of an election for the purposes of compiling data on people's political opinions.

The processing is authorised by Regulations made by the Minister.

No such authorisations have yet been issued.

The processing is necessary for the purpose of collecting taxes and other revenue.

The Government does not need explicit consent to process personal data for tax collection.

How do you obtain explicit consent?

There is no definition of "explicit consent" but clearly what is envisaged is a clear and unambiguous indication from the person that he agrees to the proposed processing. Written consent is ideal but not always possible, for example in the telesales environment. Where written consent is not possible then you should ensure that there is a record of the information supplied to the individual and the fact of their consent. In the telesales context, for example, there might be a recording of the conversation with the customer and/or a mandatory script to be read to the customer. The operator could then be required to confirm on the application form that the customer has indicated their agreement.

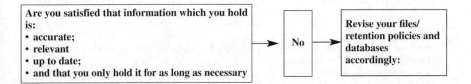

How do you ensure that the information is accurate, relevant and, where necessary, kept up to date?

You can only process information which is relevant to your dealings with an individual. All application forms (or other sources of personal information) should only request details which are necessary. You should conduct regular reviews of electronic and paper files to ensure that information is kept up to date (and to ensure obsolete information is deleted). The requirement to update applies particularly to information which by its nature should reflect a current status. For example an up-to-date credit rating will affect an individual's ability to obtain further credit. Businesses should also ensure that contact details, names, addresses and telephone numbers are kept up to date and any obsolete information is erased (subject of course to any legal requirements to retain the information).

This rule will not apply to information stored by the controller as a mere record of the fact of a transaction with the person nor does it apply to back-up data.[26]

Businesses should ensure that staff engaged in file management update information regularly and should devise an information management policy where necessary.

How can you ensure that information is not be kept for longer than is necessary?

Technology allows for the indefinite storage of a vast amount of information. However, you must ensure that personal information is not kept for longer than necessary. As long as you can point to an objective reason for keeping information, then the continued processing will be legitimate. For example, a controller may need to keep information in order to:

• bill a client;

• operate a credit control system effectively;

• comply with a legal requirement[27];

• defend actual or anticipated legal claims.

Controllers and processors need to balance this general principle against specific legislation which may require them to keep certain information for particular periods. For example, where a disciplinary investigation leads to the termination of employment, even though there may have been no explicit threat of proceedings, an employer is at risk of an unfair dismissals claim for six months after termination (12 months in exceptional circumstances). Such

---

[26] Back-up data means data kept only for the purpose of replacing other data in the event of their being lost, destroyed or damaged. (Section 1(1)(b)).

[27] *e.g.* under tax legislation there is the statutory requirement to keep such "records" as are necessary to enable true tax returns to be made. These records must be retained for at least 6 years after the completion of the transactions to which they relate. Under money laundering legislation banks are required to keep certain records for 5 years.

businesses need to keep records of the circumstances leading to the termination for that period.

The controller should delete the information once the relationship with the individual has ended unless there is a specific statutory retention period or some other requirement to preserve the information. In a recent case, the Commissioner found that a company had breached its obligations by keeping a customers credit card details after a rental agreement had concluded. The company retained information to facilitate the customer in future transactions but the customer objected to the retention of his details without his consent (case 4/01).

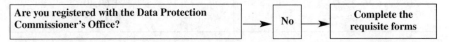

Registration – Do you need to register?

All businesses (save for those exempted from registration by Ministerial order)[28] must register either as a controller or a processor with the office of the Data Protection Commissioner. The enactment of this section has been delayed and is expected to come into force in late 2003, early 2004. Therefore, until the new s.16 is enacted the following controllers are required to register under the Act:

- Public Sector Bodies

- Financial Institutions

- Insurance Companies whose business consists wholly or partly in direct marketing providing credit rererences or collecting debts

- Controllers who process information on racial origin, political opinions, physical or mental health (other than that used for routine HR purposes), sexual life criminal convictions.

- Internet Access Providers who are wholly or partly in the business of providing individuals with connections to the Internet and who keep personal data about their customers

- Telecommunication Service Providers (holding a licence under Section 111 of the Postal Telecommunciations Services Act, 1983)

- Data Processors whose business consists wholly or partly in processing data on behalf of data controllers

Where a data controller wishes to register for processing personal information for more than one purpose a separate registration will need to be lodged in respect of each purpose. It is an offence to process information without the required registration.[29]

A controller/processor must register all purposes for which he processes information. Processing for any other reason is unlawful.

---

[28] No such regulations have been made at the date of publication.
[29] Section 19(4).

How do I register?

Registration is simple and involves completion of an "Application for Registration" form. The forms are available from the Office of the Data Protection Commissioner at The Irish Life Centre, Dublin 1 or online at *www.dataprivacy.ie* (see Appendices A1 and A2).

The fee at time of publication is as follows:

Number of employees	Registration fee €*
1–5	€ 25.37
6–25	€ 63.49
26+	€371.43

Registration is renewable annually. If a business needs to use data for different purposes in the interim they should immediately amend their registration (see Appendix B).

* Currently under review

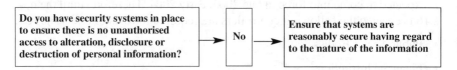

What measures should you take to ensure that the information is secure?

You must take measures to protect the information against unauthorised access, alteration, disclosure or destruction.[30] The legislation does not specify particular security measures or standards. You should assess your security requirements taking into account the circumstances of your business, the nature of the information and the resources available to you. Higher security standards are required for information held electronically or information of a sensitive nature such as medical records. You must also put organisational security measures in place. Measures you might consider include:

- ensuring that paper files are stored securely in filing cabinets or other locked apparatus;

- ensuring that files holding sensitive information (such as medical information) are stored in a secure area accessible only by relevant personnel;

- ensuring that electronic files are password controlled;

- ensuring that access to that part of the business premises which houses personal information is password/card controlled;

- ensuring that where computer screens (including laptops) are located in public areas (such as waiting rooms, showrooms), measures are taken to ensure that personal information is not inadvertently disclosed to members of the public.

---

[30]　Section 2(1)(d).

- drawing up an Information Handling Policy which is brought to the attention of all employees responsible for handling personal information.

- ensuring that all staff have been adequately trained to respect the privacy of personal information and are aware of the security standards which you have adopted.

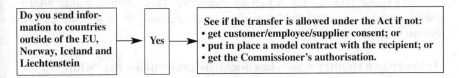

Many businesses frequently send data overseas. Multinationals may want to share employee and customer data with colleagues around the world. Because data protection laws within the European Economic Area[31] are broadly harmonized and data is similarly protected, transfers to the UK and other EU countries are permitted. You can only transfer information outside the EEA in the following circumstances[32]:

- the destination country has been approved for transfer by the EU; or

- the transfer is allowed by an exemption under the Act; or

- the individual has consented to the transfer; or

- the company importing the information enters into a contract in a form prescribed by the EU; or

- the specific transfer is approved by the Commissioner; or

- the transfer is of a type which has been approved by the Commissioner.[33]

What is a transfer?

"Transfer" is not defined but includes the transmission of the personal data to a third country.

Information published on the internet is particularly significant in terms of "transfer". Such information is accessible globally, therefore any entry of information onto the web or any other internationally accessible computer network could amount to a transfer for the purposes of the Act.

Transfer occurs even where the transferor and transferee are within the same entity. For example, where an Irish subsidiary sends information concerning employees to its parent in the US or Australia then the transfer has to be dealt with in the same fashion as if data were being transferred to an unrelated company.

---

[31] Austria, Belgium, Denmark, Finland, France, Germany, Greece, Ireland, Italy, Liechtenstein, Luxemburg, Netherlands, Norway, Portugal, Spain, Sweden, United Kingdom, Iceland.
[32] It is important to note that the restriction relates to "personal data" therefore transfer of anonymised (for example clinical data), or data relating to a Company can take place without any further investigation as there is no applicable prohibition under the Regulations.
[33] Section 11.

"Transit" will not be a transfer. Therefore, there will be no "transfer" if information, sent electronically, goes from one EEA country to another but via a country outside of the EEA. For example, if an Irish company transfers employee information to its parent in France, and if the message, in the course of electronic transmission through the telecommunications network, transits through, say the Isle of Man, there would be no transfer of the information as its entry to the Isle of Man is merely transitory. This position would alter if there were any processing of the information carried out in the Isle of Man before onward transmission to France.

Transfer to a country which has adequate protection – the "white list"

The EU Commission has identified countries regarded as having adequate data protection in place. This is referred to as the "white list". Irish companies can export information to a white-listed country without taking any further steps. The following countries have been white-listed to date:

- Hungary;

- Switzerland;

- Canada (approved only where transferred to an entity subject to the PIPED Act).[34]

- Argentina

Australia has been adjudged to have inadequate laws. Currently under examination are Isle of Man, Guernsey,[35a] New Zealand.

Transfer to the US – "safe harbour"

The US and the EU have agreed to a set of privacy standards known as the "safe harbour" principles. European companies can freely transfer data to US companies who sign up to these principles.

Relatively few US companies have signed up to the safe harbour scheme as some find the obligations too onerous.[35] Any Irish business transferring or intending to transfer data to the US should check to see if the US company is a safe harbour company. The list of safe harbour companies is available at *www.export.gov/safeharbor*. You can proceed with the transfer if the company is on that list. If not, you can only proceed if one of the other criteria outlined below are satisfied.

---

[34] The Personal Information Protection and Electronic Documents Act 2002 ("the PIPED Act") only applies to regulated private sector organisations that process personal data in the course of commercial activity. If the Canadian organisation to which you wish to send information is not subject to the PIPED Act then you cannot transfer the information unless you put adequate safeguards in place.

[35] They are required to provide a right of access to the data subject, submit to the jurisdiction of the Irish courts, inform the data subject of any change in purpose with regard to the processing, and warrant not to onward transfer the information without the data subjects consent. The safe harbour scheme does not apply to financial services companies

[35a] Guernsey has been approved by the article 29 committee and will be added to the "white list" in the coming months.

What if the country to which you want to transfer is not white-listed or safe harbour?

If the transfer is to a country which is not white-listed or a safe harbour then the next step is to see if the transfer is exempt. The transfer is exempt from the statutory restriction if:

• it is made to comply with international law; or

• it is made in connection with a legal claim; or

• it is made to protect the vital interests of the data subject; or

• the transfer is of information held on public registers; or

• the transfer is necessary for the performance/conclusion of a contract; or

• the transfer is necessary for reasons of substantial public interest.

Made in connection with a legal claim

Transfers can be made where they are (i) necessary in connection with any legal proceedings (ii) necessary for obtaining legal advice, or (iii) necessary for establishing or defending legal rights.

It is worth noting that "legal compulsion" is not an exception. Therefore where a controller is required by a foreign law or a foreign regulator to transfer information there is no exemption expressly allowing for such transfer.

Made to protect the vital interests of the data subject

This exception points to life and death situations and transfers can be made only where it is essential to prevent injury or damage to the individual. For example, while the transfer of medical information to a non-EEA country would normally be prohibited unless the patient consents, clearly if that patient has had an accident rendering him incapable of giving consent, a doctor or hospital can send the patient's details abroad without breaching the Act.

The transfer is of information held on a public register

Transfer of information to a non-EEA country is permitted where personal information forms part of a register available to the public. For example you can transfer extracts of the register of solicitors or from the register of medical practitioners or from the accounts of a company identifying directors or officers. The transferor must impose any obligation on the transferee as to access to the register which is imposed by national law.

The transfer is necessary for the performance of a contract

Transfers are permitted without consent if necessary for the performance of a contract. Whether the transfer is necessary for the performance of a contract will depend on the nature of the goods or services provided under the contract. "Necessary" is not defined and we will have to await guidance from the Commissioner and/or the courts as to the parameters of this exception. Clearly the transfer must be necessary and not just convenient for the transferring entity. Therefore, information may be transmitted, for example, where a customer books a hotel in Barbados through an agent in Dublin and it is necessary for the performance of the contract for the data to be transferred to Barbados. However, where the hotel in Barbados wishes to put the information onto a marketing database then the consent of the customer will be needed. If an Irish-based company were to process its payroll through a US parent company then this transfer, being for the convenience of the transferor, would not be strictly necessary for the performance of the contract of employment and might not therefore come under the exception.

If none of the exemptions apply can you proceed?

If none of the exemptions apply and the destination is not white-listed or is not a safe harbour company you can only transfer information abroad with the individual's consent, the authorisation of the Commissioner or through contracting with the recipient.

The Directive specifies that consent should be "unambiguous"[35b] and the individual must be made aware:

- that their personal information may be transferred; and

- the reasons their information might be transferred; and

- that the transfer may be to a non-EEA country; and

- the transfer may be to a country which does not have the same data protection laws as in Ireland or the EU.

Ideally where the data controller is aware in advance of the countries to which the transfers of information will be made, this detail should be specified.

If getting the consent is not possible or practical. Can you proceed?

Transfers abroad may be made even though there is inadequate protection in place, if the data controller secures the necessary level of protection through contractual obligation.

The EU has approved model contract clauses for transfers. Where an Irish company enters into a model contract with a foreign entity then the transfer can take place and you don't need to notify the Commissioner. It is not possible to pick and choose from the model clauses. All of the terms should be incorporated into any agreement.

In some circumstances the contractual model will not be appropriate, for example where the exporter and the importer form part of the same legal entity (such as a partnership or a branch), or the contractual terms may prove unacceptable to some foreign entities. One alternative favoured by some multinationals is to draft a Global Privacy Policy containing principles akin to but not as onerous as those contained in the model contracts. At present these policies require the authorisation of the Commissioner.

[35b] The Act requires a simple "consent". The Act will be interpreted in light of the Directive and therefore it is likely that any consent will need to reach the "unambiguous" threshold.

If none of the above apply can you transfer the information?

If you cannot facilitate your transfer by using one of the mechanisms outlined above then you can still transfer if you get prior authorisation from the Commissioner. The Commission is currently considering "Global Company Policies" as a means of legitimacy transfers. This would be particularly useful for multinationals who transfer information to a large number of countries.

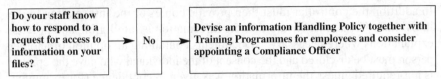

| Do your staff know how to respond to a request for access to information on your files? | → No → | Devise an information Handling Policy together with Training Programmes for employees and consider appointing a Compliance Officer |

Data protection law allows every individual to demand access as of right to information which any organisation or business holds on him.[36] People can look for their files for many reasons and dealing with such requests can be expensive and time consuming for any business. It may involve the assembly of information stored in a variety of locations, for example all e-mail communications or HR records referring to the individual throughout your business. Businesses should include a training and a data access policy as part of their overall compliance programme because it alerts staff to their responsibilities as to information management and retrieval.

An individual generally has a right to:

- a list of all information which the controller holds about them;

- access that information;

- rectify, block or erase the information;

- require the controller to cease processing or not to commence processing their information

Right to establish that you hold personal information on the individual

The controller must, within 21 days of a written request by the individual, give the individual a description of the nature of information processed by the controller, and the purpose(s) for which it is processed. Such a request for a list of information is generally a prelude to a request to access the information itself.

Right of access to the information

In order to access his information the individual must make a request in writing. A description of the following should be provided within 40 days:

- the categories of data which the controller processes in the course of its business;

- the type of information processed on that individual;

- the purposes for which you process the individual's information;

---

[36] Section 4.

- the third parties (or categories of third parties) to whom that information is disclosed;

- details of the source of the information (unless identifying the source would be a threat to the public interest); and

- details of the logic behind any automated decision.[37]

In addition the controller must then provide copies of the information to the individual.[38] You must ensure that the information is intelligible and provide explanations where necessary.[39] Documents containing an opinion of another person must be disclosed and the consent of the individual who gave the opinion is not required unless the information was given in confidence (for example a character reference). However, where a document contains information relating both to the person requesting the information and another party, the controller must delete the reference to the other person before allowing the individual to access the information.

If you need to verify the identity of the person seeking the information or to seek clarification in respect of the request, then you should write to the maker of the request seeking the additional information. The 40 days deadline is suspended until such additional details are provided. It is good practice to verify the identity of any party seeking access to personal data unless this is not necessary in the circumstances, for example when dealing with a current employee.

Can you charge for dealing with an access request?

You can charge an administration fee for dealing with any request. The maximum charge is currently €6.35. If information is held on a person for a number of different purposes the data controller is entitled to charge a separate fee for each purpose.[39a]

Can you refuse an access request?

You can refuse access in the following circumstances[40]:

Where the data is kept for the purpose of preventing, detecting or investigating offences or where the data is kept for the purpose of apprehending or prosecuting offenders or assessing or collecting any tax, duty or other monies owed or payable to the State, local authority or a health board.

For example, an employer could refuse to give an employee access to their records if they included internet traffic data collected to investigate a possible infringement

---

[37]   You will not be required to provide any technical information which is a trade secret or relates to intellectual property such as details of any software which is protected by copyright.

[38]   You have to provide a copy of each piece of information to the individual. If it is not possible to make a copy or if making a copy would involve disproportionate effort or expense then you will not be required to provide such a copy. In these circumstances you would still be required to provide the individual with a detailed description of what the record contains.

[39]   *e.g.* a glossary explaining any abbreviations or code words.

[39a] s. 4(2).

[40]   Section 5.

of the Child Trafficking and Pornography Act 1998. The investigation must relate to an offence or potential offence. Therefore the employer could not refuse access to internet traffic data collected for management purposes.

Where the access is likely to prejudice the security of, the maintenance of, good order or discipline in a prison, place of detention.[41]

To protect members of the public against financial loss occasioned by dishonesty, incompetence or malpractice on the part of persons concerned in the provision of banking, insurance, investment or other financial services in the management of companies or similar organisations or the conduct of persons who have been at any time adjudicated bankrupt.

Where the access would be contrary to the interest of protecting the international relations or security of the State.

Where the information consists of an estimate of, or kept for the purposes of estimating, the amount of liability of the Data Controller whether in respect of damages or compensation, in any case and to allow access would be likely to prejudice the interest of the Data Controller in relation to the claim.

In respect of a claim where privilege could be maintained in proceedings in a court in relation to communications between a client and his professional legal advisors or between those advisers.

Legal privilege attaches to documents which contain legal advice provided by a lawyer to his client or other communication from the client to his advisor. Documents created by either lawyer or client in anticipation or furtherance of litigation will also be privileged. Sometimes a document will be created for a number of reasons, for example an interview with an employee may be recorded to ascertain and record the facts of an allegation of misconduct, to brief others within the business and to brief solicitors in order to seek an opinion on the matter. In these circumstances the document will attract privilege if the dominant purpose in creating the document is to obtain legal advice.

Where the information consists of an expression of opinion and it was given in confidence or on the understanding that it would be treated as confidential.

This may allow an employer to refuse access to a reference obtained from an employee's previous employer without the consent of the previous employer. See Chapter 4.

Anonymised/statistical data

Backup data

Health information where it is the opinion of a health professional that disclosure would damage the mental or physical health of the individual. If you hold medical information and you are not a medical practitioner or a social worker you should

---

[41]   Military prison or detention barracks or St. Patrick's Institution.

seek medical opinion as to whether there are sufficient grounds to justify the concern that this would damage the individual's mental or physical health.[42]

Dealing with multiple requests[43]

Where an individual makes repeated requests for access to similar information, the controller can refuse to deal with further requests until a reasonable time period has elapsed since the last request. "Reasonable time period" is not defined. However, in most circumstances requests made within 6 months of each other would seem unreasonable.

Right to rectify, block or erase

An individual has a right to insist that information held on him is blocked, rectified or erased where the information is inaccurate, out of date or has been collected without his knowledge or consent in contravention of the Act.[44] Any such request must be made to the data controller in writing. A data controller must comply or indicate a refusal to comply with the request within 40 days. The individual can appeal any refusal to the Commissioner. If the individual requests that his information be rectified on the basis that it is inaccurate or out of date, then the controller can comply with his obligations by putting a supplementary statement on the individual's file which updates the information.[45]

Where an individual requires the controller to modify any information the controller must notify the changes to anyone to whom he has disclosed the information during the preceding 12 months, unless this proves impossible or involves a disproportionate effort. What is a "disproportionate effort" will depend on the circumstances of each case.

Right to require the controller to cease using information for direct marketing.

We have seen that the individual has a right to "opt out" of direct marketing at the point where their information is collected. However at any point the individual can insist (by making a request in writing)[46] that you remove their details from your marketing database. Within 40 days the controller must cease processing the data for marketing purposes and must notify the individual within 20 days that they have done so or that they intend to do so.

Right to require the controller to cease processing information for direct marketing or for other purposes

The individual can insist that you cease processing if you have not obtained their consent to process their data and:

- the processing is likely to cause substantial damage or distress to the individual; and
- the damage or distress is unwarranted.

---

[42] S.I. No. 82 of 1989; S.I. No. 83 of 1989.
[43] Section 4(10).
[44] Section 6.
[45] Section 6(1).
[46] Section 6A.

However even where there is a likelihood of distress or damage you can refuse the individual's request to cease processing if:

- the data subject has given their explicit consent to the processing; or

- the processing is necessary for the performance of a contract with the data subject; or

- the information is held to take steps at the reasonable request of the data subject prior to his entering into a contract; or

- the information is held in order to comply with legal obligations of the Data Controller or the individual; or

- the information is held to protect the vital interests of the individual; or

- processing is carried out by political parties or candidates for election, or holders of elective political office in the course of their activities; or

- where specified by regulations.[47]

Devising a Data Handling Policy

A Data Handling Policy will ensure that you can react effectively and efficiently to any request for access to personal data. A policy could include the following:

- Inform staff of your obligations under the Act and the right of employees/others to access personal information.

- Staff should arrange personal information on customers/employees, etc. in a way which facilitates efficient retrieval.

- Use of public electronic folders should be encouraged.

- Private password-controlled folders should be limited to private e-mail communications to allow access to electronic files where employees are on extended leave.

- Staff should regularly audit their files to ensure that information is accurate and up to date.

- All requests for access to file information should be referred to a central person designated to deal with such requests.

- Staff should deal with requests to provide information in response to a request quickly and efficiently.

---

[47] To date the Minister has not issued regulations under this section.

COMPLIANCE CHECKLIST

■ Put in place a Data Handling Policy to ensure that access requests are dealt with efficiently.

■ Appoint a Compliance Officer to handle requests.

■ Ensure that your files hold information which is accurate and up to date.

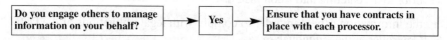

| Do you engage others to manage information on your behalf? | Yes | Ensure that you have contracts in place with each processor. |

Where you engage others to manage information on your behalf you must put a written contract in place with these outside companies to ensure the ongoing safety of the personal information. Where you engage a data processor you continue to be the manager or controller of the information and your legal obligations under the Act continue. Where you transfer "control" of the information you will not need to enter into such a contract; however, you will need to ensure that your disclosure is lawful. For example, where you engage a company to process payroll information then you remain the controller and you need to put an agreement in place. On the other hand if you arrange a group Bupa Ireland Healthcare Insurance scheme for employees, you won't need an agreement with Bupa Ireland as the employee will deal directly with Bupa Ireland who will be the controllers.

A Data Processor Agreement must contain undertakings from the processor that:

• it will only process information as instructed by the controller and for no other purposes; and

• it will ensure that there are adequate organisational and technical measures in place to ensure against unauthorised access to or loss, alteration or destruction of any of the information.

The controller has an ongoing obligation to ensure that the processor is complying with its obligations and may therefore wish to include a term in the contract allowing for ongoing inspection of security systems and/or records.

2. WHO IS THE DATA PROTECTION COMMISSIONER AND WHAT ARE HIS POWERS?

THE ROLE OF THE DATA PROTECTION COMMISSIONER

Appointment[1]

The Commissioner is appointed for a renewable five-year period and is the supervisory authority in Ireland. The Commissioner has the following functions:

- monitoring the processing of data within Ireland;

- liaising with the European Commission in relation to the implementation of the Directive;

- providing information/guidance to data controllers;

- promoting compliance with the Act and enforcing its provisions;

- maintaining a public register of data controllers and data processors.

Search and seizure powers[2]

The Commissioner has the power to investigate any breaches of the Act including the power to conduct "dawn raids".[3] This means that the Commissioner or his authorised officers can arrive at your business premises and conduct an audit of your information management systems. The Commissioner and his officers can:

- enter your premises, inspect any files and examine, operate, or test any electronic or other equipment;

- require you and your employees to comply with any reasonable request to produce information;

- inspect and copy any document, either on the premises or elsewhere and the originals can be taken away or copies can be made;

- interview any director, manager or any other employee of your company to ascertain the nature and extent of any data processing carried out by your business.

It is an offence to obstruct or impede the commissioner or his officers in carrying out their functions or providing them with misleading information. It is important

---

[1] Schedule 2.
[2] Section 24.
[3] Section 24(2).

that your staff are fully acquainted with the procedures to be followed if the Commissioner comes knocking at the door.

How likely are such search and seizure raids?

Investigations by the Commissioner will usually be instigated on foot of a complaint. In practice dawn raids will probably be rare except in response to serious complaints. The Commissioner in his Annual Report 2002 states that he intends to conduct "privacy audits" upon data controllers at random on a targeted sectoral basis. The Commissioner is constitutionally bound to exercise any powers (including search and seizure) in a fair and reasonable manner.

In 2001, 233 complaints were received by the Office of the Commissioner from Data Subjects. In 2002 189 complaints were recorded. Many complaints may be capable of resolution through correspondence with the Commissioner but if this does not prove to be the case, or if the complaint suggests that a very serious data protection abuse is taking place, then an immediate search and seizure operation may be considered.

Notices

The Commissioner has the power to issue the following[4]:

• an Information Notice;

• an Enforcement Notice;

• a Prohibition Notice;

• A decision/opinion;

He can also issue guidelines and is empowered to draw up and/or approve industry sector codes of practice.

Information Notice

At any stage (including at the registration stage) the Commissioner can issue an Information Notice requiring you to provide details (or further details) of your processing activities. An Information Notice served on foot of an application for registration must be served within 90 days of receipt of the application. There is a right to appeal an Information Notice.

Enforcement Notice

These are issued where the Commissioner is satisfied there has been a contravention of the Act by either a controller or a processor. An Enforcement Notice must set out the relevant section of the Act which the Commissioner

---

[4] Sections 10, 11, 12, 13.

believes has been contravened together with the reasons for his opinion. To date the authors are not aware of any Enforcement Notices having been issued by the Commissioner.

The Enforcement Notice can require a controller or processor to block, erase, rectify or destroy any information by a certain date. This Notice may also require that the information be supplemented with a statement relating to the information. Any such supplementary statement must be approved by the Commissioner.

An Enforcement Notice can be appealed to the Circuit Court within 21 days of the service of the Notice (see below).

If you have to significantly alter the information to comply with the Notice you are then obliged to contact anyone to whom you have disclosed the information in the 12 months preceding the Notice. Complying with this requirement may prove difficult and expensive. The Act specifies that where compliance would involve a disproportionate effort, businesses would be justified in not complying with this requirement. Unfortunately "disproportionate effort" is not defined so it may be important to liaise with the Data Protection Commissioner's Office to ensure that you come within the exemption, as failure to comply with an Enforcement Notice is a criminal offence.

Restriction on transfer Notice

The purpose of a Restriction Notice is to prevent the transfer of data outside the EEA where necessary safeguards have not been put in place. This Notice will prohibit the transfer either absolutely or until certain specified steps are taken by the controller by a certain date (the controller must be given a minimum of 7 days to comply). The grounds for restricting the transfer should be set out in the Notice. You can appeal this Restriction Notice to the Circuit Court within 21 days.

Decisions/Opinions

The Commissioner can also issue decisions and opinions in relation to complaints or enquiries.

Guidelines

The Commissioner can issue guidelines to be followed in respect of various aspects of data protection law.

Codes of practice

Codes of practice can be drawn up by trade associations or by the Commissioner. The objective is that certain categories of controllers comply with the codes in dealing with personal information. The codes need to be approved by the Commissioner. They can then be laid before the Oireachtas and at that stage they become binding on all data controllers within the sector, even if the data controller is not a member of the respective body that drafted the code.

In the UK the Information Commissioner (equivalent to the Irish Data Protection Commissioner) has been active in drafting codes of practice guidelines which have been very useful particularly in the employment law area.

Service of notices

The Commissioner can serve notices in a number of ways depending on whether the intended recipient is an individual or a company.

An individual may be served by:

• personal service, (*i.e.* by handing it to the individual directly);

• posting it to his usual or last known place of residence or business;

• by leaving it for him at that address.

A body corporate or non-incorporated body may be served by:

• sending it to the body by post;

• addressing it and leaving it at the company's registered office;

• addressing it and leaving it at the company's principal place of business.

Annual reports

The Commissioner must produce an annual report (s.14). Annual reports have been published since 1997. The report details the financial status of the office of the Data Protection Commissioner, reports on the number of complaints that have been made and for certain cases gives detailed case notes on decisions that the Commissioner has made. These reports attract absolute privilege from the law of defamation. The Commissioner's report can be accessed at *www.dataprivacy.ie.*

3. OFFENCES, PENALTIES AND LIABILITIES

OFFENCES

Certain breaches of the Act amount to a criminal offence:

- Requiring a job applicant to make an access request (*e.g.* to a current or ex employer) to support their application[1];
- Failing to comply with a Prohibition Notice[2];
- Failing to comply with a requirement specified in an Enforcement Notice[2a];
- Failing to comply with an Information Notice issued by the Commissioner[3];
- Failing to register with the office of the Data Protection Commissioner or processing data for an unregistered purpose[4];
- Disclosure of data by a processor without prior authorisation of the controller[5];
- Disclosure of data by a person whom obtains it without the authority of the data controller or data processor[6];
- Obstructing or impeding an authorised officer exercising his power under the Act or providing false information or misleading information.[7]

Summary proceedings may be brought and prosecuted by the Commissioner within one year from the date that the offence allegedly occurred.

PENALTIES

The penalties on conviction are as follows:

- On summary conviction in the district court to a fine not exceeding €3,000;
- On conviction on indictment in the circuit criminal court to a fine not exceeding €100,000;
- The court can also order the forfeiture, destruction or erasure of any data connected with the commission of an offence. If the breach is very serious the court could foreseeably make an order that an entire database be erased. This could have catastrophic consequences for any business.

---

[1] Section 13(a).
[2] Section 11(15).
[2a] Section 10(9).
[3] Section 12(A)(7)
[4] Section 19(6).
[5] Section 21.
[6] Section 22(1).
[7] Section 24(6).

Apart from the financial implications arising from a conviction, businesses could also be adversely affected by the publicity generated by a prosecution or an investigation (or indeed by a mere complaint) by the Commissioner.

As in all criminal cases there is a right to appeal any conviction, penalty or order handed down by the District Court or Circuit Criminal Court.

LIABILITIES OF DIRECTORS AND OFFICERS

A director (including a shadow director), manager, secretary or other company officer (or a person purporting or holding them out to acting in such capacity) can be prosecuted for an offence under the Act. If the offence was committed by a body corporate but with the consent, connivance or neglect of an officer of the company then that officer may find themselves liable to prosecution.

CAN THE DATA SUBJECT TAKE A CIVIL ACTION FOR BREACH OF THE ACT?

Yes. Data controllers and data processors owe the data subject a duty of care. A data subject can sue for damages in negligence or other relief for any breach of this duty of care. Such an action would be independent of any liability under the Act.

4. THE LAW — WHERE DO I FIND IT IF I NEED IT?

Unfortunately data protection and privacy laws are not found in one single document and if you need to consult the actual law then you may have to look in a number of places. We set out below the main sources of the law.

The Irish Constitution

The Irish Constitution provides individuals with a limited right to privacy.[1]

Acts of the Oireachtas

Two Irish Acts deal with data protection, the Data Protection Act 1988 ("the 1988 Act") and the Data Protection (Amendment) Act 2003 ("the 2003 Act"). Appendix C contains the 1988 Act with amendments made by the 2003 Act.

Directives

Several European Directives deal with data protection and privacy. Ireland is obliged to implement all European Directives. However, unlike European Regulations, which automatically become law here, there is some latitude in how the Directive is implemented. There are therefore slight differences in data protection laws throughout the EU despite the fact that they come from the same Directives.

Directive 95/46/EC – the Data Protection Directive ("the 1995 Directive")

The 2003 Act implements the 1995 Directive in full. The 1988 Act already contained the basic principles set out in the Directive. The 2003 Act has amended the 1988 Act to implement the remaining provisions of the Directive. The main changes which the 1995 Directive has brought about are:

- extending the application of the rules to paper files;

- regulating the transfer of information outside the EEA;

- requiring consent to process personal information;

- extending the registration requirements of data controllers and processors;

- extending the powers of the Commissioner to monitor compliance.

---

[1] Article 40, Irish Constitution 1937.

Directive 97/66/EC – the Data Protection Telecommunications Directive ("the 1997 Directive")

The 1997 Directive addresses privacy issues in the telecommunications sector. The 1997 Directive was implemented in May 2002 by way of Regulation.[2]
The main features of the Regulations are:

- Records of telephone calls may only be kept as long as necessary to enable bills to be settled.

- Telephone users have the right to block their phone number, so that it is not displayed to other telephone users.

- Individuals have the right to be excluded from public phone directories, or to have their address and gender omitted to protect their privacy.

- Individuals can sign up to a central "opt out" register, to indicate that they do not wish to receive unsolicited telephone calls.

- The Commissioner is responsible for the enforcement of the regulation and the Office of the Director of Telecommunications Regulation is responsible for ensuring compliance with some technical and practical elements of implementing the Regulation.

Directive 2002/58/EC – The e-Communications Directive ("the 2002 Directive")

The 2002 Directive was published in July 2002. When implemented this Directive will replace the 1997 Directive and will strengthen data protection rules in the telecommunications sector. It will:

- regulate the use of unsolicited communications (*i.e.* email, SMS messaging);

- prohibit direct marketing without the customer's prior consent;

- allow for the creation of an "opt in" Register for direct marketing.

Statutory Instruments

A number of Regulations have issued under the 1988 Act, the most significant of which are detailed below.

Data Protection Act, 1988 (Restriction of Section 4) Regulations 1989 (S.I. No. 81 of 1989)

These Regulations provide that confidentiality rules, relating to the Adopted Children Register and the Ombudsman, should outweigh the right of access to records under section 4 of the 1988 Act.

---

[2] The European Communities (Data Protection and Privacy in Telecommunications) Regulations 2002 (S.I. No. 192 of 2002).

Data Protection (Access Modification) (Health) Regulations 1989 (S.I. No. 82 of 1989)

These Regulations restrict patient access to health information where this is likely to cause serious physical or mental harm. Such information can only be communicated following consultation with an appropriate "health professional" (normally the patient's doctor).

Data Protection (Access Modification) (Social Work) Regulations 1989 (S.I. No. 83 of 1989)

These Regulations restrict access to social work information where this is likely to cause serious physical or mental harm. Such information can only be communicated following consultation with an appropriate social worker or health professional.

Data Protection Act, 1988 (Section 5(1)(d)) (Specification) Regulations 1993 (S.I. No. 95 of 1993)

These Regulations restrict access to personal information where the data is held by certain financial institutions such as the Central Bank and the Irish Stock Exchange. Access to information is restricted where it would prejudice or comprise the responsibilities of such bodies to prevent dishonest or fraudulent financial practices.

European Communities (Data Protection and Privacy in Telecommunications) Regulations 2001 (S.I. No. 192 of 2002)

These Regulations implement the 1997 Directive (see above).

Some other relevant sources of law

European Convention on Human Rights 1950

This Convention sets out a framework for Human Rights. Ireland has incorporated the Convention into Irish law through the European Convention on Human Rights Act 2003. This gives Irish citizens the right to rely on the rights set out in the Convention. Articles 8 and 10 of the Convention provide a right of privacy and freedom of expression.

Freedom of Information Act 1997

The Freedom of Information Act 1997 allows an individual (and companies) to access information including personal information held on record by designated public bodies. This is almost identical to the rights granted to the individual under Data Protection Law. However, the Data Protection Acts, unlike the Freedom of Information Act, is restricted to personal information and applies to information held by all data controllers not just public bodies.

PART 2
SECTORAL ISSUES

5. EMPLOYMENT AND HUMAN RESOURCES

INTRODUCTION

All employment relationships involve the supply and collection of personal information, including sensitive personal information. This process of supply and collection begins with recruitment and it continues throughout employment for purposes ranging from paying wages and deducting taxes and union dues through to complying with health and safety standards and other laws, and assessing performance. Data protection obligations survive the termination of the employment relationship. A chart showing the flow of a variety of employment information across different departments and managers is shown overleaf.

In addition, email and the internet are now an integral part of most employment environments, sometimes blurring the line between the employee's home and work life. Controversial privacy issues arise on the monitoring of employee's email and internet access.

Most HR practitioners already understand that best practice requires them to treat information which they receive and hold about employees confidentially and in a discreet manner, no matter what the source or nature of that information. Data protection legislation, in Ireland as in the rest of Europe, supplements the common law and best practice in this area and places more formal obligations on employer organisations about how they handle employee information.

This chapter considers practical data protection management and privacy issues that often arise in employment situations.

RECRUITMENT AND SELECTION

The collection of personal information begins with recruitment. This collection gives candidates rights and imposes duties on employers. No company can ignore these issues when recruiting. The need for awareness of data protection obligations is increased because of the obligations imposed on employers on other fronts by the ever increasing volume of employer legislation, including the Employment Equality Act 1998. Employees or unions can use data protection access rights as a tool to gather information designed to support a claim under this or other legislation.

Advertising

Advertising a vacancy is the first opportunity for an employer to ensure it meets its data protection obligations. When advertising vacancies, if you don't disclose your identity initially (*e.g.* where applicants are asked to respond to a P.O. Box), you should do so as soon as you begin to process the application, *i.e.*

Flowchart of Employment Information

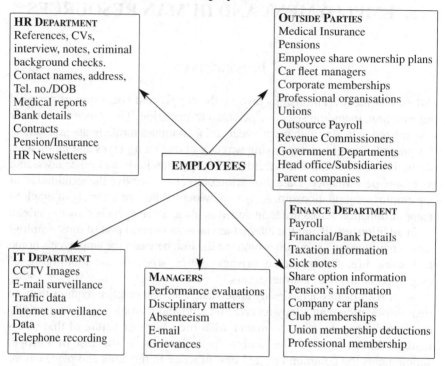

HR DEPARTMENT
References, CVs,
interview, notes, criminal
background checks.
Contact names, address,
Tel. no./DOB
Medical reports
Bank details
Contracts
Pension/Insurance
HR Newsletters

OUTSIDE PARTIES
Medical Insurance
Pensions
Employee share ownership plans
Car fleet managers
Corporate memberships
Professional organisations
Unions
Outsource Payroll
Revenue Commissioners
Government Departments
Head office/Subsidiaries
Parent companies

EMPLOYEES

IT DEPARTMENT
CCTV Images
E-mail surveillance
Traffic data
Internet surveillance
Data
Telephone recording

MANAGERS
Performance evaluations
Disciplinary matters
Absenteeism
E-mail
Grievances

FINANCE DEPARTMENT
Payroll
Financial/Bank Details
Taxation information
Sick notes
Share option information
Pension's information
Company car plans
Club memberships
Union membership deductions
Professional membership

start to consider it.[1] You should also explain the intended use of the information where necessary, *e.g.* disclosing that it might be passed on to a related company or third party, if that is the case.[2]

Recruitment agencies

Recruitment agencies advertising positions or shortlisting candidates also have duties.

- They should tell the applicant if they intend to keep their details on file for future reference.

- They need not identify the employer in advertisements but once they give the employer information identifying particular applicants, they should then, as soon as practicable, inform the applicant of the employer's identity and any proposed uses of the data unless they are self evident.[3] For example, passing the employee details to an associated company might not be self evident in which case it should be disclosed.

---

[1] Section 2D(2)(a) requires "so far as is practicable" that the data subject be informed of the identity of the data controller.
[2] Section 2D(2)(c) requires "so far as is practicable" that the data subject be informed of the purposes for which the information will be processed
[3] Section 2D.

- If the employer does not want its identity revealed to the applicant until some advanced stage in the recruitment process, the agency should only send anonymised information about the candidate to the employer.

Applicants and CVs

Employers should be aware of the need to justify, on non-discriminatory grounds, the request for information sought from applicants. For example, the decision of *Equality Authority v Ryanair*[4] shows the dangers of seeking information about an applicant's age. The Employment Equality Act 1998 highlights the importance of only seeking personal data which is relevant to the recruitment decision. The Data Protection Act reinforces this. As employers you must take into account the following:

- The application form should say to whom the information is going and, if it will be used in a way other than what would be expected, the form should be set out how it will be used.

- You should be able to show why such information is needed for the recruitment decision.

- You should consider the appropriate time to seek particular information. For example, it may be legitimate to seek information about an individual's age or marital or family status on their admission to the company pension scheme. However, such a request is only legitimate once the candidate has been recruited, as it is not necessary for the recruitment process.

- You may also need sensitive personal information from potential applicants; for example, details of criminal convictions or health problems. Such sensitive data in the employment relationship is considered at pp. 55–58 below but you should be aware, when recruiting, that it may not be appropriate to ask the same questions of all prospective employees. For example, details of offences involving fraud or dishonesty may be relevant for a sensitive or senior position involving the handling of money within a bank, but may or may not be relevant for the recruitment of a bank receptionist. We consider these issues at pp. 55–58 below.

- You must also consider what to do with application forms and CVs from unsuccessful applicants. You need to keep them long enough defend a potential claim of discrimination under the Employment Equality Act. The Act provides for equality reviews and information being sought from employers about certain employment equality practices. A discrimination claim may be brought

---

[4] DEC–E2001–14. This case involved a complaint to the Equality Authority about a job advertisement seeking "a young and dynamic professional . . . ". The Equality Officer determined that the advertisement breached the Employment Equality Act 1998 and constituted discrimination on the ground of age. Of particular interest is the concern expressed by the Equality Officer about the absence of "other written criteria for the position". This concern highlights the importance of keeping and retaining information (sometimes personal information) in order to demonstrate compliance with equal opportunities legislation. However, the very keeping of that information raises data protection issues.

within 6 months of the alleged discrimination (*e.g.* refusal of the job) but this period may be extended to 12 months in certain circumstances.[5] You should therefore keep all recruitment information, including application forms, for at least 12 months. After that, the need to show compliance with equality law could be met by retaining statistical or anonymised information. It is doubtful that the Employment Equality Act would provide justification for retaining applications or CVs for substantially longer than the timeframe within which a complaint could be brought, *i.e.* 12 months.

- Employers should have a policy with respect to the return or destruction of application forms. This includes unsolicited application forms. This is further considered at pp. 51 and 61 below.

Interviews

Employers retain records and notes of interviews as an aide memoire for the interview panel and to show good recruitment practice. The interview notes may be in electronic form or they may be manual notes held on a filing system within the meaning of the Act. While it is good employment practice to retain these notes, you should be aware that in either case, they will be generally accessible to both successful and unsuccessful job applicants. Unsuccessful applicants, particularly those considering a discrimination claim, are likely to seek such access. You should therefore follow the following basic guidelines:

- Ensure that any personal information which is recorded and retained following the interview can be justified as relevant to the recruitment process.

- Train everybody conducting interviews about data protection principles and alert them to the possibility that the applicant may seek access to such notes. The importance of proper records of the interview should be emphasised.

- Interviewers should appreciate the dangers inherent in "doodling" on interview notes or making irrelevant or personal notes about an applicant. For example, a note about a candidate's appearance (balding/glasses), innocently intended only as an aide memoire to recall which candidate was which, could be portrayed in an entirely different light in a discrimination claim.

- You might wish to consider the use of standard forms against which all applicants are marked. This allows the collection of information in relation to all applicants under the same headings and may avoid the dangers inherent in a more flexible method. (This can also assist in the comparison of the different candidates during the selection process.)

Verification and vetting

You may need to verify information provided by an applicant and make subsequent enquiries before making any final decision. This involves liaising

---

[5] *i.e.* if the Director of Equality Investigations or the Court is satisfied that exceptional circumstances prevented the complaint being made earlier (section 77 of the Employment Equality Act 1998).

with other parties about an applicant's personal information. For example, you may want to verify an applicant's qualifications or experience with an educational establishment or previous employer. Data protection issues arise with such verification. Employers should consider the following:

- Any verification process should be transparent. Applicants should be told *what* information may be verified and *how* it may be verified.

- Be aware that certain organisations, in order to comply with their own data protection obligations, will not release any personal information without a signed approval from the person concerned. This may be the case with universities and other educational institutions. You should therefore seek signed approval forms from the individuals for this purpose.

- The Act makes it illegal for an employer, either during recruitment or ongoing employment, to get the applicant or employee himself to make a data protection access request to another party or to provide information obtained through an access request from another party. It is interesting, however, that the provision banning such enforced access requests will not come into force with the rest of the Act in 2003.

- Some pre-employment vetting such as background criminal checks is more intrusive than simply verifying information given by the applicant himself. You will have to be able to show particular justification for this type of intrusive enquiry of other parties. It will depend on the risk which you are trying to prevent by vetting the employee; for example, the risk of employing a convicted paedophile to work with children, or a thief to run a bank. Employers also face practical problems in obtaining this information, because although convictions are a matter of public record the information is only accessible where the enquiring employer already knows a certain amount about the conviction, *e.g.* dates and court. The Gardaí may provide assistance but usually only where there the risk which the employer is seeking to protect is relatively high.

- A discrepancy between information provided by the applicant and information received following a verification or vetting exercise does not always mean that the applicant has been untruthful. Depending on the circumstances fair procedures may require that the applicant is informed of the discrepancy and given a chance to make representations, especially if the information could be relevant to a discrimination claim.

The Act specifically provides for regulations about processing personal information about the commission of offences and other matters.[6] No such regulations have yet been made. Hopefully, such regulations will be introduced so as to give employers some clarity in this area rather than requiring them to constantly consider whether such information can be justified in a particular matter.

---

[6] Section 2B(3).

Selection

Employers sometimes use computer software to sort or select candidates on the basis of preset criteria, such as qualifications. The Act provides for a general ban on decision-making based solely on such automated processing.[7] An automated decision is one which does not involve human input or consideration. However, the Act does permit such a decision to be made about a person in one of the following limited circumstances:

*   if the person has consented to the processing;

*   where the decision is taken while entering or performing a contract at the request of the data subject;

*   where such a decision is authorised or required by law AND the effect of the decision is to grant a request of the data subject or adequate steps have been taken to protect the data subject's interests

So what does this mean in the context of short-listing? First, when is a decision "based solely on processing by automatic means"? Software exists to allow CVs (or job applications) to be scanned onto a computer system. Such a system might involve a simple word search technique matching certain key words or phrases in the CV against those in the job specification, for example only applicants who hold a particular qualification would be short-listed. The UK Information Commissioner in her code of practice on recruitment and selection[8] suggests that a simple decision, for example to reject all applicants who do not have a third level qualification, is not prohibited. The Irish Commissioner's stance on this issue has yet to be determined.

As set out above, employers may be able to rely on an automated decision "made in the course of steps taken for the purpose of considering whether to enter a contract with the data subject; or while performing such a contract". This is an exemption of potential relevance in the context of entering into an employment contract.

What exactly does the exemption mean? In a report by Robin E.J. Chater, Director of the Personnel Policy Research Unit for the UK Information Commissioner,[9] Mr Chater concluded that it is difficult for employers to be confident in an assessment that a decision is not made "solely" on processing by automated means and that "a much more sound approach" is to legitimise a decision based on automated processing on the grounds that it was taken for the purposes or with a view to entering into a contract with the individual or in the course of performing such a contract (for existing employees).

Normally the use of an automated process will be only one of a range of factors taken into account as part of a decision-making process. In that case, the complex issues set out above will not apply. Once the decision process has a

---

[7] Section 6B.
[8] *www.dataprotection.gov.uk/dpr/dpdoc.nsf.*
[9] The uses and misuses of Personal Data in employer/employee relationships which is available on *www.dataprotection.gov.uk/dpr/dpdoc.nsf/ed1e7ff5aa6def30802566360045bf4d/5d6ee9d84e72 7202802568d9005384c6?OpenDocument.*

clear element of human involvement, for example by using qualified individuals to review and analyse the score resulting from an aptitude or psychometric test, it will not fall within the type of automated decision specifically addressed by the legislation.

Retention of recruitment information

While this is relevant to all employment information, specific issues arise in the context of applications and CVs because not all applicants will become employees. You should consider this issue specifically in your policy dealing with the retention of recruitment records.

Information may be gathered during recruitment which has no ongoing relevance once a recruitment decision has been made. Where possible, only information relevant to the ongoing employment relationship should be transferred to the new employee's personnel file. It may sometimes be impractical to separate information which has ongoing relevance from other information provided as part of the recruitment process.[10] Clearly, there is a reason for keeping a successful applicant's CV as part of his or her personnel file but the UK Information Commissioner suggests that it is more difficult to justify a need to keep character references once an applicant has been recruited. However, one can envisage circumstances where the correctness or otherwise of a reference which was relied on could be relevant so this issue is by no means clearcut and should be dealt with on a case-by-case basis.

You need to retain application forms of unsuccessful applicants for a period in order to comply with legislation such as the Employment Equality Act 1998. This does not mean that you can use the retained information for any other purpose. Unless you have indicated otherwise, it would be usual to assume that an applicant has only applied for the vacancy advertised. The details should not therefore be kept on file for any future vacancies unless the applicant has specifically been told that this is one of the purposes of collecting the information.

EMPLOYMENT RECORDS

Types of employee information

Many of the issues which arise in relation to recruitment also apply to employment records collected and processed once individuals become employees.

The personal information typically on a (manual or computer) filing system will include:

- an employee's name, address, home telephone number/mobile number and next of kin;

- banking and taxation details;

---

[10] Section 2(1) stipulates that the information which is processed be "adequate, relevant and not excessive".

- sickness and absence details;

- performance assessments;

- details of any disciplinary or grievance investigation.

Some information is likely to be sensitive,[11] giving rise to additional obligations on the employer.

You generally don't need to seek an employee's express consent to keep employment records. However, employees should be told what information you hold about them, where it came from, how it will be used and who it might be disclosed to. This may be done by an information sheet to each employee. Employee information must be accurate and up to date. This means that employers need a system for updating details which are likely to change. Elements of a personnel file which may become out of date, such as spent disciplinary warnings, should be removed as appropriate from the file. Disgruntled employees may well seek access to their personnel files and other files which may contain information about them so as to bring claims against their employer.

Sickness and absence records

There is a difference between the information kept recording an employee's absence and the information recording details of particular reasons for absence. An absence record usually only records the fact of the absence. It might give the reason, such as sickness or annual leave or compassionate leave, but should not refer to a particular medical condition. A sickness or an accident record, however, is a record which contains details of a particular illness or condition or injury. It includes information about an employee's physical or mental health and therefore involves the processing of sensitive information and must satisfy additional conditions. For this reason, employers should consider keeping such records separately.

You will often be entitled to keep information about an employee's specific illnesses or injuries because you need them to comply with other laws concerning employment. For example, the Safety, Health and Welfare at Work Act 1989 requires records to be kept of any accident at work. Employers also need to keep up-to-date details of any illness or injury which impacts on employer's ability to do the job and any special treatment or facilities which are necessary. The Employment Equality Act 1998 requires such records to be kept. This information should be appropriately secured because of its private nature, since a higher standard of security applies to sensitive information.[12] It may be appropriate to limit the information about such employees which is provided to other employees or managers.

---

[11] Sensitive information includes information relating to racial, ethnic origin, mental or physical health, sex life, trade union membership, religious or philosophical beliefs, criminal convictions or proceedings.

[12] Section 2C.

Health insurance and pension schemes

Many employees enjoy the benefit of private medical insurance or permanent health insurance schemes ("PHI") or an entitlement to join a pension scheme. Some schemes are controlled by an outside entity but administered in house, while others, although they may be funded by the employer, do not require any administration by the employer. For example the employer might have arrangements with VHI or BUPA Ireland for private medical insurance for staff. In such a case, claims by an employee go directly to the insurer, without involving the employer. The employer does not handle any information and is not therefore a data processor for this purpose (save in relation to any arrangements for deduction of premium).

Different issues arise with permanent health insurance schemes. The entitlement usually arises where the employee is unable to do the job. The insurer may ask the employer about other suitable employment for the employee. This may mean revealing medical information to the employer which it would not otherwise have. You need to take care with respect to the exchange and use of this information. One of the conditions allowing the processing of sensitive information is where the processing is necessary for medical purposes and is undertaken by a health professional or similar person.[13] An employer won't usually meet this criterion and so PHI insurance companies are likely to insist on the employer signing a medical confidentiality agreement before passing on this information which is another means of satisfying this sensitive data condition. In any event, the employer can only use such information for the purpose for which it was provided, *i.e.* ascertaining whether work is available for the employee in light of his incapacity. It may not be used for disciplining or dismissing the employee and should not be matched against medical information which has been provided by the employee as part of his compliance with any absence policy of the employer.

Similarly, an employer may have indirect access to information being processed by the trustees of a pension scheme, particularly where the trustees are also employees. Any information, including medical information, obtained for membership of the pension scheme cannot be used for other purposes, such as decisions about eligibility for sick pay or compliance with the absence policy.

Grievance, discipline and dismissal

Most employers appreciate the importance of records demonstrating a thorough investigation of any grievance raised by an employee or disciplinary investigation against an employee. Both processes usually involve personal information.

An employee has a right to access files containing information about disciplinary procedures or grievances about them, even if the disciplinary investigation is ongoing or the subject of legal proceedings such as an unfair dismissals claim. All managers involved in investigating disciplinary and grievance issues should receive training about the making and keeping of records. They should be aware that the employee has a right to access any

---

[13] Section 2B(1)(b)(vii).

records. You must also consider what records should be kept about allegations investigated and found to be without merit. In this regard managers who are involved in creating and keeping such records should be aware of when the records might be legally privileged and therefore not accessible by the employee. This issue is more fully explored at p. 59.

Employers also need a clear procedure for dealing with expired warnings. The disciplinary procedure should set out what happens when a warning expires. If the procedure provides that the warning is to be removed or deleted, employers need a system to make this happen. In reality, an Employment Appeals Tribunal would place little weight on an expired warning so the justification for retaining it is dubious once it expires.

The need for accurate information is one of the fundamental data protection principles. The UK Information Commissioner in the Code of Practice on Records Management[14] states that:

> "A breach of the Act's requirement of accuracy could arise, for example, where a worker has been allowed to resign but, because he or she is being left with little choice, the employer has recorded 'dismissed'. Particular care should be taken in distinguishing resignation from dismissal."

While it is not known whether the Irish Commissioner would adopt a similar approach, there is very often, in many dismissal cases, a discrepancy between what actually happens and the way in which information is relayed to colleagues or subsequent employers. With increased rights of access, employees can see, and exploit, any discrepancies. Of course, there will be circumstances where as part of a negotiated exit it is agreed to present the termination in a particular light. Where this is the case, however, you should try to obtain a legally valid waiver of employment rights from the employee.

References

Employers are often asked to give references about past employees and similarly rely on references about prospective employees given by a past employer. Such a character reference involves the disclosure of personal information. Unlike its UK equivalent, the Act does not expressly restrict an employee's right to gain access to such confidential job references. Irish employees may be able to seek access to a reference by request either to the maker or recipient of the reference. Employers providing references should be aware of this and of the need for accuracy to protect themselves, otherwise an employee could bring unfair dismissals proceedings or other claims against a former employer by relying on a reference given by that former employer. If such a reference gave a favourable impression of a dismissed employee, it calls into question the merits of the dismissal. If it gave an unfavourable impression, it may reinforce a discrimination or dismissal claim. Similarly, unsuccessful applicants may seek to access references from former employers with a view to framing a legal action.

---

[14] *www.dataprotection.gov.uk/dpr/dpdoc.nsf.*

Accuracy is a defence to a claim in defamation proceedings, although not one which is always easy or cost effective to maintain. With the increased rights of access, however, employers should have an eye to the risk of a defamation claim in making any record, including giving a reference. This highlights the importance of taking a prudent approach and training those employees who may be called upon to give references.

There is a possible limitation in the Act on an employee's ability to access references which have been given and received on a confidential basis.[15] The Act states that an expression of opinion about a person can be disclosed to that person without the consent of the person who expressed the opinion. Many references will contain at least an element of expression of opinion. However, if the expression of opinion is given in confidence it seems that it cannot be disclosed without the consent of the person expressing the opinion (*i.e.* the referee). To maximise the chances of relying on this provision, references should be stated to be given on the understanding that they will be kept confidential. Expressions of opinion should also be clearly distinguished from matters of fact about the employment such as dates of employment.

Disclosure of employment information (other than to the employee)

Employers receive requests for information about employees. Sometimes there is a legal obligation to disclose in the context of a criminal or tax investigation. Such situations pose few problems. Other cases will be less clear cut and disclosure may contravene the legislation. A fundamental data protection principle is that of "fairness" in processing any personal information. As a general rule of good employment practice, unless there is a good reason for not doing so, the employee should be informed about the request for disclosure and allowed to make representations.

Any employer who receives such requests for disclosure should be cautious in responding and should verify the identity and authority of the person making the request. If employers are approached by individuals seeking information on individuals to which they are not entitled, such as debt collection agencies or private investigators then, employers should have a policy to deal with any telephone calls seeking such information. The question of disclosure of information outside the EEA is considered further at p. 23.

SENSITIVE PERSONAL DATA

What constitutes sensitive personal data is explained at pp. 16 and 17. Sensitive data in an employment context could include:

* criminal convictions to assess suitability for employment, for example driving convictions for a lorry driver;

---

[15] Section 4(4A).

- information about any disability to ensure that special needs are catered for at an interview or in the workplace or to ensure that the individual can do the job;

- details of person's physical symptoms following a workplace accident to comply with the Safety Health and Welfare at Work Act 1989.

Chapter 1 sets out the conditions on which personal information can be processed. The conditions particularly relevant in an employment context are as follows.

Processing related to any legal rights or obligations regarding employment

This condition is significant because employment law imposes many obligations and rights on employers and employees. For example:

- The Safety, Health and Welfare at Work Act 1989 places a general duty on every employer to ensure the safety, health and welfare at work of all of its employees. This inevitably requires processing certain information about an employee's physical or mental health.

- The Employment Equality Act 1998 prohibits discrimination on nine grounds (gender, marital status, family status, sexual orientation, religion, age, disability, and race and traveller community). Employers need records about both applicants and employees to defend claims for discrimination in terms of access to or terms and conditions of employment.

- It is an offence to employ a non-EU resident without the appropriate work permit. Employers may therefore need records demonstrating that an employee has an appropriate work permit before taking him or her on.

- The Unfair Dismissals legislation may also be relied on to enable an employer to keep sickness records on the basis that they are necessary for the employer to ensure that it does not dismiss employees on the grounds of absence if it would be unfair to do so.

- The European Communities (Safeguarding of Employees' Rights on Transfer of Undertakings) Regulations 1981 and 2000 may also require the processing of sensitive data in certain circumstances concerning a merger or transfer of a business (see also Chapter 9).

There are some limitations on an employer's ability to rely on this sensitive data condition. First, such collection of the sensitive personal data must be "necessary" for the exercising or performing of the legal right or obligation. An employer must always therefore query whether the particular processing is "necessary". For example, certain information may only become necessary once a decision is made to take on an employee, but would not be necessary for the purposes of making a selection. Even if it is useful or convenient to have particular information, this will not suffice. It must be necessary.

One area of particular complexity is the appropriate level of health information to be gathered during recruitment and subsequently during employment. Employers must bear in mind the wide definition of "disability" in the Employment Equality Act and the fact that the disability can cover a current condition, a past condition, or a pre-disposition to a certain condition or illness. The Act specifically obliges an employer to provide special treatment or facilities for disabled employees so as to allow them to take up the job or take part in the selection process, as long as that special treatment is not more than a nominal cost.[16] This assessment clearly envisages employers obtaining a significant level of personal information about the individual's disability and health. Employers, however, should not abuse this or any other legal condition and must always be able to link the information sought with the decision being made, whether it is to recruit, facilitate or dismiss.

Processing necessary to prevent damage to health or property or otherwise to protect an individual's vital interests AND consent either cannot be obtained or the employer could not reasonably be expected to obtain the consent

This exemption could be relevant in an emergency where consent cannot be given by the individual (or the employer could not be expected to obtain such consent). For example, if an employee were taken suddenly ill and it was necessary to process certain sensitive medical information without his or her consent, this would be permitted. It could also be relevant where an employer had a concern about the mental stability of an employee and needed to release certain sensitive personal information to a family member with a view to protecting the employee.

Processing required to obtain legal advice or for legal proceedings or prospective legal proceedings

This exemption would be relevant where a claim of unlawful discrimination were made against the employer. It may also be necessary to process sensitive information in the context of any unfair dismissal proceedings or court proceedings for wrongful dismissal. The sensitive information would have to be relevant to the claim being defended. Many employers also seek legal advice about how to manage a difficult employment situation long before any proceedings issue and in circumstances where no proceedings might ever issue. It is permitted at any stage to disclose sensitive personal information to a legal advisor for the purposes of obtaining legal advice, regardless of whether litigation is contemplated. We will consider below the restrictions on an employee's ability to access such advice.

Processing necessary for medical purposes, including preventative medicine and undertaken by a health professional or someone else subject to an equivalent duty of confidentiality

This may arise in emergencies where information is held by a company doctor or similar person. It could also apply to information provided for a permanent health or occupational health scheme.

---

[16] Section 16 of the Employment Equality Act 1998.

The individual explicitly consents to the processing

Explicit consent is a primary condition which justifies the processing of sensitive data. It is sensible to include appropriate data protection consent clauses in every contract of employment. However, there is a some doubt as to whether such consent is freely given. A basic tenet of most employment protection legislation is the fact that there is a perceived power imbalance between employers and employees. This is why the law generally does not allow employment contracts to contain clauses which would deprive employees of statutory protection.[17] Many commentators have expressed doubts about the reliability of consent in an employment context.[18] They argue that if the employee faces the withdrawal of a benefit or dismissal if he refuses to consent, such consent is not freely given. In the early stages of recruitment, an individual may be regarded as having greater freedom whereas at an advanced stage of the recruitment process where a direct consequence of the employee not consenting would be the withdrawal of any job offer, it might again be argued that the consent was not freely given. Alternative views are possible and the point has not yet been authoritatively resolved by the courts in Ireland or elsewhere.

In addition, the consent must be explicit in order to satisfy the sensitive information processing condition. As discussed in Chapter 1, it is likely that this means that the individual should be told clearly what personal information is involved and what use would be made of it. Ideally, the individual should also give positive indication of agreement such as a signature.

Other sensitive information conditions

The other conditions permitting the processing of sensitive personal information are of limited relevance to employers as they assume the existence of a substantial public interest or processing connected with the prevention or detection of a crime. Such issues will only rarely arise in an employment context.

RIGHT OF ACCESS

Extent of right of access

The Commissioner has ruled that a request for access must be answered no matter "how inconvenient or disagreeable"[19] to a data controller unless the statutory restrictions apply.

Employers are no exception to this rule. Employers should consider a subject access procedure, informing employees of their right to access and the procedure to access information kept about them. This is not legally required but such a procedure helps ensure (and evidences) compliance with good employment practice and fairness to the individual. It also allows the employer organisation to retain an element of control over the process and to deal with frivolous or repeat requests.

---

[17] Section 13 of the Unfair Dismissals Act 1977.
[18] Including the UK Information Commissioner and the Article 29 Working Party.
[19] Case 3/97 in which employees sought access to a consultant's study.

Statutory restrictions on right of access

The statutory restrictions[20] on the right to access will be of limited relevance to employers. They can deny access where the information was kept to prevent or detect a crime. This may be useful for data gathered in monitoring or surveillance activities where a crime was suspected. The restriction on access to legally privileged information is more relevant. There are two main categories of legal professional privilege recognised by Irish courts[21]:

- Confidential communications between a person and his lawyer seeking or giving legal advice and documents created by either party to provide or to obtain such advice are privileged. This is known as "legal advice privilege".

- Documents created by either lawyer or client in anticipation or furtherance of litigation will also be privileged. Therefore, communications between a person and his lawyer which provide legal advice or assistance and documents created to obtain or produce such advice assistance will be privileged if given or created in anticipation or furtherance of litigation. This is known as "litigation privilege".

As set out earlier, many employers take legal advice about how to manage a difficult employee or employment situation. It is not always clear whether particular documents are legally privileged and it is important to bear this in mind when creating documents. One issue is the *purpose* when creating the document, specifically whether it was created in anticipation of legal proceedings or to obtain legal advice or whether the main purpose behind its creation was something else. It is clear, for example, that confidential correspondence with a lawyer to obtain legal advice is privileged. However, there may be situations where a document contains a mix of information, some of which is legally privileged and some of which is not. This is often the case with internal documents which may have been created with two purposes in mind, for example to provide a record of a disciplinary meeting and also to brief a lawyer. Managers need to be aware of the complexities of legal professional privilege if it is hoped to rely on it and to deny an employee access to certain documents on that basis.

Emails

Emails are also personal data and therefore employees are entitled to access emails about them. Given the volume of mail in any such organisation such a request could have huge practical issues. The UK code of practice gives some useful guidance to UK employers about this:

> "Employers are not though required to search through all email records merely on the off chance that somewhere there might be a message that relates to the worker who has made the request. For information to fall within the Data Protection Act's subject access provisions, the worker must be the subject of the information. This means, for example, that an email about a worker must be

---

[20] Section 5.
[21] *Smurfit Paribas Bank Ltd v AAB Export Finance Ltd* [1991] 1 I.R. 469 and *Gallagher v Stanley & the National Maternity Hospital* [1998] 2 I.R. 267.

provided. However, an email that merely mentions a worker, perhaps because his/her name appears on the email address list need not be provided. Employers should check wherever there is some likelihood that messages might exist, for example, in the mailbox of the worker's manager. In doing so, they should take into account any details the worker has provided to assist them in locating the information about him or her".[22]

This seems a sensible approach given the volume of emails which could exist in any workplace in which an individual employee's name might feature. The Irish Commissioner may well follow this approach when the issue arises here.

Information which identifies another person

Information which identifies another person presents a difficulty for employers when dealing with an access request, especially in the investigation of disciplinary matters on foot of a complaint by another employee. Some disciplinary investigations may be particularly sensitive where, for example, the allegation is of bullying or sexual harassment. Others are also entitled to have their personal information protected and the employer must balance the individual employee's right to access and others right of the other person to privacy. This involves an analysis of the particular circumstances. For example, if the disclosure of information would identify a fearful complainant in a bullying case, it may be permissible to refuse access. However, this argument is unlikely to have the same weight in a situation where a line manager is sensitive about the part which he or she played in a decision about a subordinate's promotion. If the employer can remove the other person's name, this should be done and the information disclosed. In an employment context, however, this will often not be the case as the other person will often be identifiable by other factors such as position or involvement in a particular issue.

Managing subject access requests

Although not a legal requirement, it is good practice to put in place a subject access procedure explaining to employees how any access request they may make will be dealt with and setting out in advance the fact that access requests must be formulated in a particular way and will be dealt with according to specific guidelines. Some employers may be concerned that the very existence of such a policy as an encouragement to employees to use the subject access mechanism. However, experience suggests that disaffected or disgruntled employees will avail of their access rights anyway and an employer who faces this and makes an effort to put in place some control mechanisms will be better placed than an employer with no policy at all.

Apart from introducing a subject access procedure, all organisations should advise and train managers and others about the nature and extent of information which an individual employee may be able to access.

---

[22] Available at *www.dataprotection.gov.uk/dpr/dpdoc.nsf*.

RETENTION OF EMPLOYMENT RECORDS

We considered this issue in the context of recruitment and selection at p. 45. All organisations should have a policy as to the retention of all personal information, including employees' information. Employment records, however, raise specific issues because of the wider range of information involved and the statutory requirements to retain certain records. For example, the Safety, Health and Welfare at Work Act 1989 and related regulations require employers to keep accident and injury records for 10 years. Similarly, the risk of an employee claim under contract or tort makes it sensible to retain other employment records for the six-year limitation period. If possible, employers should group together different types of information which need to be kept rather than retaining all personnel files where there is little or no reason for doing so. Unless there is a clear statutory requirement, the Data Protection Commissioner could query the risk which is being protected by retaining the records.

OUTSOURCING DATA PROCESSING

Outsourcing is becoming ever more common and extends to the management of employment information and functions to other organisations. Businesses often outsource payroll processing. Sometimes, an employer might engage a private investigator or other agent to collect personal information about an employee, for example where an employee is suspected of working elsewhere while in receipt of sick pay. In such situations, the private investigator and the payroll processor are "data processors" for the purposes of the Act. The employer remains the data controller and must implement appropriate security measures.

The employer should ensure that it has a written contract with the data processor. Such a contract should set out the technical and organisational measures taken to protect the personal information and obligations with respect to the personal information.

If the outsourcing involves a transfer of personal data to a country outside the EEA, particular issues arise. Those are dealt with at p. 23. However, the contract should also deal with this issue.

MERGERS AND ACQUISITIONS

This issue is dealt with fully in Chapter 9.

MONITORING AND SURVEILLANCE AT WORK

The privacy debate

Monitoring and surveillance of employees is a controversial issue, depending as it does on the balance between an employee's privacy rights and the employer's legitimate business interests. Advancing technology has further complicated the issue. On the one hand these advances have increased the risks to an employer through misuse of email and internet by employees. On the other hand the chances of intrusion into private communications or activities are increased.

In May 2002, the Article 29 Data Protection Working Party published its report on the issue of monitoring and surveillance of electronic communications in the workplace. Having considered the different rights and interests at stake, it recognised that balancing those different rights and interests:

> "takes a number of principles into account, in particular proportionality. It should be clear that the simple fact that a monitoring activity or surveillance is considered convenient to serve the employer's interest would not solely justify any intrusion in worker's privacy".[23]

Normal data protection principles apply to information collected by monitoring and surveillance. Monitoring and surveillance will therefore generally require the consent of individual employees or need to be permitted on one of the other grounds on which processing are permitted. Such practices will often be justified on the basis that monitoring is necessary to protect the employer's legitimate interests or to prevent or detect crime. Monitoring generally needs to be undertaken for a specified and legitimate purpose which has been made clear to the employees.

Practical implications

- If the stated purpose of monitoring internet access is to ensure the integrity of the organisation's computer systems, it could be incompatible with that purpose to use it for the purpose of disciplining an employee for excessive use of the internet.

- The employer should provide information, through a policy disclosing what monitoring may take place and why. This is true of telephone monitoring as well as email and internet access monitoring.

- The organisation's practice must match its policy. Any difference between the two could give rise to legal difficulties under both data protection and employment law.

- Employees should be told the consequences of any breach of their policy, and how the policy interacts with the company's disciplinary policy.

- Employees have a right to access personal information held about them and collected by monitoring and surveillance in the same way as they have a right to access any other kind of personal information. However, the Act specifically excludes a right to access any back-up data.[24]

- Data from an employee's email account or concerning his use of the internet must be accurate and kept up to date and not kept for longer than necessary. Employers should specify retention period for emails in their servers based on a business need.

---

[23] Available at *http://europa.eu.int/comm/internal_market/privacy/docs/wpdocs/2002/wp55_en.pdf.*
[24] Section 5(1)(i).

- The employer must also implement appropriate technical and organisational measures to ensure that the personal information is kept secure and safe from intrusion.

- Monitoring should be designed to prevent rather than detect misuse. This is particularly relevant with respect to the internet. It is preferable from a data protection perspective for employers to block access to inappropriate sites by using web filtering software rather than monitoring on an ongoing basis.

- Employers should try to prevent misuse by analysing levels of email traffic or recording time spent on the internet rather than monitoring the content or actual sites visited.

- Employers should consider targeting monitoring at areas of highest risk rather that in all areas of the business. If an employer can show a considered analysis of a risk before monitoring then the Commissioner is more likely to accept its reasonableness.

Covert monitoring

Covert monitoring is the most intrusive type of monitoring and surveillance. This usually involves hidden cameras or audio devices in the workplace or elsewhere. The data generated by the covert monitoring is covered by the Act and must therefore be processed fairly. Fair processing involves making the employee aware of the fact that information about them is being processed and why. This means that covert monitoring is unlawful except in certain limited circumstances, for example to prevent or detect a crime.

Care should be taken if a private investigator is used to collect the information on behalf of the employer that a contract is in place between the employer and the private investigator.

In a 1996 case,[25] the Commissioner looked at the privacy implications from the use of closed circuit TV (CCTV) systems and set out the importance of making clear the purpose of the CCTV and that the information collected must be adequate, relevant and not excessive. Given this concern, there is no doubt that the Commissioner would have a high level of concern about any footage collected by way of covert cameras in the workplace.

ALCOHOL, DRUG AND GENETIC TESTING

These specific types of monitoring involve sensitive personal data. Many employers operate alcohol and drug testing policies. For example, safety concerns for employers in the transport or construction industries clearly make such testing reasonable. Normal data protection principles are equally applicable and should be borne in mind in drawing up any policy. Few employers in Ireland carry out genetic tests and this is unlikely to change because the definition of "disability" under the Employment Equality Act 1998

---

[25] Case 14/96.

covers a predisposition to a disease or condition. Data collected through genetic test data is sensitive health data and since it will be difficult to justify the necessity for such screening, the Data Protection Act is an additional barrier to an employer's ability to conduct such testing.

FUTURE DATA PROTECTION DEVELOPMENTS FOR EMPLOYMENT LAW

The EU has been involved in a consultation process regarding the development of data protection law in the employment environment. The Commission has concluded that the specific issues which arise in an employment context mean that:

> "a European framework of common principles and rules is needed aiming at the protection of worker's personal data while striking a balance between the employer's legitimate interest and the worker's right to privacy".[26]

The scope and content of the proposed framework is not clear. However, the Commission's proposals cover the following points:

- Employee consent should not be relied upon to legitimise the processing of personal data because of the difficulties in ensuring it is genuine free consent, given the inherent power imbalance in the employment relationship. This particularly applies with respect to sensitive data.

- Processing of health data should be stringently restricted in an employment context and only permitted in three circumstances:

  - to determine whether the employee is fit to do the job;
  - to comply with the requirements of occupational health and safety;
  - to determine entitlement to social benefits.

- The Commission proposes particularly stringent rules with respect to drug testing and genetic testing because they are so intrusive and suggests that systematic generalised drug testing should only be necessary in particular safety-sensitive jobs. It is proposed that individual drug testing would only be justified where there is a reasonable suspicion that the particular employee was using drugs, regardless of the existence or otherwise of consent and that genetic testing should be limited to very exceptional circumstances where it is necessary to protect health and safety of the employee concerned or third parties.

- The Commission also proposes additional safeguards and guidelines with respect to the monitoring and surveillance of employees including a specific prohibition on an employer with respect to opening private email and/other private files regardless of whether the employer allows the use of work tools for private purposes. The Commission also proposes the prohibition of routine monitoring of each individual's email or internet use.

---

[26] Second Stage Consultation of Social Partners on the Protection of Workers' Personal Data (available on *http://europa.eu.int/comm./employment_social/news/2002/Oct/data_prot_en.html.*

Already a number of EU member states have specific legislation dealing with data protection in the workplace and Ireland may well follow suit.

COMPLIANCE CHECKLIST

All organisations should take certain steps to comply with the Act and to minimise industrial relations and other employment issues:

1. Conduct an audit of all personal information held about employees.	
2. Identify those in the organisation, including line managers, who may be collecting or processing data also.	
3. Train those individuals on the relevant implications of the Act including whether conducting interviews, performance appraisals, or investigating disciplinary issues.	
4. Eliminate the collection of personal data that is not relevant or excessive. Bear in the mind the justifiable reasons for processing data and specific conditions applicable to sensitive personal data.	
5. Give someone responsibility for data compliance including ensuring that all other employees who process data receive training on their responsibilities.	
6. Ensure that all employees who collect and process data (whether at recruitment or selection stage) through performance management of their own team or otherwise are aware of the provisions of the Act.	
7. Tell all employees of the nature of the data held about them and why it is processed. Give similar benefits to new recruits.	
8. Implement a data protection policy dealing with the type of personal data held, any sensitive personal data held, the purposes for which it is processed, to whom it is disclosed, whether there are any transfers abroad, whether disclosure might be necessary in the context of any merger or acquisition, and how it is stored. Each employee should sign the data protection policy consenting to the collection, processing, disclosure and transfer of their personal information.	
9. Implement a subject access procedure setting out how any access request will be dealt with and what circumstances an access request may be refused.	
10. Implement data processor agreements with any entities that process data on your behalf, e.g. payroll processors.	

CONCLUSION

An organisation will be better able to defend its position if it can show that it has considered and analysed its data protection employment issues thoroughly. The obligations of any employer can be summarised under three headings.

1. Audit every employment activity from a data protection compliance perspective

Such an audit involves a systematic review of a category of information obtained, held or passed on about employees, the sources of such information, the purpose for which it is processed and with whom it is shared.

2. Put in place processes to ensure compliance

Any process has a number of elements. It requires a series of policies, the most important of which is the data protection policy, published to all employees. However, it also requires guidelines and operating procedures such as data protection procedures, subject access guidelines and a disclosure policy. Every document produced or used by the organisation in an employment context should also be reviewed and a suitable form of wording included. The types of documents which should be amended to include data protection wording are job application forms, employment contracts, contracts with third party processors, contracts with recruitment agencies, interview forms, and CCTV and monitoring notices. A privacy statement should also be included on the employer's website to deal with any contact made or applications received in that way. The appropriate place to include any data protection wording is at the point of collection of information. The chart overleaf gives some examples of the standard operating procedures to be considered from an employment perspective.

3. Provide appropriate training and communication on data protection issues

Ideally workplace policies, such as the data protection policy, should be available to everybody in the organisation. The flowchart at the beginning of this chapter identified the range of staff and departments who might handle or manage employment information. All of these people need to be trained on the aspects of data protection which are relevant to them. This includes all those involved in performance management, disciplinary issues, recruitment, Human Resources, referees, etc. The following chart suggests who, within your organisation, should be trained on particular procedures or processes.

Standard operating Data Protection Procedures

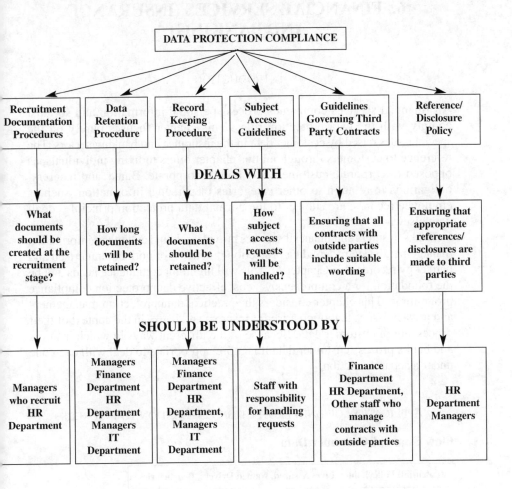

6. FINANCIAL SERVICES (INSURANCE AND BANKING)

INTRODUCTION

All financial services companies process personal information and so must comply with the data protection rules. This chapter focuses purely on the special issues raised by customer data in the insurance and banking sectors. The reference to customers throughout this chapter refers to living individuals, as opposed to corporate customers, *i.e.* bodies corporate. Banks and insurers' obligations in relation to other categories of personal information, such as employee records, are subject to the normal data protection principles dealt with elsewhere in this book.

Banks, insurers and financial services providers should audit their information management systems and data protection practices for both computerised and hard copy records (see Chapter 1). This will highlight compliance needs and be the foundation for a comprehensive, cost effective data protection compliance programme. This chapter considers the practical data protection management and privacy issues that often arise for insurers and banks in the context of their processing of customer data. Because of the different ways in which insurers and banks process customer data it is more appropriate to deal with each one under a separate section.

APPLICATION OF DATA PROTECTION LEGISLATION TO INSURERS

Flow Chart of Customer Data

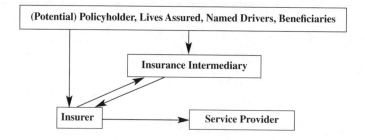

Jurisdiction and application of the Act

Insurers need to comply with Irish data protection law if they are established in Ireland or use equipment in Ireland for processing personal information (other than for the purposes of transit via computer through Ireland). "Establishment" is a broad concept and includes any insurer having an office, branch agency or regular practice in Ireland. In effect any insurer with any sort of presence in

Ireland is likely to be subject to the regime because insurers process personal information.

Insurers request specific and detailed personal information from their customers (*i.e.* policyholders and potential policyholders) in order to provide quotations and put insurance policies in place for them. They also request information to enable them to continue to administer their customers policies and/or (usually at the customer's request) amend their policy terms from time to time. Such information often includes sensitive personal information, such as medical information, particularly when a life insurance contract is being effected and/or quoted for. Insurers retain such customer data on their computer and manual record systems and process it for various purposes in the course of their business. Insurers, therefore, fall within the definition of data controller as they control the contents and use of customer data. We have discussed in Chapter 1 in more detail the meaning and consequences of being a data controller. In this section we only focus on its consequences in the context of insurers processing customer data.

Registration

All insurers processing personal information must register with the Commissioner's office. In practice it is hard to imagine any insurer who would not process at least some personal information. Processing of data without registration is illegal and an offence. The procedure for registration is straightforward and the process and costs associated with registration are discussed at p. 21.

When making an application for registration an insurer should list each purpose for which it intends to process customer data for example, the administration of insurance policies, processing claims and marketing new products to customers. A separate registration can be made with the Commissioner for each particular purpose for which the data is used. The insurer cannot use the customer data in any manner which is incompatible with the purposes for which it has registered. It is essential that the Data Protection Compliance Officer or whoever is responsible for the registration ensures the registration is clear, comprehensive and updated regularly to take account of any changes. Registrations must be renewed annually.

Registration of an intention to use personal data for a particular purpose does not overcome the need for insurers to comply with the general data protection rules, discussed in Chapter 1 and below.

Compliance issues

Insurers' management and staff may be subject to civil and criminal liability if they fail to comply with data protection laws. This is considered in Chapter 1.

The key compliance issues for insurers are:

- telling customers how and why their information will be used;

- getting consent to such use;

- the transfer of information to other parties and to countries outside Ireland;
- security.

Each of these issues is considered in more detail below. As explained in Chapter 1 an audit of an insurer's information management systems is the most straightforward means of identifying gaps in current practices and highlighting any breaches. By remedying such gaps and breaches a company minimises the risk of enforcement action being taken by the Commissioner and/or complaints from customers.

Processing or providing information to customers – the need for consent

Before processing, insurers must ensure that:

- the nature and extent of the processing has been explained to the (potential) policyholder; and
- the (potential) policyholder has consented to the processing of such information.

The insurer can only process the data if both of these criteria are met (unless one of the exemptions discussed in Chapter 1 applies, for example, where the processing of the personal information is necessary for the performance of the contract). Both of the criteria mentioned above are discussed in more detail below. The general data protection principles relating to the processing of personal information have been discussed in Chapter 1.

The nature and extent of the processing must be explained to the (potential) policyholder

This means insurers must tell (potential) policyholders the following:

1. Who is processing their information

The person who controls the data must be clearly identifiable to the customer. This will be the insurer itself but may also be the insurance intermediary who initially contacted the customer. (How this impacts on the use of insurance intermediaries is discussed below.) In recent times insurers (and indeed insurance intermediaries) are using diverse marketing channels to sell insurance, for example, motor car dealers, supermarkets and mobile telephone shops. Therefore, it is important that the customer understands who in the marketing chain is processing his personal data. The means by which insurance is being sold nowadays and its regulation is outside the scope of this text, but the above examples indicate that it may not be obvious to a customer who controls his personal data.

2. The nature of the information being held and the purpose(s) for which it is being processed

In most cases the (potential) policyholder will control the nature of information which is processed because he completes an application form. Sometimes, however, information may be obtained indirectly, for example, when an insurer obtains a medical report from a (potential) policyholder's doctor. In these circumstances an insurer must tell the (potential) policyholders what information they hold on them. More specific details about the nature of the information are required if sensitive data is processed and this is dealt with in more detail in Chapter 1 and below.

Examples of other information held by insurers

If it has not already been carried out, insurers (but generally not non-life insurers) are required to request certain documentation in order to satisfy money laundering identity checks, such as passports, utility bills, etc. The insurer should explain to the customer that it may only hold such documentation in order to verify customers' identity and verify a home address in accordance with the money laundering guidelines set out by the Irish Financial Services Regulatory Authority. Any additional information disclosed in such documentation cannot be processed by the insurer.

Where a medical report is required when taking out a life insurance policy the insurer must explain to the customer why the information is required and that it will be retained on the customer's file. The insurer should request the customer's consent to obtaining such a report from the customer's doctor. Such a report will constitute sensitive data. Explicit consent is needed for the processing of personal sensitive data. In processing personal sensitive data the insurer must outline to (potential) policyholders how this will be processed.

If an insurer wishes to carry out a credit check through a credit reference agency, it is important that the (potential) policyholder is informed of this fact and what the insurer does with such information.

An insurer may gather information through its website and some insurers' websites contain text files known as "cookies" which store information about a user. If cookies are used, the user should be informed of the information to be stored on the cookies, the purpose for which it is intended and the period for which the cookie is valid.

It is important for insurers to bear in mind that the insurer can only process information which is relevant for the purposes for which it was obtained. It cannot obtain information on the basis it might become relevant or useful in the future. Because insurers can generally only process information for the purposes known or explained to the individual, all possible uses of the information should be anticipated at the time of data capture if possible. Specifically any prospective uses of the data which would not be obvious to the (potential) policyholder (for example, direct marketing) should be disclosed. Any subsequent use for a non-disclosed purpose could require the policyholder to be contacted again which can have significant practical, commercial and financial consequences.

3. Who the data is to be disclosed to and other relevant information

Insurers must tell (potential) policyholders the persons/companies to whom they will disclose their data. Such persons may include other companies in the insurer's group, re-insurers, service providers, and regulatory authorities.

Additional relevant information which the (potential) policyholder should be made aware of might include, whether his data is to be sent outside the EEA.

If this is the case, and consent can be obtained, the (potential) policyholder should be told of the country(ies) to which it will be sent and the purposes for which it will be sent abroad. This is discussed in more detail in Chapter 1.

How should this information be communicated to (potential) policyholders?

The Act does not specify how this should be done. The easiest way to do this is to ensure insurer's documentation, *e.g.* marketing materials, proposal forms and consent forms (discussed below) contains such information. Insurers should check their existing forms and notices and, if they are not adequate, they should:

- revise their documentation;

- consider whether they need to circularise existing policyholders;

- consider placing information notices in future correspondence with existing policyholders.

Has the (potential) policyholder consented to the processing of such information?

The most convenient way to provide the information set out above and obtain consent is in application/proposal forms and fact finds, reflecting current market practice.

The wording on insurers' application forms and fact finds must be compatible and consistent with the insurers' registration with the Commissioner. There are certain situations when consent is not required and these are discussed in the context of the insurance industry below and in more detail in Chapter 1. The following are some situations where consent may not be required by an insurer from a (potential) policyholder:

- *If the processing is necessary for the performance of a contract or in order to take steps at the request of the data subject prior to entering into a contract.* When dealing with potential policyholders seeking quotations, insurers may be able to rely on the above statutory exemption. However, this exemption does not apply to sensitive personal information or to individuals other than the person making the request about whom the insurer requires information in order to give a quote, e.g. a named driver. On its face this exemption appears to limit insurers to using data to provide quotations to the individual customer and to no one else and for no other purpose. This also means that insurers should erase all personal information if a customer does not proceed to take out a policy (unless there is an objective justification for retaining it).

- *If the processing is carried out in compliance with a legal obligation to which the data controller is subject other than a duty imposed by contract.*

- *If the processing is necessary for the administration of justice or for the performance of any other public function.* This exception could be relied on if, for example, the Revenue Commissioners or the Criminal Assets Bureau were investigating tax evasion or money laundering offences.

Notwithstanding the above exemptions, it is best practice for an insurer to obtain consent to the use and processing of personal data in the insurer's documentation (e.g. application form or other relevant documentation).

One of the principal aims of the Act is to ensure that the data subject consents to the processing of his personal data. The requirement that a fully informed consent is obtained is designed to ensure that the individual controls and is fully informed how the data is used. The consent should be drafted to include explicit consent to the processing of customers' sensitive personal information where applicable. Other issues relevant to the issue of the data subjects consent are direct marketing and automated decision making discussed below.

Insurers will often receive personal information about individuals other than the person completing the proposal form. For example, an applicant might provide details of other individuals who are to be named drivers, lives assured or beneficiaries. In some of these limited circumstances it may be sufficient for the (potential) policyholder only to sign the consent wording in the proposal form. However, the information relating to the other party(ies) being provided to the insurer must be relevant and minimal. This must be considered on a case by case basis and will depend on the information being provided (for example, this would not apply where detailed financial information relates to another individual.)

The Act does not specify how consent should be obtained. Written consent is most desirable from an evidentiary point of view, and as stated above written consent in the proposal/application forms or fact finds (for quotations) is the easiest way to obtain this. Any consent wording should be drafted in clear intelligible language so that a (potential) policyholder can understand what he or she is agreeing to in respect of his or her personal information.

If consent cannot be obtained in writing but is obtained orally, for example, over the telephone, a detailed policy statement should be read to the (potential) policyholder and his acknowledgement and agreement obtained. A record of this should be kept by the insurer. Similarly, where consent is obtained over the internet, a detailed policy statement should be displayed on the screen and the (potential) policyholder requested to accept by clicking on an accept option on the screen.

An audit of an insurer's information management systems should allow it to formulate a comprehensive consent wording. Such wording should include:

- who holds the data;
- the purposes for which it will be held;
- the persons to whom it will be disclosed; and
- whether it will be sent outside the EEA. It should also include wording to deal with sensitive data (discussed below) and refer to direct marketing and, if appropriate, automated decision making (also referred to below).

Direct marketing

Insurers wishing to market new products to (potential) policyholders must allow them to opt out or object to receiving such mailings. The easiest way to do this is to include "opt out" wording in the application/proposal form and in "fact finds" (in the case of potential policyholders) by providing a box which the policyholder can tick to object to the mailing. The Irish Direct Marketing Association (IDMA) has published a data protection code of practice which binds is members. Many insurers are members of IDMA.

If an insurer receives a request from a customer not to use his personal information for marketing purposes in the future (for example if he didn't opt out previously or has changed his mind) the insurer is obliged to comply with such a request and must within 40 days erase such data. If the data is retained for other purposes, the insurer must refrain from further processing the data for marketing purposes.

Automated decision making

Subject to very limited exemptions (see p. 16) decisions concerning policy-holders or potential policyholders cannot be made by insurers solely on the basis of automated decision making.

The provision relating to automated decision making is of particular relevance to insurers in today's market which demands speedy and often semi-automated processing of applications. The Act provides that insurers may not stipulate the terms of a policy purely on the basis of, for example, the age, medical history, gender or other personal attributes of the individual without making further inquiry and without allowing for the input/clarification of the proposed policyholders. Unless the exemptions discussed in Chapter 1 can be relied on (for example, where the customer has consented), insurers cannot fully automate the compilation process and produce a decision as to whether and on what terms the customer would be insured. Legal advice should be obtained by insurers if they wish to implement any such systems.

Sensitive data

Explicit consent of the customer is required by an insurer in order to process sensitive data. Sensitive data means details of:

• racial or ethnic origin, political opinions or religious or philosophical beliefs of the data subject;

• physical or mental health or condition or sexual life of the data subject;

• trade union membership;

• the commission or alleged commission of any offence by the data subject;

• any proceedings for an offence committed or alleged to have been committed by the data subject, the disposal of such proceedings or the sentence of any court in such proceedings.

Explicit consent means a clear and unambiguous consent must be given by the (potential) policyholder to the processing of their sensitive information. Insurers often obtain sensitive data in the context of life insurance applications where they require a potential policyholder to undergo a medical examination by their doctor and the doctor's report is sent to the insurer's actuary to assess whether the risk will be covered and if so at what premium. Non-life insurers may also obtain medical reports when claims are being assessed. Therefore, it is important to ensure that explicit consent is obtained from all individuals about whom the insurer will hold such data.

Service providers

It is increasingly common for insurers to outsource certain back office activities, such as premium processing, claims handing, marketing and payroll processing. It is often more cost effective for insurers to engage third party administrators (TPAs) to provide such services so insurers can concentrate on their core business. In such cases, the TPA is a data processor for the purposes of the Act. When an insurer engages a TPA the insurer retains control of the personal information it passes on to the TPA to process and the insurer is obliged to ensure that appropriate security measures are put in place. In such cases, the insurer must enter into a contract with the TPA to ensure the TPA processor:

- acts only in accordance with the instructions of the insurer;

- guarantees that appropriate organisational and technical measures are in place to protect unauthorised access to the data or loss/destruction of the data.

The insurer must take reasonable steps to ensure that the TPA processor complies with its undertakings and this obligation is ongoing.

Transferring policyholder data abroad

Insurers often transfer personal information outside Ireland, particularly if their head office is overseas and/or they seek to have data processed by a sister company.

Transfers within the EEA are permissible because these countries are deemed to have adequate data protection laws. Normal data protection principles (which are discussed in Chapter 1) must still be followed. The rules for transfer are discussed in detail at p. 23.

In summary transfers cannot be made outside the EEA unless:

- the country to which the personal information is being transferred is white-listed by the EU Commission;[1] or

- a model contract in a form approved by the EU Commission is put in place with the provider; or

- the Commissioner approves the transfer of the data; or

- one of the statutory exemptions (see p. 25) applies to the transfer; or

- there is consent to the transfer.

Insurers usually deal with this issue by obtaining the unambiguous consent to the transfer of personal information outside the EEA in application/proposal forms. However, if that is not feasible and no other exemptions can be relied on, in certain circumstances the insurer should seek the approval of the

---

[1] At present Hungary, Switzerland, Argentina, some Canadian companies and US companies who have signed up to the safe harbour principles have been "whitelisted".

Commissioner. It is important to bear in mind that even transfers between group companies are subject to the prohibitions on transfer in the Act.

Security

Insurers must take reasonable security measures against unauthorised access to or unauthorised alteration, disclosure or destruction of personal information and against all other forms of processing, especially if personal information is transmitted over a network.

The Act says in such circumstances the insurer may consider the state of technological development and the cost of implementing measures. In determining "reasonable security measures" the insurer must ensure that the measures provide a level of security appropriate to the harm that might result from unauthorised or unlawful processing.

Insurers should take all reasonable steps to ensure that their employees and others working on their premises understand and comply with the relevant security measures which have been put in place.

The Commissioner has made some helpful comments on these security obligations. In one case[2] he recommended that computer screens which displayed personal information should be placed in private and secure positions away from public scrutiny and that the data controller's staff should be reminded to be careful when accesing or displaying such customer personal information. In another case[3] the Commissioner (commenting on laptop passwords) stated that data controllers should ensure that personal information does not become more widely accessible than is necessary. He commented that restricting the availability of personal information is one of the "appropriate security measures" that data controllers should consider.

Another case[4] concerned an ex-employee of a life assurance company who failed to return a laptop computer containing customer data (despite numerous attempts by the company to get it back). The ex-employee, who was then working for another insurer, contacted a customer of his previous employer. The customer complained to the Commissioner. The Commissioner upheld the complaint and emphasised the need for insurers as data controllers to have firm and enforceable procedures in place to ensure that they do not lose control of personal information for which they are legally responsible. This duty extended to circumstances when employees left an organisation. He recommended that companies provide for the automatic deletion of records (which the life assurance company subsequently did).

Obligation to keep data up to date and rights of customers

The obligations of data controllers to keep customer information accurate, complete and up to date were discussed at Chapter 1. Insurers hold a wide range of personal information (for example details of current employment, salary, next of kin, and medical records) and must ensure systems are in

---

[2] Case 6/96.
[3] Case 1/98.
[4] Case 2/99.

place to enable customer records to be updated appropriately. Out-of-date information should be deleted.

The rights which policyholders and potential policyholders enjoy under the Act include:

- a right of access to the data;
- a right to have their data blocked, rectified or erased;
- a right to have processing stopped in certain circumstances;
- a right to complain to the Commissioner.

Right of access

The following are some observations as to how this will affect insurers:

The right of access (unless it is restricted – see Chapter 1) gives customers an opportunity to ascertain what information is held on them and to obtain a copy of this. The customer is entitled to be informed of the type of data held, the recipients of the data and the purposes for which it is held, and to be provided with these details in an intelligible form. If the processing is by automatic means and this was or was likely to constitute the sole basis for any decision affecting the customer, then the customer is entitled to be informed for free of the logic involved in the processing. Requests must be complied with within 40 days of the request. It is open to insurers to charge a fee of up to €6.35 for such a request (except in the case of automatic processing where individuals are entitled to be informed for free of the logic involved in such processing). The only obligation on the individual is to apply in writing. The insurer may request further information if necessary to comply with the request. If repeated requests are received and the insurer has already responded the insurer can refuse until a "reasonable interval" has elapsed.

Policyholders' and potential policyholders' rights of access can put a considerable administrative burden on insurers and lead to increased costs. To streamline the process we recommend putting an access policy in place and training staff in respect of such policy. A data protection compliance officer should be put in charge of all such requests and ensure that the access policy is being adhered to.

Restrictions on rights of access

The restrictions on customers access rights have been discussed in chapter 1, but it is worthwhile mentioning one of these in the context of the insurance industry as it may be a useful exemption in refusing an access request, namely:

> "[where the data is] kept for the purpose of preventing, detecting or investigating offences, apprehending or prosecuting offenders or assessing or collecting any tax, duty or other moneys owed or payable to the State, a local authority or a health board, in any case in which the [access application] would be likely to prejudice any of the matters aforesaid."[5]

---

[5] Section 5(1)(a).

It is important to note that insurers cannot release a medical report unless they have obtained an opinion from a medical practitioner that the release of information is not likely to cause harm to the individual.

The rights of policyholders to have their data blocked, rectified or erased

Customers have rights to insist that data held is blocked, rectified or erased where the information is inaccurate, out of date or has been collected without their knowledge in contravention of the Act. Such request must be made in writing to the insurer. The insurer must respond within 40 days indicating compliance or a refusal to comply. Customers can appeal to the Commissioner. Insurers can comply with requests that their information be rectified on the basis that it is inaccurate or out of date by putting a supplementary statement on their files updating the information. Where the customer requires insurers to modify any information held by them, insurers must notify the changes to anyone to whom they disclosed the information during the preceding 12 months (unless its proves impossible or involves disproportionate effort.)

Records and retention of documents

The Act does not set out specific periods for which documents containing personal information should be retained by insurers. However, insurers must not keep personal information for any longer than necessary for the purposes for which it was obtained subject to any relevant statutory retention periods. In addition, insurers must keep personal information up to date. Insurers must take these obligations into account in the context of their document retention policies. All insurers should have a clear document retention policy in operation complying with statutory retention periods.

Where there are no specific legislative provisions, documents should be retained for a "reasonable" period, that is as long as there is an objective business reason for their retention. (Some documents of course should be retained indefinitely, for example, property title documents.)

Other relevant matters

Transfer/sale of insurance business

The sale of an insurance business can take place either by way of share transfer or asset transfer. An asset transfer includes a transfer of the portfolio of insurance contracts, and if the head office of the insurer is in Ireland it requires the sanction of the High Court. If there is a full or partial portfolio transfer, the personal information held by the transferor insurer will be passed on and "disclosed to the transferee insurer on the effective date of the transfer". A number of issues arise in this context and legal advice should be taken at the time of considering the transfer on this point.

If the transfer takes place by way of a share transfer, there is no transfer or disclosure of personal information as there is no change in the data controller (i.e. the insurance company is the data controller and all that is changed is the ownership of the company but it is still the same legal entity). The sale of shares in an insurance company raises other legal and regulatory issues outside the scope of this text.

Insurance intermediaries

Insurance intermediaries (that is insurance brokers, agents and tied agents) be they individuals, bodies corporate, partnerships or other entities are subject to data protection law.

All data controllers and processors must register unless exempt under the legislation. Insurance intermediaries must register because they are data controllers in respect of the personal information they collect and hold in relation to their customers and employees.[6] Sometimes the relationship between the insurer and the insurance intermediary may mean that the intermediary is also a processor, *e.g.* if it processes claims for the insurer.

The relationship between the intermediary, the insurer and their customers means that the processing of personal information can be divided into three areas, namely:

* the personal information which the intermediary collects and uses about its customers;

* the personal information which the insurer collects and uses about the intermediary; and

* the personal information the insurer collects and uses about its (potential) policyholders.

Each of these is considered briefly below.

Intermediary processing personal information about its customers

The intermediary must ensure that it has the appropriate authority to process the personal information it holds about its customers, that is the personal information it holds in its own right.

An intermediary usually holds personal information about its customers so it can advise them as to the various types of insurance policies available. Intermediaries should get the customer's consent to holding that customer's personal information at the initial consultation, either through the intermediary's own customer form, a fact find or a similar document in writing. If this is not possible, oral consent should be obtained and recorded on a telephone call. Similarly where consent is obtained over the internet the potential policyholder should be requested to click on an "accept" button. The same considerations as discussed in the context of insurers obtaining consent apply. The intermediary will usually then provide the customer with the insurer's application form (which ought to contain seperate consent wording) for a specific product which the customer will complete. That form containing the personal information of

---

[6] For the registration process see Chapter 1.

the customer will then be sent to the insurer who is the data controller in respect of that information.

The insurer processing personal information about the intermediary

Information held about a company is not personal information but personal information held about the directors or staff would be personal information and data protection law will apply to this information.

Data protection laws will also apply if the intermediary is an individual or group of individuals. The insurer should ensure it has the individual's consent to process their personal information. This consent is usually dealt with in the agreement appointing the intermediary. The consent wording in the agreement should be sufficiently broad to cover all of the processing to be carried out by the insurer.

The Insurer processing personal information on its policyholder

We have mentioned that the insurer requires consent from policyholders (and from others about whom they hold personal information, e.g. lives assured and beneficiaries), in order to process their personal information. Where an intermediary is involved consent will also be necessary. The consent wording should include a provision allowing the insurer to pass information to the intermediary. This is to ensure that the insurer has the requisite authority to pass on any additional information which it holds over and above that obtained by the intermediary initially so that the intermediary obtains such information fairly.

Insurers often ask intermediaries to carry out certain administrative duties for them, for example claims processing. The policyholder should have consented to this in appropriate terms and the intermediary must comply with its obligations as a processor. As discussed in Chapter 1 the insurer should also enter into a written data processor agreement with the intermediary. This contract should include the following provisions:

- the intermediary will only process the policyholder information as instructed by the insurer;

- the intermediary will put adequate technical and organisational measures in place to ensue the security of the (potential) policyholders' information.

COMPLIANCE CHECKLIST

Key points for insurers to consider in the context of their audit.

1. Has information about the processing of the customer's data been given to him and have the necessary consents been obtained to process the data and/or do application/other forms (e.g. fact finds) need to be revised?	
2. Is the data used for direct marketing purposes? If so is there appropriate "opt out" wording in the application form/elsewhere?	
3. Is data transferred to countries outside of the EEA and if so have appropriate measures been taken to comply with the law?	
4. Are service providers engaged to assist with processing? If so are appropriate contracts in place with them?	
5. Is there a designated Data Protection Compliance Officer who deals with the compliance with the, Act including responding to access requests and training staff?[7]	
6. Is the insurer registered and has this registration been renewed and updated?	
7. Are the security systems in place to protect the personal information satisfactory in the circumstances?	
8. Has an appropriate system been put in place to deal with access requests and to carry out audits of data protection compliance procedures on a regular basis?	
9. Has a document retention policy been put in place in compliance with the law?	
10. Are staff aware of the consequences of non-compliance with the Act and have they been adequately trained?	

---

[7] There is no legal requirement to appoint a compliance officer. However, this can be an effective means of monitoring and ensuring ongoing compliance as well as dealing with customers' requests.

IMPLICATIONS OF THE DATA PROTECTION ACT
FOR THE BANKING SECTOR

Flow of Personal information

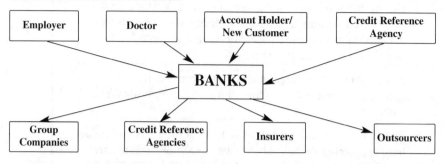

Registration

Banks request specific and detailed personal information about their customers in order to open and administer customer accounts, approve applications for personal loans, credit cards or mortgages, and generally to provide normal banking services. Such information is retained by banks on customer's files (both electronic and paper)[8] and processed for different purposes. Banks therefore fall within the definition of data controllers as they have control over the nature and content of the data, the uses of the data and the parties to whom it may be disclosed. As data controllers, banks must register with the Data Commissioner.[9]

The procedure for registration is a simple process whereby a bank completes an application form and submits it to the Data Commissioner together with a minimal fee. This process is set out in detail on p. 21.

When making an application for registration, a bank should list each purpose for which it intends to hold customer information; for example, the administration of bank accounts, the establishment of a credit history, or the marketing of new types of savings accounts or investment plans.

Banks cannot use customer information for any purpose other than the purposes registered with the Data Commissioner. A separate registration can be made with the Data Commissioner in respect of each purpose for which customer information is held. Although separate registrations for different uses of customer data are not required under the Act, they will allow a bank to reflect a clear distinction between different uses of customer data in different areas of banking business, *e.g.* information used for the purposes of deposit taking and secured lending, information to be transferred to data processors[10] such as marketing agencies, information to be transferred to different entities

---

[8]   See p. 5.

[9]   Banks (as financial institutions) were required to register under the 1988 Act. They are required to register under the amended legislation which provides for universal register for all data controllers.

[10]   See p. 21.

within the banking group such as car finance or life assurance entities. Each purpose notified to the Data Commissioner will be noted in a register.

Registrations with the Data Commissioner should be renewed annually. Failure to register is a criminal offence.[11]

Jurisdiction and application of the Act

The Data Protection Act applies to banks that are "established in Ireland". Banks that maintain an "office, branch or agency in Ireland, through which [they] carry on any activity or a regular practice" will be deemed established in Ireland.[12]

Accordingly, banks from elsewhere in the EU which have passported into Ireland in accordance with the Banking Consolidation Directive[13] and have established a branch in Ireland will be subject to the Irish data protection laws.

An audit of a bank's information management system

As explained at p. 8, an audit of a banking information system is a useful procedure to identify the type of information that is collected from customers through the sale/promotion of banking products, etc. The following sections outline the obligations of a bank in obtaining, managing and processing such customer information under the Act and highlight areas where a bank should be mindful of current practices to ensure that it does not fall foul of the provisions of the Act. This section can be used by banks when carrying out an audit of its information system to help identify discrepancies in its data control and to help identify areas where its data protection procedures could be improved or updated.

Obtaining and processing data lawfully and fairly

A relationship between a customer and a bank usually begins with a request from an individual to open a bank account. It is from this point on that a bank should ensure that its procedures in relation to data protection are in place and adequate. The Act provides that in order for the collection of information to be fair and lawful and for a bank to be compliant, it must ensure that all personal information obtained from customers is obtained fairly and transparently, that customers are aware of all information held, the uses for which it is intended and the parties to whom it will be transferred or disclosed.

An audit of the type of information that can be elicited from customers from the sale and/or maintenance of different banking products, including products offered by other members within the banking group such as car insurance or life assurance, will greatly assist a bank in identifying whether or not its existing consent declarations and registrations with the Data Commissioner are broad enough to capture all types of information held and the uses of such information. Such an exercise may also highlight areas where a bank may be

---

[11] See Chapter 3.
[12] Section 1(3B)(b)(iv)(I) and (II).
[13] EU Banking Consolidation Directive 2000/12/EC.

gathering information about a customer of which the customer is not aware and indeed a type of information of which the bank is not aware, for example, sensitive data. In order for a bank to validly process such information, a customer's consent may be required and a revised registration may have to be made with the Commissioner.

Data controller to be clearly identifiable

The person who controls the information must always be clearly identifiable to a customer. In the majority of cases this will be the bank itself. Increasingly, however, banks are entering into joint ventures and affinity arrangements with other commercial businesses, such as supermarkets, to offer products such as credit cards. For example, the joint venture company may promote the credit card offer through the supermarket and then process the customer information on the application form. The customer should be aware of the identity of the joint venture company and that the joint venture company is the data controller of his personal information.

The nature of the information which is held and the purposes for which the data will be processed

As stated above, an audit of information to be obtained from customers in respect of different banking products is a useful exercise to identity the nature of information held and its uses in order for this to be disclosed to a customer. In most situations, however, the customer will be in control of the information disclosed to the bank and therefore will be aware of the nature of the information held by the bank. The type of information held on a customer file and each of the purposes for which a bank intends to process that information should be made absolutely clear to the customer.

Examples of the nature of information held by a bank include the following:

- Banks are required by law to request certain documentation in order to satisfy anti-money laundering requirements, such as a passport, utility bills, social insurance documentation and/or other specified documentation. Customers may occasionally be reluctant to produce such documentation and may question its necessity. A bank should explain to its customer that it is obliged by law to request such documentation and that it may only hold such documentation in order to verify the customer's personal identity and home address in accordance with money laundering guidelines issued by the Money Laundering Steering Committee.[14] Banks should note that any additional information that may be disclosed in such documentation, *e.g.* a personal public service (PPS) number, cannot be isolated from the documentation provided specifically for money laundering purposes and processed by the bank for its own purposes.

- Before approving a loan application, is it usual for a bank to carry out a credit check through a credit reference agency in order to establish a customers' credit rating. It is important that the customer is aware that

---

[14] The Criminal Justice Act 1994; Guidance Notes for Credit Institutions, November, 2001.

such a search will be performed and the information obtained will be retained by the bank and used in deciding whether or not to approve such loan application.

- A bank may also gather information on its customers and other users through its website. Some banking websites contain text files (cookies) which store information about a user, *e.g.* pages viewed and advertisements clicked and can be used to create a detailed user profile. If cookies are used on the website, the user should be informed of the information to be stored on the cookie, the purpose for which it is intended and the period for which the cookie is valid. The user should be given the option to accept or reject the sending or storing of the cookie. This principal equally applies to other software applications such as JavaScript.

Other relevant information

If a bank intends to engage a data processor to process information on its behalf, this should be disclosed to the customer. This might involve, for example, engaging a marketing firm to target certain customers in respect of a new type of savings account or equity based investment account.

Similarly, if the bank wishes to transfer the data to other companies within the banking group, to countries outside the EEA, to credit rating agencies, to insurers or to regulatory authorities, this must also be disclosed to the customer.

Obtaining customer consent to use data and disclose data to third parties

One of the principal aims of the Act is to strengthen an individual's position with respect to his personal information and how that information is to be used. By obtaining a valid consent from an individual, that individual is provided with an opportunity to control what happens to his personal information.

Is consent actually required?

The Act provides for certain situations in which consent may not be required and these have been discussed in detail at p. 12.

As a general rule, banks must obtain customer consent before processing information in respect of a banking product. However, there are certain limited circumstances in which a bank may "process" information without customers consent. Examples of such situations are set out below:

If the processing is necessary for the performance of the contract or in order to take steps at the request of the data subject prior to entering into a contract.

On a strict interpretation of this provision, where personal information is obtained from an individual in order to assess the possibility of entering into a contract with them, consent is not required.

Therefore, in a situation where an individual approaches a bank with which that individual has no previous banking relationship and applies for a credit card, is the bank obliged to obtain the individual's consent to process the application?

No consent is required to process the individual's information until the bank has made a decision as to whether or not it will approve the credit card application. However, once such approval is given, consent of the individual will be required and the bank will have to follow up with the individual to obtain the appropriate consents. A more practical, less costly and time consuming alternative is to obtain the appropriate consents at the outset when the individual is completing the application form.

Clearly, however, if consent is obtained at the outset and the credit card application is not approved, the bank would not be entitled to retain the information and such information should be deleted.

If the processing is carried out in compliance with a legal obligation to which the data controller is subject other than a duty imposed by contract.

As stated above, in order for a bank to open a customer account, it must ensure that the provisions relating to money laundering are complied with as set down in the money laundering guidelines. If a customer fails or is unable to provide all the information necessary to verify personal identity and address, the guidelines provide other methods of verification that a bank could utilise. Such methods include a search on the electoral register, a credit reference agency check or a check of a local telephone directory or street directory. These search methods can be undertaken by a bank without the consent of the individual because such searches are necessary to satisfy legal obligations with respect to anti-money laundering before a bank account can be opened in the name of the customer.

Banks should be mindful that although the money laundering guidelines also state that methods such as telephone contact at home or work or an employer will suffice to verify personal and address identity, where such contact is made to satisfy money laundering requirements in order to approve a loan/credit agreement which falls within section 46 of the Consumer Credit Act 1995, the written consent of the customer must be obtained.

If the processing is necessary for the administration of justice or for the performance of any other public function.

This exception relates to the processing of data at the request, for example, of the Revenue Commissioners or the Garda Bureau of Fraud Investigation in order to detect or investigate claims of money laundering, tax evasion or other crimes.

How is consent to be obtained?

The most appropriate method of obtaining customer consent to hold, use, process and disclose data is at the initial application stage for a product. The Act does not specify that consent must be obtained in any particular format. Written consent is obviously the most desirable form of consent but may not always be appropriate. In order for consent to be valid, the extent and nature of that consent must be clear.

Bank account, mortgage, personal loan, or credit card application forms are the most appropriate means to obtain a valid consent and should contain a data protection statement which is broad enough to encompass all of the purposes for which the bank intends to use information. Provision should be made on the application forms for a customer's signature to confirm that he specifically consents to all such processing of his information.

Where consent is to be obtained over the internet, a detailed policy statement on data protection should be formulated by the bank and the customer should able to acknowledge and agree the policy statement by clicking an option on the computer screen.

Similarly, where consent is to be obtained over the telephone, a detailed policy statement should be read out to the customer and the customer requested to acknowledge and agree such terms and conditions. An application form should then be posted to the customer to be filled out and returned with the consent declarations acknowledged and signed by the customer.

Specific issues to be addressed when drafting consent declarations are discussed below.

Direct marketing

A data protection statement should be drafted in such a way as to give a customer the option to decide which information can be processed for certain uses and which may not.

This distinction is particularly relevant in the area of direct marketing. A data protection statement should contain a separate consent declaration for the use of data for the purposes of direct marketing and the customer should be able to specifically "opt-out" of such use (see wording provided at p. 15).

If a bank receives a customer request not to use his personal information for marketing purposes, the bank is obliged to comply with such a request and must, within 40 days, erase such data. If the data is retained for a number of purposes, only one of which is marketing, the bank must refrain from further processing such data for marketing purposes.

Automated decision making – consent required

The Act prohibits data controllers from making decisions using processes based solely on automatic means and which decisions would significantly affect an individual and are intended to evaluate certain matters relating to that individual, such as creditworthiness.

This provision will have an impact on banks as automated decision making tools are commonly used in deciding whether or not to approval personal loans or mortgage applications. Computer software programs are used to apply credit scoring techniques using data such as an individual's current and potential earning capacity, expenses and lifestyle, current borrowings and loan history, etc. in order to assess the suitability of an applicant for a particular product and determine the ability of the individual to make monthly repayments.

There are two cases in which decisions made by way of automated decision making processes will be deemed "exempt decisions" under the Act[15]:

Case 1: The decision is to be made in order to decide (a) whether or not to enter into a contract with the individual or in the course of performing such a contract; **or** (b) the decision is authorised by law and the individual has been informed of the proposal to make the decision;

---

[15] Section 6B.

AND in the case of (a) or (b) either

(i) the effect of the decision is to grant the request of the individual; **or**

(ii) adequate steps have been taken to protect the interests of the individual, for example, allowing for representations to be made on behalf of the individual.

Case 2: The individual has consented to the automated decision making process.

In what circumstances will a decision by a bank made using automated means be deemed an "exempt decision"?

Example:

An individual approaches a bank and fills out a mortgage application form. The bank uses automated tools to apply a credit scoring technique in order to assess the suitability of the applicant.

Case 1: The bank has satisfied the first part of the exemption as this automated process has been applied for the purpose of deciding whether or not to enter into a contract with that individual, *i.e.* whether or not to approve the mortgage application. The bank, alternatively, can inform the customer that credit scoring techniques will be used to assess his application.

In order to satisfy the second part of the exemption, (i) the decision of the bank must be positive and the mortgage application must be approved, or (ii) if the decision is negative, the bank must take steps to ensure the applicants legitimate rights are protected, *i.e.* allow representations on behalf of the applicant to be made.

If the decision of the bank is not to grant the mortgage and no representations could be made by the customer, the bank would not be able to rely on the automated process solely as a means of determining the customer's suitability for a mortgage.

Case 2: The customer must have consented to the use of credit scoring techniques as the sole factor in determining whether his mortgage application form will be approved.

In general, results of an automated process are only one factor in a range of factors used to determine whether to approve a loan/mortgage application and therefore may fall outside the automated decisions specifically prohibited by the Act. However, if a bank does rely solely on an automated decision making process for certain products, the results of which would significantly affect the applicant, such processes should then be structured so as to include a right of representation for the applicant in a situation where the application is initially denied.

Specific issues for consent declarations

After having reviewed the types of information gathered as part of an information audit for a banking system, it would be advisable to conduct a review of all documentation such as account opening documentation, credit card, loan or mortgage application forms, and any other documentation which requires personal information to be disclosed by a customer and which information will be processed. This exercise would provide an opportunity to ensure that all documentation contains a data protection statement which is broad enough to encompass all of the purposes for which the bank intends to use customer information and for which purposes it is registered with the Data Commissioner.[16]

If customer information is held for purposes other than those notified to the Data Commissioner, an amended registration may be necessary and if appropriate, customer consent should be obtained.

A bank should consider the following issues when drafting consent declarations:

* consent to contact and/or mail the customer for direct marketing purposes;

* consent to disclose data to other parties (including other companies within the same group);

* consent to transfer data to countries outside the EEA;[17]

* explicit consent if sensitive data will be processed.

Sensitive data

Sensitive data is dealt with at p. 16 and includes information in relation to racial or ethnic origin, information on health or sexual life, trade union membership, religious, political or philosophical beliefs.

Sensitive data may arise, for example, in the context of a life assurance policy that is required in order to approve a mortgage application where a customer is required to answer questions in relation to his health and a doctor is to submit a medical report (if appropriate). However, this requirement will usually come from a life assurance company and it is the responsibility of that insurance company rather than the bank to obtain the appropriate consents to process sensitive data as data controller.

An area where a bank may unwittingly be recording sensitive data is by way of a customer's credit card statements or bank account statements. Such statements may record details such as subscriptions to certain charitable organisations, trade unions or political parties that may suggest a particular ethnic origin or political belief. This type of information constitutes sensitive personal data.

As part of an information audit, again it is advisable for banks to consider the type of information recorded in respect of each of its products to determine if sensitive data is being recorded and if so, put procedures in place to ensure the appropriate consents are obtained.

Retention of data that is accurate complete and up to date

The Commissioner has emphasised in a case study[18] that the Act places a clear and active obligation on data controllers to ensure that data is kept accurate and up to date and has said that this is especially important in the case of credit records where inaccuracies can have a significant bearing on people's livelihood.

---

[16] See p. 21.
[17] The EEA consists of countries within the EU, Norway, Iceland and Liechtenstein.
[18] Case Study 6/99.

Banks must ensure that customer records are accurate, complete and up to date and must take all reasonable steps to ensure that any data that is inaccurate or incomplete is erased or rectified. The type of information that may be held in respect of a customer would include the following details:

- customer name, address, age and next of kin;
- current employment, salary level;
- past borrowings, repayments made, loans cleared, loans refused;
- any credit cards held;
- any credit agency searches.

Banks should have a system in place that will enable customer records to be updated appropriately. Any information in respect of a customer that is out of date should be deleted.

Customers are entitled to make an application to review information held on their file (see p. 27) and if the recorded information does not accurately reflect a customer's banking history or is out of date, the customer is entitled to take a civil action against the bank where the customer has suffered damage as a result of the bank's failure to comply with the Act. In addition, failure by a bank to update its customers' information could have consequences for the future credit rating of a customer and may result in a prosecution of the bank under the Act.

The Commissioner has reported on an investigation into claims by a complainant who had difficulty in getting a mortgage that his record with a credit reference agency was incorrect.[19] The credit agency's record related to a hire-purchase agreement and showed that part of the complainant's loan had been written off and that litigation had been pending against him. This was disputed by the complainant.

The Commissioner established that the loan in question had been for a term of four years but the complainant had only been given a repayment book for three years in error. The complainant stopped making payments in the fourth year of the loan in the mistaken belief that the loan had been paid off. The Commissioner reported that at that stage proceedings could have been taken against the complainant for non-payment but no such proceedings were ever initiated. The Commissioner found that the complainant's record was inaccurate in stating that proceedings had been pending against him.

Negotiations ensued between the finance company and the complainant and a settlement was reached whereby the complainant paid the 12 outstanding payments due under the hire purchase agreement and the finance company agreed to write off the outstanding interest. The Commissioner found that the complainant's record was not inaccurate in that part of the loan had been written off. However, the Commissioner expressed concerns that the information had not been "processed fairly" and said that the obligation to obtain data fairly requires a high degree of transparency, particularly so where loans are settled

---

[19] Case Study 8/97.

by agreement with amounts written off. The Commissioner also referred to section 6(1) of the Act[20] and said that the implication of the provision was that an individual, whose information has not been obtained fairly, can apply to have such information deleted.

Banks are obliged to exercise due diligence in the way and form in which a customer's data is presented or may be interpreted. If the data is misleading or is in a form that cannot be properly interpreted by a third party, for example a credit reference agency, a bank may be in breach of its obligations. This issue was examined by the Commissioner in the following case study which provides some helpful guidance.[21]

The Commissioner investigated a situation whereby a customer requested access to his personal records and thereafter disputed his credit rating. The bank in question claimed that the credit rating was correct on the basis of its internal guidelines. The Commissioner reviewed the bank's guidelines and concluded that the rating was fair in the circumstances. However, the Commissioner pointed out that section 1(2) of the Act states that data are inaccurate "if they are incorrect or misleading as to a matter of fact".

If the information were expressed in a way that would not be properly understood by a third party, the data controller would not be meeting its obligations. In this particular instance the bank was not in default of its obligations because the credit rating was used for internal purposes only and would only have been seen by persons who had access to the guidelines and were in a position to interpret the guidelines correctly but this example is a warning to banks to ensure that data provided to third parties is fair, accurate and not misleading.

The Data Commissioner was quoted in that case study as saying "if the information, albeit factually correct, were expressed in a way that would not be properly understood by a third party then the data controller would not have been meeting its obligations."

Right of access

The Act provides that banks are required to have regard to an individual's right to access to his records. This is another example of the greater protection now afforded to an individual in the area of data protection and provides the individual with an opportunity to ascertain what personal information is held by the bank on him and to ensure that information is accurate and up to date.

The Data Commissioner has ruled that provided that none of the restrictions laid down in the Act apply to an individual's right of access, that the request must be responded to, no matter how inconvenient or disagreeable it may be for the data controller to do so.[22]

---

[20] Section 6(1) states that "an individual shall . . . be entitled to have rectified or, where appropriate, erased any such data in relation to which there has been a contravention by the data controller of section 2(1) of this Act; and the data controller shall comply with the request as soon as may be and in any event not more than 40 days after it has been given or sent to him."

[21] Case Study 2/96.

[22] Case Study 3/97.

A customer has a right to:

- a list of all information held by the bank about him;
- access to that information;[23]
- to opportunity to rectify, block or erase the data; and
- require the controller to cease processing or not to commence processing the data.

Where a request is made by a customer, the bank as data controller is obliged to give details of the customer's personal information, the purpose of the processing and the recipients of such information or to whom it may be disclosed or transferred. Similarly, if the processing of the information is by automatic means and a decision will be solely based on this process, the bank must inform, free of charge, the customer of the logic involved in the processing. A more detailed analysis of the information to be provided to a customer is at p. 27.

A bank must comply with a customer request to access his information within 40 days of receipt of such request. Banks can charge up to €6.35 per request and are entitled to seek verification of the customer's identity before responding to an access request. Banks should note that the only obligation on the individual is to make the request to access certain specified information in writing to the bank. The bank cannot delay the process by, for example, requesting that the individual fill out an access request form. The Data Commissioner recently ruled on such a response by a bank to a written request by a customer and stated that "where an individual supplies [the bank] in writing with sufficient information to process the access request . . . then the request is valid and must be complied with."[24]

A bank is, however, entitled to request further information from the individual where the nature of the information to which they require access is unclear.

In circumstances where a bank has received multiple requests from a customer to access records and where the bank has previously responded to a request, the bank is entitled to refuse the request until a "reasonable interval" has elapsed. "Reasonable interval" has not been defined by the Act but factors such as the nature of the information, the purpose for which the information is processed and the frequency with which the information is altered should be taken into account.

Although responding to access requests from customers may be a time-consuming and costly exercise for a bank, it is also an opportunity for a bank to build up customer confidence through such open communication. It is therefore advisable for a bank to formulate procedures and guidelines to instruct employees on the handling of customer requests to access records, the persons to whom such requests should be directed and what information is to be disclosed.[25]

---

[23] Right to access back-up data is specifically excluded by the Act, section 5(1)(i).
[24] Case Study 3/98.
[25] See p. 31 on devising a Data Handling Policy.

Statutory restrictions on rights of access

A detailed analysis of statutory restrictions on rights of access is dealt with at p. 27. However, two restrictions which are of particular significance to banks are listed below and represent circumstances in which a bank would be entitled to refuse a request from a customer to access particular records:

- where data is kept for the purpose of preventing, detecting or investigating an offence or where the data is kept for the purpose of apprehending or prosecuting offenders or assessing or collecting any tax, duty or other monies owed or payable to the State, a local authority or health board; and

- to protect members of the public against financial loss occasioned by dishonesty, incompetence or malpractice on the part of persons concerned in the provision of banking, insurance, investment or other financial services in the management of companies or similar organisations or the conduct of persons who have been at any time adjudicated bankrupt.

Right of an individual to rectification or erasure

Customers have a right to demand that information held by a bank in respect of themselves be blocked, rectified or erased.[26] Where a customer requests a bank to rectify his data, the bank must to comply with the request within 40 days of receipt of the request and amend the data held as directed. This issue was highlighted by the Commissioner in Case Study 8/97.[27]

The bank must notify the customer whether or not his request has been complied with within 40 days of the request. If compliance with the request materially alters the data held in respect of that customer, the bank must notify all parties to whom the data has been disclosed during the immediately preceding 12-month period of that alteration unless such a notification is impossible or involves a disproportionate effort.

Customers are also entitled to demand that banks refrain from processing their personal information for other unauthorised purposes, *e.g.* direct marketing.

Security measures to protect the data[28]

The Act requires that banks implement appropriate technical and organisational measures to ensure that customer data is protected and secure and to prevent unauthorised access by bank employers and others.[29]

The Commissioner recently addressed a situation where a file containing staff members' performance ratings were accessed by unauthorised staff members. The "access permissions" had been inadvertently set up to allow members of the staff outside the management team to access the information. The Commissioner found that failure to implement appropriate security measures and access restrictions and the resulting dissemination of the file to

---

[26] Section 6(1). See also p. 27.
[27] See n.8 above.
[28] See p. 22 for a more detailed analysis.
[29] Chapter 1 outlines suggested measures to be implemented in order to protect data.

other unauthorised staff members contravened the Act and amounted to an incompatible disclosure of data under the Act.[30]

Banks must have regard to the state of technological development and must ensure that the measures implemented are proportional to the harm that may result in unauthorised or unlawful dissemination of customer information.[31] Due to the sensitivity surrounding an individual's financial information, there is a particularly heavy onus on banks to ensure that all details relating to an individual's financial affairs are protected from unauthorised access and the curiosity of other bank or group company employees.

It is also advisable for a bank to arrange appropriate training for all staff involved in the processing of information and ensure that staff members understand the consequences of failure to adhere to data protection rules. The Data Commissioner has held that failure by staff members to alert their superiors immediately to the fact that information can be accessed, potentially resulting in an unauthorised dissemination of information, would amount to an incompatible disclosure of information under the Act, an offence which could be criminally prosecuted.[32]

Independent data processors

Increasingly, independent data processors are being employed by businesses to process information in relation to customers and employees, etc. on its behalf. In the banking sector, a bank may employ a marketing agency to prepare and issue circulars to its customers in relation to new banking products. In such cases, the marketing agency would be a data processor for the purposes of the Act. Another example of a data processor would be a group company providing insurance services to customers of the bank such as life cover.

Where a bank employs a data processor, the bank as data controller is obliged to take all reasonable steps to ensure that the appropriate security measures are in place. For example, the bank should enter into a contract with the data processor whereby the data processor will undertake to:

- act only in accordance with the instructions of the bank who should specify the parameters; and

- guarantee that the appropriate organisational and technical measures are in place to protect unauthorised access of the data or loss or destruction of the data.

The bank is also obliged to take reasonable steps to ensure that the data processor complies with its undertakings and this obligation is ongoing.[33]

Transfer of information abroad

A detailed analysis of the provisions relating to transfer of information under the Act is set out at p. 23.

---

[30] Case Study 3/2001.
[31] Section 2C.
[32] See Case Study 3/2001 and section 2(1)(c)(ii).
[33] Section 2C(3).

A bank will need to consider the rules of transfer in the following circumstances:

- transfer by a subsidiary of its customers' data to its parent outside of the EEA;

- transfer by a branch or representative office of its customers' data outside the EEA;

- transfer of data to service providers located outside the EEA.

Transfers of data between companies within the same banking group but outside of the EEA are also subject to the transfer provisions under the Act.

A bank should consider each of the following questions before transferring a customers' data:

(i) Has the bank registered with the Commissioner the transfer of such information to another person or country as one of its uses of customer information? Transfer of data to another person or country must be specifically stated in a bank's registration.

(ii) Has the customer been notified that his data may be transferred to other parties and has the appropriate consent been obtained? This issue has been discussed at p. 12 .

If (i) and (ii) have been satisfied:

(a) Is the transfer:

- to a country within the EEA; or

- to a company in the US that has signed up to the "safe harbour" principles; or

- to a country that has been placed on the "White List" approved by the EU Commission?[34]

If so, transfer can take place. The explicit consent of a customer of a transfer to such a jurisdiction is not required.

(b) If the proposed transfer does not fall within any of the categories listed at (a) above, the bank should endeavour to obtain customer consent to such a transfer. The consent required is unambiguous consent and the customer must be made aware that the transfer may be to a non-EEA country and to a country that does not have the same data protection rules as in Ireland.

(c) If customer consent cannot be obtained or it is not practical to obtain it, the bank could consider entering into a model contract with the proposed recipient of the data.[35]

(d) If none of the above options are feasible, the bank should seek authorisation from the Commissioner to transfer the data.

---

[34] Hungary, Switzerland, Argentina, some Canadian companies and US companies which have signed up to the safe harbour principles have been "white listed".
[35] Model Contract Clauses approved by the EU, see p. 26 for more details

Internet banking

Where a bank conducts its business over the internet, it is vital that a comprehensive policy statement in relation to data protection is drafted which covers all of the issues referred to above and includes:

• the identity of the data controller and any representatives of the data controller should be clear;

• the paying of particular attention to the type of information collected, for example, through the use of cookies;[36]

• the purposes for which data is collected, the recipients of the information, the countries where the information may be transferred; and

• the users' rights such as to reject the use of cookies.

By the very nature of internet banking, customer information will be transferred from one country to another. Any entry of data onto the web or any other internationally accessible computer network will amount to a transfer for the purposes of the Act. Banks operating through the internet should pay particular attention to the transfer provisions referred to above and ensure that the appropriate consents are obtained from customers at the application stage, if possible.[37]

Banks conducting business in this way should pay particular attention to drafting their online application forms in order to ensure that:

• the customer acknowledges the data protection policy and accepts its terms and conditions; and

• the customer gives all appropriate consents to allow the bank to process and/or transfer data as its business may require.[38]

A greater onus is placed on a bank that conducts its business over the internet to ensure that the appropriate technical and organisational measures are in place to protect against accidental or unlawful destruction or accidental loss, alteration, unauthorised disclosure or access to data where such data is transmitted over a network. The level of security should be proportional to the nature of the information and the harm that may result from such unauthorised access, loss or disclosure.

---

[36] See chapter 8.
[37] See p. 23.
[38] See chapter 1.

COMPLIANCE CHECKLIST

When conducting an information audit, the following list should help to identify areas where a bank may or may not be in compliance.

1. Are you registered as a data controller with the Data Commissioner?	
2. Is your registration with the Data Commissioner broad enough to encompass all of the purposes for which you hold customer data including sensitive data and the transfer of data to third parties/other jurisdictions?	
3. Does your existing notification to the Data Commissioner need to be extended to cover additional purposes for which you hold customer data?	
4. Do your application forms include consent declarations that are broad enough to encompass all the purposes for which you hold data?	
5. Have customers specific consent to the processing of his data been obtained?	
6. Do you need to obtain further consent from your customers to process data in a particular manner?	
7. Do your application forms provide for an "opt-out" option in respect of direct marketing?	
8. If so, have your customers made such an election?	
9. Is there a procedure in place to ensure that customer data is updated and obsolete data deleted as and when necessary?	
10. Are there adequate security measures in place to ensure that customer data is protected from unauthorised access or tampering?	
11. Are staff aware of the consequences of unauthorised dissemination of data and failure to comply with data protection rules?	
12. Do you have procedures in place to deal with access requests for information from customers?	
13. If you transfer data, have you considered each of the provisions relating to the transfer of data set out at p. 23?	
14. Do you engage the services of a data processor?	
15. If so, do you have a contract in place with that data processor?	
16. Are employees of the bank who are involved in the processing of data familiar with the provisions of the Act and are they aware of the consequences of a breach of the Act?	
17. Have you considered appointing a Data Compliance Officer?	

7. HEALTH CARE

INTRODUCTION

Health care professionals will already be familiar with issues of privacy and confidentiality *vis-à-vis* patient information. The common law duty of confidentiality imposes a general duty on health care professionals to protect medical information from inappropriate disclosure. Data protection law does not replace this duty but supplements it in placing formal obligations on data controllers in the health care sector. In practice these obligations will require data controllers to put compliance systems in place. Compliance with data protection law is mandatory and a breach of the legislation may amount to a criminal offence (see Chapter 3).

The Act imposes strict compliance requirements for processing "sensitive information"[1] (see Chapter 1), *i.e.* details of an individual's:

- physical and mental health;

- sexual life;

- political, religious or philosophical beliefs;

- racial or ethnic origin;

- criminal convictions or proceedings

- clinical trials

This type of information is routinely processed within the health care sector. Individual practitioners, hospitals and clinics will also process "non-sensitive" information relating to patients, such as their name and address and employment details. They will also process a range of other information relating to their business such as details on employees and suppliers. The rules for processing this type of information are set out in Chapters 1 and 4. This chapter deals exclusively with sensitive patient information (this will mostly consist of information relating to a patient's physical and /or mental health).

We consider the issues arising in the context of:

- practitioners in private practice;

- hospitals and clinics;

- telemedicine.

---

[1] The Act applies only to living individuals, and sensitive information on the deceased is not subject to data protection law.

FLOWCHART OF HEALTHCARE INFORMATION

Practitioners in private practice

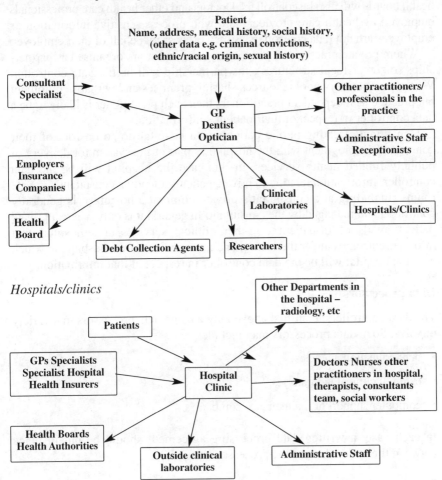

Identifying the data controller

We have seen in Chapter 1 that the main compliance obligations under the Act rest with data controllers.[2] A data controller is the individual or entity who collects information from the individual and manages and controls it in order to provide the required services. Data processors act on behalf of a data controller. Although data processors may be required to register and ensure that their security systems are adequate, their obligations will usually be prescribed by their contract with the controller.

---

[2] Where information is managed by more than one person or entity there may be two or more "joint data controllers".

Health care professionals working as sole practitioners are data controllers as clearly they manage, control and have primary responsibility for their patients' information. Legal entities such as hospitals, clinics, research bodies and health boards will also be controllers. Doctors and other health care professionals employed by health care providers and who process sensitive information as employees are not data controllers as they process on behalf of their employer.

Where private practices in the primary care sector are organised as partnerships (or other legal structures), the partnership will be the data controller. Where practitioners pool resources sharing premises and perhaps equipment but practice as independent practitioners then each practitioner is likely to be a data controller in respect of their patient's information.

Consultants treating public patients in a hospital do so on foot of their contract of employment with the hospital as part of the system for delivery of publicly funded health services. In this case the hospital will be the data controller. Information relating to private patients attending consultant's private rooms (including at a consultant's private clinic at a hospital)[3] is generally controlled and managed by the consultant. In general it is only where a private patient avails of in-patient or other clinical services at a hospital that information comes under the control and management of the hospital, in which case the hospital will be the data controller in respect of that information.

Data processors

The data controllers identified above may engage data processors in a variety of ways. Such data processors may include:

- debt collection agencies;
- external clinical laboratories;
- computer support or maintenance companies.

In each case, a written data processing agreement should be put in place between the controller and the processor (see p. 32).

Information notices – what patients must be told

As explained in Chapter 1, data controllers must be transparent in their dealings with individuals. When processing sensitive information such as medical data it is vital that patients are fully informed as to how their information will be used and disclosed and who will be allowed to access it. There is an obligation to provide this information even where consent is not required (see below). Some "purposes" for which sensitive information may be used will be obvious to the patient. Where a patient gives information to his general practitioner, dentist, or a hospital it will be obvious that his information will be used by the practitioner to treat him. However, some uses and disclosures (even where routine) may not be so obvious to a patient unfamiliar with medical practice

---

[3]   Including voluntary hospitals.

and procedure. For example a patient may not know that his sensitive information might be:

- passed to other practitioners in the hospital/practice other than for their direct treatment;

- passed to a health board for disease surveillance;

- placed on a database which is shared with other hospitals/practitioners;

- used for a clinical audit;

- passed to researchers;

- used for teaching purposes.

Any "non-obvious" uses of sensitive information such as those outlined above should be specifically brought to the patient's attention.

What form should the information notice take?

There is no prescribed form for communicating the information and the format should be considered in the light of the environment in which the services are provided. Although information can be given orally, from a practical point of view a written notice is the most effective way of achieving and proving compliance. In one case the Commissioner upheld a complaint against a hospital which had posted an information notice on the wall of the waiting room of the Accident and Emergency department.[4] The notice stated that the patients' information would be disclosed to researchers. The patients were asked to indicate to the receptionist if they did not want their information disclosed to the researchers. Some weeks after attending the A & E department a patient was contacted by researchers who knew she had attended the hospital and asked her a series of questions. The patient complained to the Commissioner's Office that her information had been unlawfully disclosed. The Commissioner found that the hospital had obtained her data unfairly[5] as it had not provided her with adequate information on how her details would be used. The Commissioner accepted that in certain circumstances an information notice on a waiting room wall would be sufficient to comply with the Act. However, he stated:

> "In this case . . . account ought to have been taken of the particular environment in which patients' data were obtained. Many patients presenting themselves to the Casualty department of a hospital may be expected to be in a state of some anxiety or discomfort. Consequently, they may not be expected to be alert to matters not relating directly to their condition. In such circumstances, there is a special need for the data controller to satisfy itself that any uses of the data which are unlikely to be anticipated by the data subject are fully explained."

Therefore, where there is a likelihood that a notice will be read by patients, this may be sufficient to comply with the Act. However, in circumstances where

---

[4] Case 1/97.
[5] The hospital's registration had included disclosure "to personnel engaged in medical research".

patients may not have sufficient time or (due to their physical or mental state) may not be expected to examine the notices, further steps have to be taken in order to ensure that they are fully informed as to how their information will be used. One alternative would be to provide each patient with a written notice and get them to indicate that they have understood its contents by signing the form.

Where there is a risk that patients may not be able to read or do not understand English then where practical (and in all cases where consent is required) the information contained in the notice should be explained to the patient in a language which they understand.

Consent – is it necessary?

In general, consent will be required to process sensitive information. We have seen at p. 16 that in certain limited circumstances consent will not be required including:

- where the information is processed to prevent injury or damage to the health, property or vital interests of the patient or other party and if it is not practical or reasonable to obtain his consent, or where the patient unnecessarily unreasonably withholds his consent; and the seeking of the consent might damage the data subject's interests[6];

- where the data controller is under a legal obligation to process the information. For example, where a registered medical practitioner discloses patient data to a medical officer of health on foot of the Infectious Diseases Regulations 1981.

In all other cases consent will be required. Where the processing is carried out by a health care professional[7] (or another person who owes an equivalent duty of confidentiality to a patient such as a social worker or a nurse) for medical purposes[8] consent can be implied. Where it is processed for purposes other than for medical treatment or by a person other than a healthcare professional, consent should be explicitly given by the patient.

Implied consent

A patient will be taken to give an implied consent to process medical data for obvious uses in the context of treatment. For example in normal circumstances a patient can be taken to consent to routine filing, disclosures to consultants in the context of referrals, disclosures to laboratories in the context of diagnostic testing or screening, and to nurses and other medical staff directly involved in their treatment. However, in the case of non-obvious uses such as referring the information to another practitioner outside the hospital (where this has not been discussed with the patient) for a second opinion or photographing or videoing

---

[6] Sections 2A and 2B.
[7] Defined as dentists, doctors or other health workers or social workers specified by Regulation made by the Minister.
[8] "Medical purposes" is defined in section 2B(4) as including preventive medicine, medical diagnosis, medical research, the provision of care and treatment and the management of healthcare services.

patients for teaching purposes, the patient's express consent will be required.[9] Processing for any purpose other than medical purposes by a health care professional will require explicit consent.

Explicit consent

Strictly speaking, a written signature is not necessary to obtain explicit consent. A firm indication that the patient agrees to the processing will be sufficient. However, from a practical point of view, a written signature is the best evidence that a patient has agreed to the processing and signatures should be obtained where possible. Where a patient is a very young child or incapacitated to the extent that he/she is are incapable of giving a written consent,[10] written consent should be sought from a parent, guardian or other relative.[11]

Consent Requirements – some typical disclosures

Routine processing for treatment and diagnosis

You will not need your patient's explicit consent to process his medical information for his ongoing treatment in a practice or in a hospital.

Sharing information with other personnel /receptionists/nurses/other doctors/ other departments

Generally you will not need explicit consent to share patient data with other personnel in the practice provided that this is necessary in the context of the patient's treatment. For example consent would not be required to send a patient's information to a dietician in a hospital for assessment. However, if the sensitive information was to be given to a visiting academic carrying out research on a dissertation then consent would be required. Receptionists and other administrative staff would not normally have a reason to access patient files and this should be avoided unless strictly necessary or consent has been obtained. In his Guidelines to medical practitioners[12] the Commissioner advises that secretaries and other administrative staff should only be allowed access to patient files to the extent necessary to allow them to do their job. Therefore for example access to a patient's complete medical history will not be necessary to draw up a bill. Medical students usually form a part of the medical team in a

[9] Unless the information is anonymised. See below.
[10] Section 2(1)(a) states that consent from a relative must be sought where "the data subject, by reason of his or her physical or mental capacity or age, is or is likely to be unable to appreciate the nature and effect of such consent." The Act does not specify the age at which an individual is capable of providing consent. The commissioner has indicated that for a child under 14 years consent from a relative should be sought. For children between 14 and 18 years the Commissioner indicates that in certain circumstances the child may be able to provide consent themselves. Section 23 of the Non-Fatal offences against the person Act 1997 deems a 16-year-old child capable of giving consent to surgical, medical or dental treatment. Where the child is capable of providing consent to their treatment, it is likely that they would be capable of giving the required consent under the Act.
[11] Relative is defined as grandparent, uncle, aunt, brother or sister.
[12] *www.privacy.ie* medical and healthcare issues page 2.

teaching hospital however this may be a non obvious use of their data and the fact that medical students may access a patient's sensitive information should be set out in the appropriate Information Notice.

Referrals to consultants and other specialists or specialist hospitals

Where a practitioner refers a patient to a consultant or other specialist or where an opinion or specialist tests are requested from another specialist hospital or external consultant, consent to disclosure of the sensitive information can be implied once the patient has agreed to the referral.

Disclosure to a locum

Explicit consent will not be required to disclose patient detail to a locum where the disclosure is to allow the locum to treat the patient.[13]

Disclosure to a laboratory

Usually the clinical laboratory will act as an agent for the practitioner or the hospital. The laboratory will undertake tests and process data on behalf of and on the instruction of the practitioner. Where information is processed by an agent to provide a service to a controller there is no disclosure and explicit consent will not be required. However, the patient should be made aware that relevant information will be passed to the laboratory with the sample for the purposes of testing. As with all processors practitioners should ensure that they have written contracts in place with the laboratories.[14] See Chapter 1, p. 32.

Disclosure to other health care professionals (within or outside the practice) for guidance on diagnosis

This is a non-obvious use of the patient's information and the patient should be informed. When sharing patient information in this way the data should be anonymised as the identity of the patient will usually be immaterial to a diagnosis.[15]

Other health care professionals (within or outside the practice) for research purposes

Where a practitioner/ hospital uses patient data for their own research explicit consent will not be required.[16] Disclosing information to anybody else for research will require explicit consent. Where patient information is anonymised consent will not be required but again the patient should be informed that their information will be used in this way where the anonymised information is disclosed to an outside party.

---

[13] *www.privacy.ie* medical and healthcare issues page 2.
[14] *www.privacy.ie* medical and healthcare issues page 3.
[15] *www.privacy.ie* medical and healthcare issues page 3.
[16] Section 2(5)(a).

Debt collection agencies

Debt collectors, like laboratories, act on behalf of the practitioner. Explicit consent will not be required to disclose patient information to them. However only such information as is necessary to allow for the debt to be processed should be revealed. A written data processor agreement will be required with all data processors.

Employers' pre-employment medicals

Examination for the purposes of a pre-employment medical does not come within the definition of "medical purposes" and explicit consent should be obtained before sending the individual's information to the employer. This is consistent with Medical Council Ethical Guidelines.[17]

Insurance companies' assessment medicals

As with pre-employment medicals, examinations carried out by insurance companies will not come within the definition of "medical purposes" and explicit consent should be sought from the individual to pass on their information to the insurance company. This in line with the Medial Council Ethical Guidelines.[18]

Notification of infectious diseases

Under the Infectious Diseases Regulations 1981, registered medical practitioners are obliged to notify a medical officer of health in a health board of an incidence of an infectious disease.[19] The health board is obliged to maintain the confidentiality of the patient's information and cannot disclose the patient's name or other identifying information without consent. The practitioner is obliged by law to notify a health board of a case of infectious disease and no consent is required. It would be best practice, however, to inform the patient that his information will be passed to the health board.

It should be noted that this exception only applies to registered medical practitioners. In a recent case the Commissioner decided that a pharmacist could not disclose sensitive information to the health authority even where requested to do by the Department of Health and Children.[20]

He stated:

> "Personal details obtained for prescription purposes cannot be subsequently used for other purposes without the express consent or, . . . a clear statutory basis."[21]

---

[17] *A Guide to Ethical Conduct and Behaviour* (5th ed). Clause 18.6 (4) states: "The significance, rather than the precise details, of the medical findings should be conveyed to any third party and then only with the patients consent".

[18] Clause 18.10 states "a doctor asked by an insurance company to complete a medical report on a patient, must ensure that this is not issued without the consent of the patient".

[19] Infectious diseases are prescribed by regulations.

[20] Case Study 11/2002. Annual Report 2002, p. 37.

[21] In this case a pharmacist sought guidance from the Commissioner on a scheme proposed by the Eastern Health Authority (sic) requiring pharmacists to assist in the surveillance of TB.

Disclosure to the National Cancer Registry Board

Consent is not required under the Act to send patient information to the National Cancer Registry Board or a hospital, health board or other body participating in any cancer screening programme.[22]

Anonymising data

As we have seen in Chapter 1, the Act only applies to information which allows an individual to be identified. There are no prohibitions on the disclosure of information from which all identifiers have been removed. This process is referred to as "anonymising data". For example where a practitioner sends an aggregate of patients presenting with a particular disease to a health board under a disease surveillance programme there is no data protection issue as no personal data is disclosed. In other cases a practitioner might remove personal identifiers but apply a code to the patient data so that he could continue to identify the patient in his own files. This is referred to as "pseudononymising" data. Disclosing information in pseudononymised form will bring the information outside the Act only if the recipient does not have, or have access to, the key to the code.

Pseudononymisation is particularly appropriate to epidemiological research. Anonymised or aggregate information can result in duplication of data (as a patient may have presented to more than one practitioner). This hinders empirical research. It is likely that coded identifiers and protocols for their use within the health care sector will emerge in the near future and will facilitate the sharing of information amongst a number of health care providers.

The Commissioner has endorsed the use of unique identifiers in his guidance to practitioners:

> "Researchers who obtain anonymised patient data are sometimes faced with the problem that they may be dealing with two or more data-sets from the same individual, received from different sources. To address this problem, it may be permissible for a data controller (such as a doctor) to make available anonymous data together with a unique coding, which falls short of actually identifying the individual to the researcher. For example, a data controller might 'code' a unique data-set using a patient's initials and date-of-birth. The essential point is that the researcher should not be in a position to associate the data-set with an identifiable individual."[23]

Registration

Data controllers within the health care sector must register with the Data Protection Commissioner's Office. Registration is a simple process (see p. 21). Controllers need to take particular care to ensure that they have given a clear

---

Pharmacists were required to disclose to the health board personal information of patients prescribed with TB drug therapies. Following the query to the Commissioner, the Department of Health and Children decided to abandon the reporting scheme.

[22] The Health (Provision of Information) Act 1997.

[23] *www.privacy.ie* sectoral issues page 3.

description of all of the sensitive information they process and that they have registered *all* of the purposes for which they anticipate patient data will be used. For example, a general description such as "for medical treatment of patients" would not cover disclosure of data to other clinicians or hospitals for research purposes and more specific detail should be given.

Security

Data controllers in the health care sector must take particular care to ensure that their security systems are adequate. The Act does not prescribe any set standard[24] and controllers will need to audit their security needs according to their own circumstances and seek expert advice as to their adequacy. Sensitive information will require a higher standard of security than ordinary information given its confidential nature and the potential harm which an unauthorised disclosure or loss of the information could cause.[25] Some of the issues which need to be addressed in the course of a security systems audit in the health care sector include:

- are paper files kept in secure locked cabinets;

- access to patients' papers/files should be restricted to those who need to consult them in the context of treatment;

- filing cabinets should never be kept in public waiting areas or other areas to which the public have access;

- as far as practicable, patients' charts should not be openly displayed or placed in areas to which the public have access;

- access to computer files should be password controlled and limited to authorised personnel;

- access to sensitive information should be restricted to information which is appropriate to the role of each member of staff in the delivery of service to the patient. A hierarchy of passwords may be appropriate in that regard.

- computer screens should not be on view in public areas[26];

- downloading to lap-top computers should be kept to a minimum and security protocols ought to be adopted in relation to the use and storage of lap-tops when taken outside of the practice or hospital;

- where computers are sold or transferred out of the practice or hospital, care should be taken to "wipe" files permanently from the hard drive;

---

[24] Section 2C provides that in determining security standards (particularly where the processing involves transmission over a network) you may have regard to (a) available technology and (b) the costs involved. Whatever measures are taken the controller must have regard to (1) the nature of the information and (2) the potential harm which a breach of security might cause.
[25] Data controllers are obliged to ensure that the sensitive information is protected from unauthorised or unlawful processing, accidental or unlawful destruction or accidental loss of, or damage to, the data concerned.
[26] Case 6/96.

- all staff should be trained in data handling practices and a staff policy ought to be devised.

- employment contracts should be revised where necessary to impose a duty on employees to familiarise themselves with and adhere to the security and data protection compliance policies drawn up by the practice or hospital.

Patients' access to their files

The Act gives patients the right to access their medical records. Applications must be made in writing and the data controller must respond within 40 days (see p. 27). Health professionals[27] must refuse[28] access to health data[29] where it is likely to cause serious harm to the physical or mental health of the patient. Refusal of access is restricted to that portion of the information which the practitioner believes would be harmful and all other information must be disclosed. For example, if a controller holds medical records on a patient which reveals details of a psychiatric condition which he believes would be harmful if revealed to the patient, he must refuse access to that information. However, if the patient's file also contains other information judged not to be harmful this must be released.

Other data controllers (who are not health professionals) who process health data cannot release any health data where they are requested to do so by an individual seeking access under the Act unless they consult with the appropriate health care professional.[30] Therefore practitioners may receive requests for an opinion from hospital administration or external data controllers such as employers or insurance companies in connection an access request.

Similarly social work data[31] cannot be released[32] if it would be likely to cause serious harm to the physical or mental health or the emotional condition of the individual making the request. Where the data has been supplied by a social worker who works as an agent or employee of the data controller, the controller will not be required to consult with the social worker in relation to the release of the information. However where the information has been supplied by a social worker or other individual who is not the controller's agent or employee the controller must consult with that individual before supplying the

---

[27] Defined in the Data Protection (Access Modification) (Health) Regulations 1989 (S.I. No. 82 of 1989) as a registered medical practitioners, dentist, opticians, pharmaceutical chemists, nurses or midwifes a chiropodist, dietician, occupational therapist, orthopist, physiotherapist, psychologist, child psychotherapist or speech therapist.
[28] Under the 1989 Regulations above.
[29] Defined in the 1989 Regulations above as personal data relating to physical or mental health.
[30] Defined as the individual's doctor or dentist currently or most recently responsible for the clinical care of the data subject in connection with the matters to which the information the subject of the request applies. Where a doctor or dentist is not the most appropriate health professional then another can be consulted if have the necessary experience and qualifications.
[31] Defined as personal data kept for, or obtained in the course of, carrying out social work by a Minister of the Government, a local authority, a health board, or a voluntary organisation or other body which carries out social work and is in receipt of moneys provided by a Minister, authority or board, but excludes any health data.
[32] The Data Protection (Access Modification) (Health) Regulations 1989 (S.I. No. 82 of 1989).

information to the data subject.[33] Access can only be restricted to that portion of the social work information which the data controller believes would be harmful and all other information must be disclosed.

A patient has a right to require the practitioner/hospital to rectify any records containing information which is excessive, inaccurate or out of date (see Chapter 1).

Codes of practice

The Act provides that codes of practice can be drawn up within industry sectors. Codes of practice should be submitted to the Commissioner for his approval or drawn up with his collaboration. Codes of practice are currently being considered by a number of data controllers within the health care sector. In his Annual Report 2002 the Commissioner welcomes the initiative by the GPIT unit at the Department of Health to draw up a code for general medical practitioners.[34]

Document retention policies

The Act specifies that information (including sensitive information) cannot be kept for longer than is necessary. Data controllers in the health care sector can keep sensitive information as long as there is an objective necessity to do so. Health care providers need to devise document retention policies which are appropriate to the different types of information which they keep. The primary purpose for which medical records are kept is the delivery of quality medical care to each individual patient. Where a patient suffers from a lifelong illness a health care provider may be justified in retaining records for the lifetime of the individual to meet the primary purpose. Examples of this would be in relation to certain psychiatric illnesses or where it is essential to be able to assess the progression of a condition or illness or measure the severity of a current episode of illness against earlier episodes. Policies in relation to appropriate retention periods should set out the objective criteria upon which they are based. In addition to the primary purpose there are also secondary purposes for which medical records are kept. These include administrative, medico-legal and insurance purposes. There are other important secondary purposes also, *e.g.* audit, research and health care planning for future service requirements. In practice health care providers frequently look to medico-legal and insurance purposes to support a retention periods which stretches beyond those which are necessary to meet the primary purpose. Frequently relevant limitation periods for potential claims will be factored into devising appropriate retention periods[35] although it is necessary to take account of medico-legal and insurance considerations this should not be to the exclusion of other important considerations.

---

[33] S.I. No. 82 of 1989, s. 4(3).
[34] Annual Report 2002, p. 4.
[35] *e.g.* the Statute of Limitations Acts, 1957–2000 and the Civil Liability Act 1961.

Issues for telemedicine

More and more health care services are now available on the internet. Sometimes services are offered through a passive site (providing information and/or advertising products), however some health care websites are interactive and the individual may supply personal information. Some sites use "cookies" to track the visitor's data thereby collecting personal information without the individual's knowledge.

A privacy notice should be posted on all websites where personal information is obtained or cookies are used and all of the purposes for which the information will be used ought to be set out and the Data Controller should be clearly identified. Where there is any marketing of goods and services the individual must be given an opportunity to "opt out" of receiving such material. Where any sensitive information is supplied online express consent to the processing should be obtained. Consent can be obtained by way of "clicking" an "I consent" button.

Clinical trials

A person's written consent must be obtained to participate in a clinical trial.[36] The ethics committee considering an application for approval of a proposed trial is obliged to consider the criteria which will be used by the person[37] intending to conduct the trial to ensure that the identity of each participant remains confidential.[38] In addition to the obligations under the clinical trials legislation organisers of a clinical trial should have regard to compliance with data protection obligations when preparing the protocol for the trial and the patient information sheet and consent by the participant. The protocol and patient information sheet should identify the data controller(s), set out the purpose for which the information is gathered, describe the uses to which it will be put and say to whom it will be disclosed. As we have seen, the definition of "medical purposes" includes medical research. Therefore it is permissible to rely on implied consent to processing of information. However it is best practice to include in the consent form signed by the participant consent to the processing of the participant's information for the purposes of the clinical trial. In a multi-centred trial specific consent must be obtained to transfer the patient's information to a country outside the European Economic Area unless one of the safeguards discussed in Chapter 1 is put in place.

---

[36] Clinical trials are regulated under the Clinical Trials Acts, 1987–1990.
[37] Only registered medical practitioners or registered dentists may conduct a trial.
[38] Section 8(4)(k) of the Clinical Trials Act 1987.

COMPLIANCE CHECKLIST

1. Draft appropriate information notices informing patients how their medical information will be used.	
2. Assess most appropriate means of communicating the notice.	
3. Do you use medical information for any purpose other than their treatment?	
4. If so have you obtained the patient's explicit consent?	
5. Have you reviewed your security systems and are you satisfied that sensitive information is adequately protected?	
6. If you disclose sensitive information in anonymised or aggregate form are you satisfied that patients cannot be identified from the remaining information?	
7. Have you provided adequate training for staff?	

8. THE INTERNET AND ELECTRONIC COMMUNICATIONS

Introduction

Many activities and transactions on the internet involve persons obtaining and processing personal information.

Principles of data protection apply to personal information obtained or processed via the internet where an individual can be identified from that information.[1]

Such information is referred to as "online personal information" in this chapter.

Personal information usually flows through different stages and parties where it is obtained on the internet. The following chart shows an example of how personal information might typically flow.

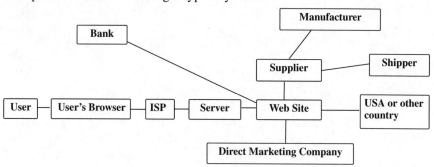

Controllers and processors of online personal information

If you control the use of online personal information, you are a data controller. Similarly, if you process online personal information on behalf of a data controller, you are a data processor. Controllers of online personal information are referred to as "online controllers" and persons that process online personal information on behalf of online controllers are referred to as "online processors" in this chapter.

Whether you control the use of or process online personal information is a question of fact and will depend on what you do with the information you receive. If you operate a website and individuals provide personal information to you which you use for your own purposes, you are likely to be a data controller. However, if you merely collect the personal information on behalf

---

[1] See Chapter 1 in relation to the criteria that need to be met in order for personal information to come within the terms of the Act.

of someone else who ultimately decides what should be done with it, you are likely to be a data processor.

For example, referring to the data flow chart, the operator of the website is usually a data controller. The ISP and operator of the server are likely to be data processors. However, if the ISP retains information and processes the information for its own purpose, the ISP could also be a data controller. These are factual issues that need to be considered in each situation.

Jurisdiction/application of the Act

As the internet can be accessed and used worldwide, it is not always clear which national laws will govern a particular transaction or activity. The Act has attempted to address this uncertainty by setting out when the activities of a data controller or data processor are governed by it.

The Act applies to online controllers and online processors that are "established in Ireland". The Act defines when a data controller is considered to be established in Ireland.[2]

The Act also applies to online controllers and online processors who, (if not established in Ireland or in any other EEA Member State, make use of equipment in Ireland for processing online personal information, except to transmit the information through Ireland[3] (see Chapter 1). An example where equipment is used for transit of information through Ireland would be the use of telecommunications networks to carry internet communications from the point where they are sent to their destination.[4] "Equipment" is likely to include personal computers, terminals and servers used to process data.

The meaning of "making use of equipment in Ireland for processing personal information" is not defined and is open to interpretation. An EU study provides some guidance on the meaning of making use of equipment for processing personal information in relation to the internet.[5] The study states that the equipment must be at the disposal of the data controller[6] and that the data controller must carry on an activity in Ireland. Therefore, the data controller must exercise some *control* over the equipment used to process the information. The necessary degree of control is established where the data controller determines what information is collected, stored, transferred and/or altered, the means of such processing and for what purpose. Ownership of the equipment used to process the information is irrelevant for purposes of this analysis.

---

2   Section 1(3B)(b).
3   Section 1(3B)(a)(ii).
4   See the Article 29 Working Group's Working Document on determining the international application of EU data protection law to personal data processing on the Internet by non-EU based web sites 5035/01/EN/Final WP 56 adopted May 30, 2002.
5   See n. 4.
6   The Article 29 Working Group advocated a cautious approach to applying the principle of making use of equipment for purposes of processing personal information and stated that not every interaction between an internet user in the EU and a website based outside the EU leads to the application of EU data protection law.

By way of illustration, if an Irish citizen enters a website operated by a US corporation and provides personal information to purchase an item, the US corporation collecting the information is an online controller. The US corporation is not, however, subject to Irish data protection law unless the corporation is established in Ireland within the meaning set out in the Act[7] or uses equipment in Ireland (for purposes other than mere transmission of data through Ireland).[8] Similarly, the processing activities of an online processor that processes personal information for or on behalf of the corporation will not be subject to Irish data protection law.

If the same US corporation uses equipment located in Ireland to process the personal information, then the corporation is an online controller whose activities are subject to the terms of the Act (as are those of an online processor that processes the information for the corporation).

If you are not established in Ireland but come within the remit of the Act because you make use of equipment in Ireland for processing data (otherwise than for transit through Ireland) you are required to appoint a representative established in Ireland.[9]

Obtaining personal information online

There are different ways in which personal information can be obtained online. Information may be actively provided by an individual, *e.g.* where an individual provides personal information while using a website or by sending an email. Personal information may also be obtained without an individual's knowledge, for example, through the use of electronic cookies.

The governing principle that you must observe if you obtain or process online personal information (with or without the individual's consent) is that you must collect the information fairly.[10] The concept of fairness in obtaining and processing personal information is discussed in detail in Chapter 1. In summary, you must provide the individual with information on how you intend to use their personal data and you should obtain their consent to do so. You must also ensure that the information which you seek from an individual is relevant to the intended transaction. For example, if you collect data for the sale of a book, it would be relevant to ask for a name and address but a question asking the individual to indicate gender would not be directly relevant.

Directly obtaining personal information

Where an individual wishes to purchase an item through a website, he is typically required to provide certain minimal information so that he can purchase the item. This information usually includes the name, email address, postal address and credit card details of the individual.

Other common practices where online personal information is obtained directly from an individual include an email from the individual requesting

---

7   Section 1(3B)(b).
8   Section 1 (3B)(a)(ii).
9   Section 1(3B)(c).
10 Section 2(1)(a).

more information from a website, where an individual completes and submits an application form online and where an individual subscribes to a website or mailing list.

If you are an online controller and obtain online personal information directly from an individual, you must ensure, as far as practicable, that the individual already has, is provided with or has made readily available to him, certain information. This information must include:

- Your identity (this may not always be obvious in the online environment);

- The purpose for which you will use the online personal information;

- Any other relevant information. This might include any third parties to whom you will transfer the online personal information, whether cookies or any other data tracking devices operate on your site and the security measures you employ to ensure the security of the online personal information (these matters are discussed in more detail below).

One practical method that you could use to show that you fairly obtain online personal information is to ensure that your website has a suitably drafted privacy statement that addresses all of the relevant data protection issues.

Your website's homepage should prominently display a link to your privacy statement and request the user to read it before progressing to another page (or at least before providing any personal information). In addition, the link should appear on every page through which you obtain personal information.

Secretly obtaining personal information

Technology facilitates the collection of information from individuals without them being aware of it. Cookies are one example of this.

A cookie is information generated by a webserver (via a user's web browser) to a user's computer. The user's web browser, if cookie enabled, receives the cookie and can store it in a file (or "cookie list"). The cookie can then subsequently be automatically transferred from the user's computer to another web server (by the user's web browser) when the user directs his web browser to display a certain web page from that server.

Cookies are generally used without the user's knowledge. They can include information about the user, the user's browsing activities or transactions effected by the user on the internet. The information stored in a cookie will comprise online personal information and you will be required to process this information in accordance with the rules laid down in the Act.

The use of cookies (and other such devices) without the user's consent and knowledge goes against what the Commissioner has described as the *touchstones of fairness in data protection* – transparency and informed consent.[11]

---

[11] See *Data Protection Act 1988. Keeping personal information on computer: Your responsibilities. Guidelines for Data Controllers*, issued by the Data Protection Commissioner. These guidelines are available on the Commissioner's website.

With this in mind, if you obtain online personal information by using cookies or similar methods, you should do the following[12]:

- Inform the individual of the fact that you are using cookies at the earliest practical opportunity. One way of doing this would be to state the fact clearly and visibly on your website.

- Inform the individual of the information to be stored on the cookie, for what purpose and for how long. Some websites provide the information in a cookies policy statement available on the website.

- Give the individual the choice to accept or reject the sending or storage of a cookie.

Disclosure of information to a third party

Online personal information can easily be disclosed by an online data controller or online data processor to a third party. For example, where an individual orders an item online and pays by credit card or similar method, there will often be a subsequent disclosure of online personal information by the online retailer to a credit card company or bank to process payment.

In addition, the online retailer may not manufacture, source, store, package or ship the item to the individual who ordered it. Where any of these steps are undertaken by someone other than the retailer, it could involve the disclosure of online personal information by the retailer to its partners in the supply chain.

If you are an online data controller and disclose online personal information to third parties, you must inform the individual about the recipients or categories of recipients of the information. This should be communicated at the time the information is obtained. Failure to notify individuals that their information could be disclosed could render the use of the information unlawful.

Transfer of data outside Ireland

Due to the worldwide nature of the internet, online personal information is quite easily transferred to another country. For example, if an item is ordered on a website, personal information may be processed by a web server in Ireland and then transferred to another country because the item in question is stored in and shipped from that other country. If the information is sent outside the EEA, the statutory requirements relating to such a transfer of personal information[13] would need to be met (see Chapter 1).

If you are an online data controller and you transfer (or anticipate the transfer of) online personal information to a country outside the EEA, you should:

---

[12] These requirements are included in an EU Directive. See n.47.
[13] Section 11.

- Inform the individual of this fact before the information is obtained. This can be done by including a statement to that effect in your website's privacy statement or terms and conditions.

- Name the country or countries to which the information is transferred.

- If the country or countries are not "white listed"[14] for transfer (see Chapter 1), inform the individual of that fact. You should also state that the data protection laws in that country may not be of the same standard as in Ireland.

Meeting your obligations in respect of disclosure or transfer

Obtaining the consent of the individual to disclosure or transfer is one way an online controller can comply with the applicable statutory requirements covering fair processing and transfer.[15]

An individual's consent to a proposed disclosure or transfer of online personal information could be obtained by following these steps:

1. Include the information outlined above relating to the proposed disclosure or transfer on your website in a suitably drafted statement. This could be contained in your website terms and conditions or privacy statement.

2. Alert the individual to the statement and have a link to the statement on your homepage and every page through which personal information is obtained.

3. Before any personal information is obtained, ensure that the individual opens and scrolls through the statement.

4. Require the individual to signify consent to the disclosure or transfer referred to in the statement by clicking an "I accept" icon or similar acknowledgment.

These steps should be completed before the individual has the opportunity to enter or provide any personal information.

Direct marketing

As mentioned in Chapter 1, specific requirements must be met where personal information is used for direct marketing and those requirements apply equally to online personal information.

If you are an online controller and use or intend to use personal information for direct marketing, you should:

- Inform the individual of any possible use of information for direct marketing purposes.[16] This can be done by referring to such use in your website terms and conditions or privacy policy.

---

[14] Hungary, Switzerland, Argentina, some Canadian companies and US Safe Harbor companies.
[15] It may be that the data controller can satisfy other criteria to legally transfer or disclose data without obtaining the individual's consent. See Chapter 1.
[16] Section 2(8).

- Obtain the individual's consent to using the information for that purpose. Your website terms and conditions should give the individual an option to "opt-out" of any such use of data by clicking on a suitable icon (such as a tick-box). The individual should be required to indicate that he accepts the terms and conditions by clicking an "I accept" or similar icon on at the end of the terms and conditions.

Again, these steps should be completed before the individual provides or submits any personal information where it may be used for direct marketing.

Security

The Commissioner has indicated that high standards of security are required for computerised personal information.[17]

The Act requires that an online controller must take appropriate security measures to prevent:

- Unauthorised access to personal information;

- Improper alteration, disclosure or destruction of personal information;

- All other unlawful forms of processing the information.[18]

If you are an online controller you must take reasonable technological and organisational steps to provide adequate security for personal information. The Act provides guidelines on what factors you need to consider:

- The level of security should be appropriate to the harm that might result from any improper or unauthorised processing or damage to or loss of the information.[19]

- The nature of the information must be considered.[20] The security appropriate to processing sensitive data would be far greater than that required for non-sensitive data, for example.

- You *may* have regard to developments in technology and the cost of implementing security measures[21] (technological security measures would include encryption and similar technology). For example, in deciding on an appropriate security system you should ensure that the security system is not outdated. At the same time, it does not appear that you would have to go to disproportionate cost to keep the system constantly in line with all new developments in technology.

In addition to meeting requirements regarding your own security system, if you are an online controller and you engage an online processor to process information on your behalf, you must:

---

[17] n.11.
[18] Section 2(1)(d).
[19] Section 2C(1)(b)(i).
[20] Section 2C(1)(b)(ii).
[21] Section 2C(1)(a).

- Ensure that the online processor takes appropriate technical and organisational steps to ensure the security of the information. As the online controller, you will be required to ensure that the processor takes these steps.[22]

- Have a written contract in place with the online processor. The contract must provide that the online processor will process the information according to your instructions and take appropriate security measures against unauthorised access to the information, and any alteration, disclosure or destruction, and all other unlawful forms of processing, of the information.[23]

Access to information

An individual has the usual rights of access[24] to personal information obtained online and may exercise his right to have such information rectified, deleted or blocked.[25]

Online controllers and online processors should consider drawing up an access request policy so as to deal efficiently and cost effectively with requests.

Registration with the Data Protection Commissioner

Internet access providers[26] are expressly required to register with the Commissioner.[27] The usual registration requirements[28] (see Chapter 1) apply to other online controllers and online processors that use, control or process online personal information.

Records and retention policies

The requirements relating to retaining and maintaining personal information apply to online personal information. In summary, online controllers must ensure that they do not hold customer information for longer than is necessary. This will need to be balanced against other requirements (including statutory requirements) to retain information. Online controllers will also have to ensure that the information that they hold is accurate and up to date.

Assessing compliance

If your activities involve obtaining and processing online personal information you should conduct an audit of your activities from a data protection compliance perspective. An audit would involve a systematic review of the type of information you obtain and process, how and for what purpose. At the end of this chapter is a checklist of items which raises preliminary matters for you to consider in that context.

---

[22] Section 2C(3)(b) and 2C(3)(c).
[23] Section 2C(3)(a).
[24] Section 4. For discussion see Chapter 1.
[25] Section 6. For discussion see Chapter 1.
[26] Persons whose business consists wholly or partly of connecting people to the internet and who hold personal information relating to those people.
[27] Pursuant to the Data Protection (Registration) Regulations 2002 (S.I. No.2 of 2001).
[28] Sections 16 to 20.

PART II – ELECTRONIC COMMUNICATIONS

Data protection issues for providers of electronic communication services

Electronic communications often contain individuals' personal information. The use by individuals of electronic communications services can itself generate information personal to them, for example where they are located.

Irish and European legislation has been enacted to regulate the use of personal information in the provision of electronic communication services. Two of the principal pieces of legislation are considered below.

Data protection in telecommunications regulations

The Irish European Communities (Data Protection and Privacy in Telecommunications) Regulations 2002[29] supplement the Act and address specific issues relating to data protection in the telecommunications sector. The issues addressed include security, privacy, directories of subscribers[30] and direct marketing.

Application of the Regulations

The Regulations apply to processing information on public telecommunications networks,[31] in particular via the Integrated Services Digital Network (ISDN) and public digital mobile networks.[32]

Specified activities of telecommunications network providers (persons who provide a public telecommunications network), telecommunications service providers (persons who provide publicly available telecommunications services) and publishers of a directory[33] come within the remit of the Regulations. These include email, WAP and SMS text services.

Jurisdiction

If you are a telecommunications service provider, telecommunications network provider or publisher of a directory your activities will only be regulated by the Regulations if you satisfy certain jurisdictional requirements. These are the same as those applicable to an online controller referred to previously in this chapter and as set out in the Act (see Chapter 1).

---

[29] S.I. No.192 of 2002. The Department of Communications, Marine and Natural Resources has indicated that the regulations will be repealed on the implementation of Directive 2002/58/EC. See n. 47.

[30] A subscriber is a person who has contracted with a telecommunications service provider for the supply by the provider to the person of telecommunications services.

[31] A transmission system and, where applicable, any switching equipment and other resources which permit the conveyance of signals between defined termination points by wire, radio, optical or other electromagnetic telecommunications services.
     Telecommunications services are services, other than radio and television broadcasting, the provision of which consists, either in whole or in part, of the transmission and routing of signals on telecommunications networks.

[32] Regulation 3(1).

[33] A directory consists of a list of persons that have contracted with a telecommunications service provider for the supply of telecommunications services (subscribers) which is available to the

Security of telecommunications services

As a telecommunications service provider you must comply with certain security requirements in processing personal information:[34]

- You must take appropriate technical and organisational measures to safeguard security of your services and, if necessary, do so in conjunction with the telecommunications network provider with respect to the network security.

- Your security measures must be appropriate to the risk presented and have regard to the state of the art and the cost of their implementation.

- You must inform subscribers about the risk of a particular network security breach, any possible remedies and the costs involved.[35]

Telecommunications network providers are required to comply with any reasonable request of telecommunications service providers using their network in order to assist them in meeting their security obligations under the Regulations.

Unsolicited calls for direct marketing

The Regulations establish a national register where subscribers can indicate that they object to receiving unsolicited calls used for direct marketing (the "opt-out" register).[36]

The Regulations prohibit the use of telecommunications services to make unsolicited calls for direct marketing in certain circumstances. Such calls may not be made to a subscriber if the subscriber has notified the relevant person that he does not consent to the call or has entered his name in the opt-out register.[37] There are similar restrictions in respect of automated calls and faxes.[38]

If you intend making calls or sending faxes for direct marketing, you will need to:

- Consult the opt-out register before making the communications to check if the intended recipient is listed. If listed, making the communication is prohibited.

- Respect the wishes of the recipient if he does not consent to receiving the call.

As a telecommunications services provider you may, with the subscriber's consent, use a subscriber's traffic and billing data[38a] for the purpose of marketing your own telecommunications services.

---

public or information from which is available to members of the public by way of a directory enquiry service.

[34] These are set out in Directive 97/66/EC of the European Parliament and of the Council of December 15, 1997 concerning the processing of personal data and the protection of privacy in the telecommunications sector. Official Journal L 024 , January 1, 1998 pp. 0001–0008. The Directive will be repealed on October 31, 2003 and replaced by Directive 2002/58/EC. See n. 47.

[35] Article 4 of Directive 97/66/EC.

[36] Regulation 10. This "opt-out" register will form part of a national central telephone directory established by the European Communities (Voice Telephony and Universal Service) Regulations 1999 (S.I. No.71 of 1999)

[37] Regulation 9(3).

[38] Regulation 9(1).

[38a] See n. 40 and n. 41.

Enforcement

The Regulations grant certain enforcement powers to the Director of Telecommunications Regulation (as opposed to the Commissioner).[39] These include the
power to enforce compliance with the security principles referred to above. The
Director may direct a telecommunications service provider or telecommunications network provider to take or refrain from certain action to ensure
compliance. Such action can be enforced through the courts if necessary.

Billing and traffic data

The Regulations also regulate telecommunications services providers' and
telecommunications network providers' processing of traffic data[40] and billing
data[41] which relate to subscribers and users of telecommunications services.

If you are a telecommunications services provider or telecommunications
network provider:

- You must erase or make anonymous traffic data on the termination of a call[42].

- You may, for the purpose of subscriber billing and interconnection payments,
  process billing data until the end of the period within which legal proceedings
  may be brought for payments due, or alleged to be due, for the relevant
  telecommunications services or, if proceedings are commenced within that
  period, until the proceedings are finally determined[43].

- You must restrict the processing of billing and traffic data to persons acting
  under your authority who handle billing or traffic management, customer
  enquiries, fraud detection and marketing the relevant provider's own telecommunications services. You must also restrict such processing to what is
  necessary for the purpose of those activities.

The Commissioner has stated that, in applying the restrictions on the
processing of traffic and billing data referred to above, telecommunications
services providers and telecommunications network providers should be
mindful of "the strong privacy impact" of logging the details of particular calls

---

[39] These enforcement powers relate to regulations 3(2), 5, 6, 7, 9, 10, 15 and 18.
[40] Traffic data is any data relating to the conveyance of calls on a telecommunications network
      and the billing of such calls (including data relating to the time or duration of calls).
[41] Billing data is certain data which is held by a telecommunications network provider or
      telecommunications services provider for the purpose of billing a subscriber or making or
      paying interconnection charges, or both. Billing data is specified in the Annex to EU Directive
      97/66/EC and consists of data containing the:
      − number or identification of the subscriber station;
      − address of the subscriber and the type of station;
      − total number of units to be charged for the accounting period;
      − called subscriber number;
      − type, starting time and duration of the calls made and/or the data volume transmitted;
      − date of the call/service; and
      − other information concerning payments such as advance payments, payments by
        instalments, disconnection and reminders.
[42] Regulation 4(1).
[43] Regulation 4(2).

made by subscribers.[44] The Commissioner recommends that (subject to certain exceptions referred to below) telecommunications companies should only store such privacy-sensitive data for a limited period of three to six months to enable routine billing queries to be addressed and not longer. However, the Commissioner takes the view that it is permissible to retain traffic and billing data for a longer period in certain cases. For example, if there is some binding legal requirement to retain the data for a longer period, the data may be retained for that period.[45]

Directories of subscribers

The Regulations set out certain data protection principles that apply to a directory[46] in either printed or electronic form.

A subscriber has rights in respect of such a directory and these include the right to request that information be excluded. In addition, the subscriber may request the telecommunications service provider not to use (or assist any other person to use) any information relating to the subscriber contained in a database upon which the directory is based.

If you are a telecommunications service provider you must:

• If you receive a request from a subscriber in the nature referred to above, as soon as practicable, send details of the request to the person who publishes the directory. That person must in turn comply with the request.

• Limit the directory information to the information necessary to identify the subscriber and his number. A subscriber may consent to the publication of additional information.

Two Case Studies of the Commissioner that relate to directories may be useful in drawing up compliance programmes.

Case Study 1/96 — Publication of subscriber list on the internet

This case concerned a professional association's intended disclosure on the internet of a list of its members. The list had already been published in a book. The Commissioner determined that internet disclosure would not have been anticipated by the members when they provided their information to the association (on the basis that the consequences for their privacy of publication on the internet were qualitatively different from publication in book form). The Commissioner advised that consent of the members to publication on the internet of their names, addresses and membership of the association would be required. The Commissioner suggested that a practical method to obtain such

---

[44] *Data Protection in the Telecommunications Sector – A Guide to the European Communities (Data Protection and Privacy in Telecommunications) Regulations, 2002* issued by the Data Protection Commissioner. The guide is available on the Commissioner's website.

[45] Other examples given by the Commissioner are where a subscriber has queried his bill and the data needs to be retained to enable the query to be resolved or if there is some other legitimate reason to believe that a query or dispute is likely to arise in a particular case.

[46] It should be noted that the principles in the Regulations relating to directories do not apply to directories that were published before April 1, 2002.

consent would be to notify the members of the intention to disclose the list on the internet when members were invited to renew their membership of the association and to seek their consent at that time.

Case Study 8/99 — Publication of a telephone directory on the internet

This case concerned the publication of a telephone directory on a CD-Rom and then on the internet. The Commissioner determined that the principal data protection issue was whether the publication of the electronic directory and the novel uses of the personal information in the electronic directory were compatible with the purposes for which the information had been obtained and were kept by the data controller. The Commissioner asked the question: what would a data subject have reasonably expected to happen to the information at the time that it was obtained?

The Commissioner determined that if a data subject was content to have personal information included in a manual telephone directory (where the option not to do so is readily available) a telecommunications company was reasonably entitled to assume that the data subject would not object to the inclusion of the same information in an electronic directory.

However, the Commissioner stated that there were additional data protection considerations where the electronic directory offered novel capabilities for the processing of the information. The Commissioner determined that the ability to search the electronic directory using address details was a novel capability for the processing of the information as this could not readily be done using the directory in book form. Data subjects could not reasonably be assumed to have consented to this new use of their personal information. The publisher of the directory agreed to modify its electronic version of the directory and removed the ability to search the directory using address details.

Wider electronic communications services

A European Directive from 2002[47] regulates processing of information in public electronic communications services[48] which are provided on public

---

[47] Directive 2002/58/EC of the European Parliament and of the Council of July 12, 2002 concerning the processing of personal data and the protection of privacy in the electronic communications sector (Directive on privacy and electronic communications) Official Journal L201, July 31, 2002 pp. 0037–0047. The Department of Communications, Marine and Natural Resources has indicated that Directive 2002/58/EC is expected to be implemented in October 2003. The Department has published Guidance Notes on the Transposition into Irish Law of EU Directive 2002/58/EC, July 29, 2003.

[48] An electronic communications service is a paid service which consists of the conveyance of signals on electronic communications networks, including telecommunications services and transmissions services and networks used for broadcasting. It does not include services providing, or exercising editorial control over, content transmitted using electronic communications networks and services.

An electronic communications network is a transmission system, and, where applicable, switching or routing equipment and other resources, which permit the conveyance of signals by wire, radio, optical or other electronic means, including satellite networks, fixed and mobile terrestrial networks, electricity cable systems, to the extent that they are used for the purpose of transmitting signals, networks used for radio and television broadcasting, and cable television networks, irrespective of the type of information conveyed.

communications networks.[49] Those services also include email, WAP and SMS text. The Directive has not been implemented into Irish law at the time of this publication. However, this must be done by October 31, 2003.[50]

The Directive is part of a wider European harmonisation of the regulation of electronic communications and associated services.[51] The Directive addresses issues similar to those addressed by the Regulations such as security, confidentiality and unsolicited electronic communications (commonly known as spam). The Directive applies to a broader range of electronic communications service providers.[52]

Security

If you supply public electronic communications services you are required under the Directive to take certain security measures similar to those required under the Regulations.

Confidentiality of communications

If you are a public communications network or electronic communications service provider, you must ensure the confidentiality of communications and traffic data[53] on your networks and in providing relevant services.[54] It is illegal for you or anyone other than the user of the service to listen, tap, store or otherwise intercept or operate surveillance of communications and related traffic data except with the consent of the user or if legally authorised to do so.

The Directive regulates the use of cookies and similar methods of collecting and storing personal information.[55] As mentioned above, you must provide certain information to a user or subscriber of your service, and offer the user or subscriber the opportunity to object to, the processing of such information.

Location data

The Directive restricts processing of location data.[56] This is data (other than traffic data) processed in an electronic communications network which indicates the geographic position of the terminal equipment of the user of an electronic communications service.

---

[49] A public communications network is an electronic communications network used wholly or mainly for the provision of publicly available electronic communications services.
[50] Article 17.
[51] See Directive 2002/21/EC of the European Parliament and of the Council of 7 March 2002 on a common regulatory Official Journal L108, April 24, 2002, pp. 0033–0050 framework for electronic communications networks and services (Framework Directive). This Directive has been implemented into Irish Law by the European Communities (Electronic Communications Networks and Services) (Framework) Regulations 2003 (S.I. no. 307 of 2003).
[52] See definition of electronic communications service – n.48.
[53] For purposes of the Directive traffic data is any data processed for the purpose of the conveyance of a communication on an electronic communications network or for the billing of such a communication.
[54] Article 5(1).
[55] Article 5(3).
[56] Article 9.

As a service provider you must:

- Inform the user or subscriber, before obtaining consent, of the type of location data which will be processed, the purpose and duration of the processing and whether the data will be transmitted to another party to provide a value added service.[57]

- Obtain the consent of the user or subscriber to the processing of this data.

- Give the user or subscriber the possibility to withdraw consent to the processing of location data at any time.

- Render location data anonymous if it is to be processed. This is not required where the user or subscriber has consented to the processing (and then only where the user is being provided a value added service).

Directories of subscribers

Where it is intended that personal details of subscribers to an electronic communications service are to be included in a printed or electronic directory of subscribers which is available to the public or can be obtained through directory enquiry services,[58] the subscribers must:

- Be told, before their personal information is included in a directory, the purpose of the directory.

- Be given the opportunity to determine whether their information is included in a public directory, and if so, to verify, correct or withdraw such information.

- Be informed of further use of their information due to search functions in electronic versions of the directory.

Unsolicited communications

The Directive specifies that the use of automated calling systems, fax machines or email for the purpose of direct marketing may only be allowed in respect of subscribers who have given their prior consent to such communication.[59]

However, if you obtain electronic contact details from your customers through a sale of a product or service, you may use those details for direct marketing your own similar products or services. Your customers must, however, clearly and distinctly have the opportunity to object to such direct marketing. The opportunity to object must be given on each direct marketing communication.

It is illegal to send an email for direct marketing which disguises or conceals the identity of the sender, or does not include a valid address to which the recipient may send a request for such communication to cease.[60]

---

[57] A value added service is defined as a service which requires the processing of traffic data or location data beyond what is necessary for the transmission of a communication or the billing for it.

[58] Article 12.

[59] Article 13(1).

[60] Article 13(4).

Registration

All telecommunications service providers[61] are required to register with the Commissioner.[62] The usual registration requirements apply in respect of other persons in the telecommunications sector who are data controllers and date processors (see Chapter 1).

COMPLIANCE CHECKLIST

All organisations should take certain steps to ensure compliance with the Act (and the Regulations and Directive, if applicable):

1. Assess whether your business activities involving use of the internet involve the obtaining, use, control or processing of personal information	
2. Are the jurisdiction requirements satisfied?	
3. Does any of the information comprise sensitive data?	
4. Do you obtain and process personal information fairly and lawfully?	
5. Do you provide the required information to an individual including all uses of the information, the recipients or categories of recipients of the information and that the information may be transferred to a country outside the EEA (if applicable)?	
6. Do you expressly and clearly provide those details in a suitable privacy statement or terms and conditions which is brought to the individual's attention before any information is obtained?	
7. Can you show that an individual has been made aware of and consented to the proposed use of his personal information?	
8. Do you use technology such as cookies to obtain personal information without the knowledge and consent of an individual?	
9. Do you make individuals aware of the use of cookies or similar technology and give the choice to opt out of the use of cookies?	
10. Do you have adequate security in place relating to the use and processing of personal information?	
11. Do you comply with the additional security requirements if you transfer personal information on a network?	
12. If you provide electronic communications services, have you met your additional obligations under the Regulations and will you meet your obligations under Directive 2002/58/EC when it is implemented in Ireland?	

---

[61] Any person holding a licence granted under section 111 of the Postal and Telecommunications Services Act 1983 (No. 24 of 1983), as amended by the European (Telecommunications Licences) Regulations 1998 (S.I. No.96 of 1998), and who holds personal data relating to a person to whom a network, service or system is provided under such licence.

[62] Pursuant to the Data Protection (Registration) Regulations 2001 (S.I. No.2 of 2001).

9. MEDIA

The Act applies to journalists, writers and publishers just as it applies to any other business.

In most cases the data controller will be the newspaper or publisher, but in the case of freelance journalists they themselves will be data controllers as they control and manage the information they receive from individuals.

The Act recognises that the statutory processing restrictions might be inappropriate where personal information is processed for journalistic or literary purposes with a view toward publication. Often journalists by the nature of their work need to process and disclose information irrespective of the wishes of the individual.

Therefore, in certain circumstances the Act provides that where journalists process personal information with a view to publishing such material, they will *not* have to:

- tell the data subject how their personal information is to be processed;

- obtain consent to process (non-sensitive or sensitive) information;

- ensure that personal information retained by them is accurate, relevant and up to date;

- ensure that they only retain personal information which is strictly relevant to the actual purpose of their article.

In addition, the individual will not have a right to access the information which the journalist holds on them or to block its use for any purpose.

To avail of this "special purposes" exemption the following conditions must apply[1]:

- processing must be carried out with a view to publication of journalistic, literary or artistic material;

- the writer must reasonably believe that publication is in the public interest;

- the writer must reasonably believe that compliance with the Act would be incompatible with that public interest.

With a view to publication of journalistic, literary or artistic material

There is no definition in the legislation of what is journalistic, literary or artistic material. The exemption may not be limited to professional journalists and publishers but could apply to any individual who publishes information in the

---

[1] Section 22A of the Data Protection Act 1998 (as amended).

public interest. This was the interpretation (of a similar provision in the Swedish Personal Data Protection Act 1998)[2] adopted by the Swedish Supreme Court in a recent case. The Court held that an individual who had published disparaging details of a group of businessmen on a website came within the "special purposes" exemption.

The writer must reasonably believe that publication is in the public interest

In deciding whether or not the publication of the relevant material is in the public interest, the journalist's compliance with codes of practice will be vital.

The following principles of the Code of Conduct of the National Union of Journalists would be relevant to deciding whether the writer believed publication to be in the public interest:

• A journalist shall only mention in passing race, colour, creed, illegitimacy, mental status, gender, or sexual orientation if this information is strictly relevant.

• A journalist shall neither originate nor process material which encourages discrimination, ridicule, prejudice or any hatred on any of the above mentioned grounds.

The English Court of Appeal recently accepted that the publication by the Daily Mirror concerning the well known model Naomi Campbell's attendance at meetings of Narcotics Anonymous was in the public interest. The Court accepted the newspaper's claims that it reasonably believed the article to be in the public interest as Ms Campbell had gone out of her way to deny the use of drugs, stimulants or tranquillisers. The Daily Mirror stressed that they had considered the public interest guidelines contained in the Press Complaints Commission Code of Conduct before making the decision to publish.

The writer must reasonably believe that compliance with the Act would be incompatible with that public interest

A journalist or publisher must reasonably believe that they would be unable to publish the work (or a substantial part of it) if they complied with the data protection principles and other provisions of the Act.

In the Naomi Campbell case the Court held it would not have been reasonably practicable for the Daily Mirror to comply with the provisions of the Data Protection Act and publish the story. In fact, the Daily Mirror was informed prior to publication by Ms. Campbell's agent that consent would not be forthcoming.

Obligations of journalists and writers under the Act

Even where the special purposes exemption applies, journalists and other writers will be obliged to comply with the remaining provisions of the Act as follows.

---

[2] Section 7 of the Personal Data Acts, 1988 to 2003 states that several of its sections shall not be applied to the processing of personal data as occurs exclusively for journalistic purposes or artistic or literary expression. The Irish and Swedish legislation both originate in the EU Directive 95/46.

Registration

Data controllers must register with the Data Protection Commissioner in respect of personal information they process (see page 21). Salaried journalists will not be required to register as their employer (usually the publisher) will be the data controller in respect of the data. Freelance journalists will, however, be obliged to register as a data controller. (See Appendix A1.)

Data security

Data controllers must ensure that appropriate organisational and technical security measures are in place to protect their paper and electronic files, film and photographic files.

There are no set standards of security and your individual obligations need to be assessed having regard to:

• the nature of the information which you store;

• the resources available to you.

The following may serve as some useful guidelines:

Physical security

• Are the PCs located in a secure area?

• Are terminal screens clean of any previous data when not in use?

• Are they logged off or switched off when not in use?

• Are the disks, photography or magnetic tapes stored and locked away when not in use?

• Is there a shredder or other reliable method to dispose of personal data printouts when no longer required?

• Are printouts kept secure and despatched in sealed envelopes and copies not left lying around?

• Have you adopted a data security policy and are staff aware of its contents and applications?

Software security

• Does the data controller maintain a proper archive of past editions (both hard and computerised copies) and online editions where appropriate?

• Is computer access password controlled?

Transferring data out of Ireland

Journalists/writers/publishers are not exempt from the prohibition on transferring personal information out of the EEA (see Chapter 1).

It should be remembered that publishing an article online may constitute a transfer of personal information as it is accessible globally.

Thus where journalists transfer information out of the EEA they should obtain the data subject's consent to the transfer.

Processing where the special purpose exemption does not apply

Newspapers, broadcasters and journalists process a great deal of information, only some of which is processed with a view towards publication.

Obviously, information processed without a view to publish does not come within the terms of the exemption and must therefore be processed as it would be by all other data controllers (see Chapter 1 and Chapter 4).

The individual's right of access

The individual has a right to access personal information held by a journalist, newspaper or publisher and the right can only be curtailed where it is incompatible with the public interest.

10. TRANSFER OF A BUSINESS OR COMPANY

INTRODUCTION

Data protection issues arise where an organisation is either buying or selling a business or where it is seeking investment. In these cases specific issues arise on data protection because the investment or sale and purchase process can involve the disclosure of personal data at different stages of that process. These issues may also arise if you are selling the company even though in that situation the holder of the data will not be changing, only its shareholders.

SELLER ISSUES

- A good data protection compliance programme may give a positive signal of a "compliance culture" in your business.

- Knowledge of your company's data protection compliance will speed up the due diligence process.

- A review of your data protection compliance programme will make you aware of weaknesses which may impact on the transaction timetable.

BUYER ISSUES

- You will need to determine if costs will be incurred post-purchase to improve compliance or begin a compliance programme.

- A data protection due diligence may make you aware of the detailed workings of the business you propose buying.

- Lack of compliance may be evidence in certain businesses of a trend of non-compliance with other areas.

Before you sell any business you should consider carrying out a data protection audit on your organisation to prepare it for the due diligence process which a buyer will carry out. This is dealt with in more detail below.

The due diligence process

Due diligence is the term given to a series of financial and legal investigations made by the buyer into the target company's business. The due diligence process can then be used as a tool to negotiate on the details of the transaction. Standard sale agreements will typically include a warranty in favour of the buyer about the seller's compliance with data protection laws.

A due diligence exercise would typically include a review of employee data, customer lists and databases. Therefore a seller needs to evaluate whether it can lawfully disclose such personal data to a prospective buyer and its advisors.

If your due diligence review shows that the target company has not been in compliance with data protection laws, and if it is your view that you as buyer will incur significant costs in putting a compliance programme into place, then you should consider whether this has an impact on the price you are willing to pay. You should also consider seeking an appropriate indemnity from the seller.

A seller and buyer will usually enter into a confidentiality agreement before due diligence begins.

EMPLOYEE DATA

Employment information may be processed in the context of a merger or acquisition.

An employee is legally protected on the transfer of a business (or part of a business) to another employer under the Acquired Rights Directive and the European Communities (Safeguarding of Employee's Rights on Transfer of Undertakings) Regulations. The Regulations effectively mean that employees transfer to the new owner of the business with their existing terms and conditions of employment and continuity of service.

Disposals of businesses may involve the disclosure of employment information to the new employer. Such disclosure of personal data is subject to the usual data protection principles which apply to the processing of sensitive and non-sensitive personal data as the case may be.

Disclosure to the potential buyer may arguably be necessary for the purposes of the legitimate interests of the employer. The stringent conditions necessary with respect to the processing of sensitive personal data are more difficult to satisfy.

Such disclosure may also arguably be compatible with the normal employment purposes for which the data may have been obtained. Nevertheless, it is advisable for employers to expressly provide in their data protection policy that certain personal information may be disclosed in the context of acquisition discussions. If possible, the employer's data protection policy should identify the nature of the data which will be disclosed.

The Irish Data Protection Commissioner has not yet issued guidelines on the conduct of due diligence exercises in acquisition situations. However, the UK Information Commissioner has set out six recommendations for data protection compliance in such situations.[1] It might be argued that similar standards would be expected of Irish companies although these are only recommendations that are not legally binding even in the UK.

The UK Information Commissioner's recommendations are as follows:

- Ensure, wherever practicable, that information handed over to another organisation in connection with a prospective acquisition or merger is made anonymous (called "anonymised" data);

---

[1] *www.dataprotection.gov.uk/dpr/dpdoc.nsf.*

- Only hand over personal information prior to the final merger or acquisition decision after securing assurances that:

    (i) it will be used solely for the valuation of assets and liabilities;
    (ii) it will be treated in confidence and will not be disclosed to other parties; and
    (iii) it will be destroyed or returned after use.

- Advise employees, wherever practicable, if their employment records are to be disclosed to another organisation before an acquisition or merger takes place. If the acquisition or merger proceeds, make sure employees are aware of the extent to which their records are to be transferred to the new employer.

- Ensure that if you intend to disclose sensitive personal data, sensitive personal data conditions are satisfied.

- Where a merger or acquisition involves transfer of information about a employee to a country outside the European Economic Area, ensure there is proper basis for making the transfer.

- New employers should ensure that the records they hold as a result of a merger or acquisition do not include excessive information, and are accurate and relevant.

Practical issues will arise with the UK Information Commissioner's recommendations. For example, it may be possible, particularly with junior employees, to anonymise data by simply providing information about the number of employees in particular in respect of the business, but this could be unacceptable to many buyers. In any event, in some cases the removal of names may not be sufficient as individuals would be identifiable by their job title, for example. Furthermore, a buyer may not be satisfied by anonymised information if it needs to do a full appraisal of the company's human resources assets with a view to rationalisation. At the very least, it may be necessary to allow some means of subsequently verifying the information given at due diligence stage, for example by keeping a record of the number allocated to the employee and subsequently checking the information post completion.

Many deals are secret until announced to the employees. Complying with best practice in data protection may involve breaching that secrecy so you should take detailed advice from your lawyers on this point before announcing anything to your employees.

Information about directors or key employees presents particular issues. Anonymisation in these circumstances is simply not possible where they are a key component in the transaction. In many cases, such key employees may consent to disclosure of their personal information, once the prospective transaction has been disclosed.

The due diligence exercise would not usually require the disclosure of "sensitive" personal data. Organisations, however, should be careful that it is not inadvertently disclosed along with other personal information.

CUSTOMER LISTS

If your customer lists contain information about *living individuals* (as opposed to companies) then this information (*e.g.* names of key contacts in customer organisations) should be blanked out before the due diligence material is handed over to the buyer. If your customers are individuals then you should anonymise the data and only hand over customer numbers to the buyer. If this is not possible then you should get the consent of your customers in advance to their data being disclosed in this way, but this may for commercial reasons not be palatable to either the buyer or seller.

PURCHASE OF A BUSINESS WITH A DATABASE

A sale of the assets of a company means that the ownership of those assets will be changing. If those assets include a database either of customer or supplier lists then data protection considerations may arise. You may not need to seek consent of the data subjects to use the data as it may be data that is necessary for you to perform any contract with them, (*e.g.* billing and contact information). If, however, in acquiring the business you have specific plans to use the data in a different way from what it has been used for before, then you should consider getting the data subject's consent. In either event, you should look for strong warranties and indemnities from the seller that in the collection, processing and storing of the data before the transfer, that all data protection laws have been complied with.

WARRANTIES

It is usual in any acquisition for a buyer to seek warranties from the sellers as to compliance with data protection laws so that the buyer can get some comfort that all is in order. Such a warranty might be more meaningful to certain types of companies than others. In a normal acquisition agreement there will be a general warranty to the effect that the target company has complied with all laws, regulations, etc. pertaining to their business. It is becoming more common to have a separate warranty which is specific to data protection compliance. At a minimum, a prudent buyer will satisfy itself that the company has complied with all data protection laws and that it has not received any notice or allegation from a data subject that if it has breached that person's data protection rights. In addition, the buyer should seek a warranty that the company has obtained all necessary consents from data subjects to permit it to process within the meaning of the Act all relevant personal data and where applicable, sensitive personal data in connection with the business of the company in the manner in which it was carried on prior to completion.

DATA PROTECTION AUDIT

Many businesses carry out frequent data protection audits on themselves in order to ascertain their level of compliance with both legislation and best practice in their industries. Such exercises are worthwhile given the complex nature of data protection law and the development of the law.

Issues to be addressed in the audit should include:

- Identifying the persons in your organisation who have responsibility for information management. If more than one person, then the head of the relevant section (*e.g.* Marketing, HR) should complete a separate questionnaire.

- Categorising the personal data your organisation holds and the purpose for which it holds it

- Recording details of what information is held (*e.g.* name, address, credit card number) and how it was obtained (orally, on an application form, etc).

- Whether the person about whom the data relates was told at the time of collection of the purposes to which the data would be put.

- Whether your organisation holds "sensitive data".

- Whether your organisation has a data privacy statement or policy.

- Whether you disclose the data to any third parties.

- How the data is stored and details of the filing system used and who has access to it.

- Whether you have a data retention policy.

- Whether you transfer the data abroad.

- Do you train your staff in relation to data protection?

- Are you registered as a controller or processor under data protection legislation?

Depending on the nature of the business a more detailed audit may be necessary – the above are examples of some of the points which should be reviewed.

The UK Information Commissioner has produced an Audit Manual to provide guidance on this matter.

Many independent companies provide data protection auditing services including staff training in particular areas (for example employment or marketing) so that an organisation can carry out regular self assessment.

APPENDIX A1

APPLICATION FOR REGISTRATION
AS A DATA CONTROLLER

Data Protection Act, 1988

Application for Registration

Form DPA1

Data Protection Commissioner
Block 4
Irish Life Centre
Talbot Street
Dublin 1
Ireland

tel: (01) 874 8544
fax: (01) 874 5405
e-mail: *info@dataprivacy.ie*
web: *www.dataprivacy.ie*

It is important that you read the accompanying GUIDANCE NOTES before completing this Form.
Use this Form if you are a data controller (or a data controller and data processor) who is required to register
Please complete this form in BLOCK CAPITALS

---

1. Name & Address
If you are an individual or sole trader, give your surname and first name(s). A partnership should include the name of the firm and the names of each of the partners. Where the data controller is a company, the name of the company should be given, along with a trading name (if different) and the address should be that of the registered office. Persons other than companies should give the address of the principal place of business.

Name(s)
....
....
....

Address
....
....
....
....

Website address (optional): ....

---

2. Contact Person
Name or job status of person to whom applications for access to personal data should be sent:

Name/Job Status
....
....

Address (if different from above)
....
....
....

---

3. Purpose(s)
Please provide a general, but comprehensive, statement of the nature of your business, trade or profession; and of any additional purposes for which you keep personal data.
Use additional sheets if necessary.

(a) ....
....
....

(b) ....
....
....

(c) ....
....
....

4. Description

Briefly list/describe each application of personal data, relating to the purpose(s) listed in section 3 above, together with the types of personal data (e.g. name, address, date of birth, e–mail address, staff ID number) kept or used in connection with that application.

Give full details also of any personal data kept in relation to the purpose(s) listed in section 3 above, but not normally associated with any of the applications you have listed.

Use additional sheets if necessary.

Application:	*Description of Personal Data:*
. . . .	. . . .
. . . .	. . . .
. . . .	. . . .
. . . .	. . . .
. . . .	. . . .
. . . .	. . . .
. . . .	. . . .
. . . .	. . . .
. . . .	. . . .
. . . .	. . . .
. . . .	. . . .
. . . .	. . . .
. . . .	. . . .
. . . .	. . . .

5. Disclosures

For each application listed in Section 4 above list the persons or bodies (or categories of them) to whom the personal data may be disclosed.

Use additional sheets if necessary.

Application:	*Disclosees:*
. . . .	. . . .
. . . .	. . . .
. . . .	. . . .
. . . .	. . . .
. . . .	. . . .
. . . .	. . . .
. . . .	. . . .
. . . .	. . . .

Note: A disclosure of any personal data to a person specified above must not be made in any manner incompatible with the purpose(s) for which those data are kept.
Otherwise, the disclosure will be in contravention of Section 2(1)(c)(ii) of the Act.

6. Transfers Abroad

For each application listed in Section 4 above, list the countries or territories (if any) to which you transfer, or intend to transfer, personal data directly or indirectly: along with a description of the data to be transferred and the purpose of transfer.

Use additional sheets if necessary.

Application:

Country	Description of data	Purpose of transfer

Application:

Country	Description of data	Purpose of transfer

Application:

Country	Description of data	Purpose of transfer

7. Sensitive Data

* other than as kept in respect of your employees in the normal course of personnel administration and not used or disclosed for any other purpose.

i) State which of these kinds of personal data you keep:

    (a) racial origin ❑

    (b) political opinion ❑

    (c) religious beliefs ❑

    (d) other beliefs ❑

    (e) physical or mental health * ❑

    (f) sexual life ❑

    (g) criminal conviction ❑

ii) State for which of the applications specified at 4 (Description) each of these kinds of data is kept:

. . . .

. . . .

. . . .

. . . .

. . . .

If you keep sensitive data, then please specify under the following headings the safeguards in operation for the protection of the privacy of the data subjects concerned: (You do not need to give these details if you do not keep sensitive data.)

PHYSICAL SAFEGUARDS

. . . .

. . . .

. . . .

. . . .

. . . .

. . . .

TECHNICAL SAFEGUARDS

. . . .

. . . .

. . . .

. . . .

. . . .

. . . .

---

8. Public Information

Does any of the personal data kept by you consist of information which you are required by law to make available to the public ?

               Yes ❑   No ❑

If 'Yes', give details:

. . . .

. . . .

. . . .

. . . .

. . . .

. . . .

9. Data Processors	Are you a data processor who is required to register? (i.e. are you a person whose business consists wholly or partly in processing personal data on behalf of others?) Yes ❑ No ❑ If 'Yes', state the countries or territories (if any) to which you transfer, or intend to transfer, such data for processing directly or indirectly: . . . .

10. Compliance Person Details of individual (if any) who will supervise the application of the Act within your organisation in relation to the personal data with which this application for registration is concerned. *Note: This is the person to whom we will address all correspondence in connection with this application for registration.*	Name/Job status: . . . . Address (if different from section 1 above): . . . . *Optional details:* Phone: . . . . Fax: . . . . E-mail: . . . .

I certify that the above information is correct and complete and apply to be registered in the register maintained under Section 16(2) of the Data Protection Act 1988 in respect of the purpose(s) specified in paragraph 3 of this application.

The fee payable is related to the number of people employed:

IR£250/€317.43 for applicants with >25 employees;
IR£50/€63.49 for applicants with 6–25 employees;
IR£20/€25.37 in all other cases.

I enclose the prescribed fee of: . . . .

Number of employees: . . . .

Signature: . . . . Date: . . . .
      *Applicant   *(*Delete whichever is inapplicable)*
      *Authorised to sign on behalf of Applicant

NOTES

1. Knowingly to furnish false or misleading information is an offence.
2. It is also an offence knowingly (a) to keep personal data not specified on your applications, (b) to keep or use personal data for any purpose, or disclose personal data to any person or body, not described in those applications or (c) to transfer personal data to a country or territory not named at 6 above.
3. The information provided by you in this application will be held on computer by the Data Protection Commissioner, in accordance with section 16(2) of the Data Protection Act, 1988. Questions 1 to 6 (inclusive) comprise the Public Register, and may be inspected by members of the public at any time. No other disclosures of the information will be made.

APPENDIX A2

APPLICATION FOR REGISTRATION
AS A DATA PROCESSOR

Data Protection Act, 1988

Application for Registration as a Data Processor

Form DPA3

Data Protection Commissioner
Block 4
Irish Life Centre
Talbot Street
Dublin 1
Ireland

tel: (01) 874 8544
fax: (01) 874 5405
e-mail: *info@dataprivacy.ie*
web: *www.dataprivacy.ie*

It is important that you read the accompanying GUIDANCE NOTES before completing this Form. Use this Form if your business consists wholly or partly in processing personal data on behalf of data controllers and you are not required to register as a data controller.

---

1. Name & Address
If you are an individual or sole trader, give your surname and first name(s). A partnership should include the name of the firm and the names of each of the partners. In the case of companies, the name of the company should be given, along with a trading name (if different) and the address should be that of the registered office. Persons other than companies should give the address of the principle place of business.

Name(s) ....
....
....
....

Address ....
....
....
....
....
....

---

2. Transfers Abroad
State countries or territories (if any) to which you transfer, or intend to transfer, personal data for processing directly or indirectly:

....
....
....
....
....

---

apply to be registered in the register maintained pursuant to Section 16(2) of the Data Protection Act 1988.

My business consists wholly*/partly* in processing personal data on behalf of data controllers.

*I do not control the contents and use of any personal data /*I control the contents and use of personal data but I am not a data controller who is required by Section 16 (2) of the Act to register in that capacity.

The fee payable is related to the number of people employed:
IR£250 /€317.43 for applicants with >25 employees;
IR£50/€63.49 for applicants with 6–25 employees;
IR£20/€25.37 in all other cases.

I enclose the prescribed fee of: ....

Number of employees: ....

Signature: .... Date: ....
       *Applicant / *Authorised to sign on behalf of Applicant

NOTE: Knowingly to furnish false or misleading information is an offence.

*Delete whichever is inapplicable

APPENDIX B

APPLICATION FOR ALTERATION IN
REGISTRATION PARTICULARS

Data Protection Act, 1988

Form DPA5

Application for Alteration in Registration Particulars

Data Protection Commissioner
Block 4
Irish Life Centre
Talbot Street
Dublin 1
Ireland

tel: (01) 874 8544
fax: (01) 874 5405
e-mail: *info@dataprivacy.ie*
web: *www.dataprivacy.ie*

1. Name & Address:

....
....
....
....
....
....

2. Registration Number: ....

I apply to have the particulars in the entry in the register relating to me under the above registration number altered as follows:

....
....
....
....
....
....
....
....
....
....
....
....
....
....
....
....

(please use separate pages if necessary)

I certify that the above information is correct.

I enclose the prescribed fee (IR£50.00, or €63.49).

Signature: .... **Date:** ....

    *Applicant   *(*Delete whichever is inapplicable)*
    *Authorised to sign on behalf of Applicant

NOTE: Knowingly to furnish false or misleading information is an offence.

APPENDIX C

CONSOLIDATION OF DATA PROTECTION ACT 1988 AND DATA PROTECTION (AMENDMENT) ACT 2003

DATA PROTECTION ACTS 1988 AND 2003

ARRANGEMENT OF SECTIONS

PRELIMINARY

Section
1. Interpretation and application of Act.

Convention for the protection of individuals with regard to automatic processing of personal data done at Strasbourg on the 28th day of January, 1981

Second Schedule

The Data Protection Commissioner

Third Schedule

(Repealed)

DATA PROTECTION ACT, 1988 AND 2003

AN ACT TO GIVE EFFECT TO THE CONVENTION FOR THE PROTECTION OF INDIVIDUALS WITH REGARD TO AUTOMATIC PROCESSING OF PERSONAL DATA DONE AT STRASBOURG ON THE 28TH DAY OF JANUARY, 1981, AND FOR THAT PURPOSE TO REGULATE IN ACCORDANCE WITH ITS PROVISIONS THE COLLECTION, PROCESSING, KEEPING, USE AND DISCLOSURE OF CERTAIN INFORMATION RELATING TO INDIVIDUALS THAT IS PROCESSED AUTOMATICALLY. AN ACT TO GIVE EFFECT TO DIRECTIVE 95/46/EC OF THE EUROPEAN PARLIAMENT AND OF THE COUNCIL OF 24 OCTOBER 1995 ON THE PROTECTION OF INDIVIDUALS WITH REGARD TO THE PROCESSING OF PERSONAL DATA AND ON THE FREE MOVEMENT OF SUCH DATA, FOR THAT PURPOSE TO AMEND THE DATA PROTECTION ACT 1988, AND TO PROVIDE FOR RELATED MATTERS.

BE IT ENACTED BY THE OIREACHTAS AS FOLLOWS:

Preliminary

Interpretation and application of Act.

1.—(1) In this Act, unless the context otherwise requires—

"'the Act of 2003' means the *Data Protection (Amendment) Act, 2003;*

"appropriate authority" has the meaning assigned to it by the Civil Service Regulation Acts, 1956 and 1958;[1]

"automated data" means information that—

(a) is being processed by means of equipment operating automatically in response to instructions given for that purpose, or

(b) is recorded with the intention that it should be processed by means of such equipment;

---

[1] Section 2 of 1956 states:

"In this Act, 'appropriate authority' means—

(a) in relation to a civil servant holding a position to which he was appointed by the Government, the Government,

(b) in relation to a civil servant who is a member of the staff of the Houses of the Oireachtas or an officer of the Attorney General, the Taoiseach,

(c) in relation to a civil servant who is a member of the staff of the office of the Revenue Commissioners, the Minister, or

(d) in relation to any other civil servant, the Minister of State by whom the power of appointing a successor to him would for the time being be exercisable . . .

Nothing in this section shall be construed as affecting the powers exercisable by the Revenue Commissioners under any enactment for the time being in force."

"back-up data" means data kept only for the purpose of replacing other data in the event of their being lost, destroyed or damaged;

'blocking', in relation to data, means so marking the data that it is not possible to process it for purposes in relation to which it is marked;

"civil servant" has the meaning assigned to it by the Civil Service Regulation Acts, 1956 and 1958;[2]

"the Commissioner" has the meaning assigned to it by *section 9* of this Act;

"company" has the meaning assigned to it by the Companies Act, 1963;[3]

"the Convention" means the Convention for the Protection of Individuals with regard to Automatic Processing of Personal Data done at Strasbourg on the 28th day of January, 1981, the text of which is set out in the *First Schedule* to this Act;

"the Court" means the Circuit Court;

'data' means automated data and manual data;

"data controller" means a person who, either alone or with others, controls the contents and use of personal data;

"data equipment" means equipment for processing data;

"data material" means any document or other material used in connection with, or produced by, data equipment;

"data processor" means a person who processes personal data on behalf of a data controller but does not include an employee of a data controller who processes such data in the course of his employment;

"data subject" means an individual who is the subject of personal data;

"the Directive" means Directive 95/46/EC of the European Parliament and of the Council of 24 October 1995 on the protection of individuals with regard to the processing of personal data and on the free movement of such data;

"direct marketing" includes direct mailing other than direct mailing carried out in the course of political activities by a political party or its members, or a body established by or under statute or a candidate for election to, or a holder of, elective political office;

"disclosure", in relation to personal data, includes the disclosure of information extracted from such data and the transfer of such data but does not include a disclosure made directly or indirectly by a data controller or a data processor to an employee or agent of his for the purpose of enabling the employee or agent to carry out his duties; and, where the identification of a data subject depends partly on the data and partly on other information in the possession of the data controller, the data shall not be regarded as disclosed unless the other information is also disclosed;

"the EEA Agreement" means the Agreement on the European Economic Area signed at Oporto on 2 May 1992 as adjusted by the Protocol signed at Brussels on 17 March 1993;

"enactment" means a statute or a statutory instrument (within the meaning of the Interpretation Act, 1937);[4]

"enforcement notice" means a notice under *section 10* of this Act;

[2] *Section (1)(1) of 1956:—*
"civil servant" means a person holding a position in the Civil Service, and includes a member of the staff of the Houses of the Oireachtas;
[3] *Section 2(I) of 1963 states:*
"'company' means a company formed and registered under this Act, or an existing company;"
[4] *Section 3 of 1937 states:*
In this Act—

"the European Economic Area" has the meaning assigned to it by the EEA Agreement;

"financial institution" means—

   (*a*) a person who holds or has held a licence under *section 9* of the *Central Bank Act, 1971,* or

   (*b*) a person referred to in section 7 (4) of that Act;[5]

"information notice" means a notice under section 12 of this Act;

"local authority" means a local authority for the purposes of the *Local Government Act, 1941*;[6]

"manual data" means information that is recorded as part of a relevant filing system or with the intention that it should form part of a relevant filing system;

"Minister" means Minister for Justice, Equality and Law Reform;

"personal data" means data relating to a living individual who is or can be identified either from the data or from the data in conjunction with other information that is in, or is likely to come into, the possession of the data controller;

"prescribed", in the case of fees, means prescribed by regulations made by the Minister with the consent of the Minister for Finance and, in any other case, means prescribed by regulations made by the Commissioner with the consent of the Minister;

"processing", of or in relation to information or data, means performing any operation or set of operations on the information or data, whether or not by automatic means, including—

   (*a*) obtaining, recording or keeping the information or data,

   (*b*) collecting, organising, storing, altering or adapting the information or data,

   (*c*) retrieving, consulting or using the information or data,

   (*d*) disclosing the information or data by transmitting, disseminating or otherwise making it available, or

   (*e*) aligning, combining, blocking, erasing or destroying the information or data;

---

the word "statute" includes (in addition to Acts of the Oireachtas) Acts of the Oireachtas of Saorstát Eireann, Acts of the Parliament of the former United Kingdom of Great Britain and Ireland, and Acts of a Parliament sitting in Ireland at any time before the coming into force of the Union with Ireland Act, 1800;

the word "instrument" means an order, regulation, rule, bye-law, warrant, licence, certificate, or other like document;

the expression "statutory instrument" means an instrument made, issued or granted under a power or authority conferred by statute;"

[5] *Section 7(4) of 1971 states:*

"Subsection (1) of this section shall not apply in relation to the Agricultural Credit Corporation, Limited, the Industrial Credit Company, Limited, the Post Office Savings Bank, a trustee savings bank certified under the Trustee Savings Banks Acts, 1863 to 1965, a building society, an industrial and provident society, a friendly society, a credit union, an investment trust company or the manager under a unit trust scheme in respect of the carrying on of the business of the scheme."

[6] *Section 2(2) of 1941 States:*

Each of the following bodies (whether corporate or unincorporated) shall be a local authority for the purposes of this Act and the Acts which may be collectively cited with this Act, that is to say:—

   (*a*) a council of a county, a corporation of a county or other borough, a council of an urban district, a public assistance authority, commissioners of a town, a port sanitary authority, and

   (*b*) a committee or joint committee or board or joint board (whether corporate or unincorporated) appointed by or under statute to perform the functions or any of the functions of any of the bodies mentioned in the immediately preceding paragraph of this sub-section, and

   (*c*) a committee or joint committee or board or joint board (whether corporate or unincorporated), other than a vocational education committee or a committee of agriculture of or appointed by one or more of the bodies mentioned in paragraph (*a*) of this sub-section."

"prohibition notice" means a notice under *section 11 of this Act*;

"the Principal Act" means the Data Protection Act, 1988;

"the register" means the register established and maintained under *section 16* of this Act and any cognate words shall be construed accordingly;

"relevant filing system" means any set of information relating to individuals to the extent that, although the information is not processed by means of equipment operating automatically in response to instructions given for that purpose, the set is structured, either by reference to individuals or by reference to criteria relating to individuals, in such a way that specific information relating to a particular individual is readily accessible;

"sensitive personal data" means personal data as to—

    (*a*) the racial or ethnic origin, the political opinions or the religious or philosophical beliefs of the data subject,

    (*b*) whether the data subject is a member of a trade union,

    (*c*) the physical or mental health or condition or sexual life of the data subject,

    (*d*) the commission or alleged commission of any offence by the data subject, or

    (*e*) any proceedings for an offence committed or alleged to have been committed by the data subject, the disposal of such proceedings or the sentence of any court in such proceedings;

(2) For the purposes of this Act, data are inaccurate if they are incorrect or misleading as to any matter of fact.

(3)(*a*) An appropriate authority, being a data controller or a data processor, may, as respects all or part of the personal data kept by the authority, designate a civil servant in relation to whom it is the appropriate authority to be a data controller or a data processor and, while the designation is in force—

    (i) the civil servant so designated shall be deemed, for the purposes of this Act, to be a data controller or, as the case may be, a data processor, and

    (ii) this Act shall not apply to the authority, as respects the data concerned.

  (*b*) Without prejudice to *paragraph (a)* of this subsection, the Minister for Defence may, as respects all or part of the personal data kept by him in relation to the Defence Forces, designate an officer of the Permanent Defence Force who holds a commissioned rank therein to be a data controller or a data processor and, while the designation is in force—

    (i) the officer so designated shall be deemed, for the purposes of this Act, to be a data controller or, as the case may be, a data processor, and

    (ii) this Act shall not apply to the Minister for Defence, as respects the data concerned.

  (*c*) For the purposes of this Act, as respects any personal data—

    (i) where a designation by the relevant appropriate authority under *paragraph (a)* of this subsection is not in force, a civil servant in relation to whom that authority is the appropriate authority shall be deemed to be its employee and, where such a designation is in force, such a civil servant (other than the civil servant the subject of the designation) shall be deemed to be an employee of the last mentioned civil servant,

    (ii) where a designation under *paragraph (b)* of this subsection is not in force, a member of the Defence Forces shall be deemed to be an employee of the Minister for Defence and, where such a designation is in force, such a member (other than the officer the subject of the designation) shall be deemed to be an employee of that officer, and

    (iii) a member of the Garda Síochána (other than the Commissioner of the Garda Síochána) shall be deemed to be an employee of the said Commissioner.

(3A) A word or expression that is used in this Act and also in the Directive has, unless the context otherwise requires, the same meaning in this Act as it has in the Directive.

(3B)(*a*) Subject to any regulations under section 15(2) of this Act, this Act applies to data controllers in respect of the processing of personal data only if—

    (i) the data controller is established in the State and the data are processed in the context of that establishment, or

    (ii) the data controller is established neither in the State nor in any other state that is a contracting party to the EEA Agreement but makes use of equipment in the State for processing the data otherwise than for the purpose of transit through the territory of the State.

  (*b*) For the purposes of paragraph (*a*) of this subsection, each of the following shall be treated as established in the State:

    (i) an individual who is normally resident in the State,

    (ii) a body incorporated under the law of the State,

    (iii) a partnership or other unincorporated association formed under the law of the State, and

    (iv) a person who does not fall within subparagraphs (i), (ii) or (iii) of this paragraph, but maintains in the State—

        (I) an office, branch or agency through which he or she carries on any activity, or

        (II) a regular practice, and the reference to establishment in any other state that is a contracting party to the EEA Agreement shall be construed accordingly.

  (*c*) A data controller to whom paragraph (*a*)(ii) of this subsection applies must, without prejudice to any legal proceedings that could be commenced against the data controller, designate a representative established in the State.

(3C) Section 2 and sections 2A and 2B (which sections were inserted by the *Act of 2003*) of this Act shall not apply to—

  (*a*) data kept solely for the purpose of historical research, or

  (*b*) other data consisting of archives or departmental records (within the meaning in each case of the National Archives Act 1986),[7] and the keeping of which complies with such requirements (if any) as may be prescribed for the purpose of safeguarding the fundamental rights and freedoms of data subjects.

---

[7] *Section 2(1) of 1986 states*:
"For the purposes of this Act, 'archives' includes—

  (*a*) such records and documents (and copies of them) as are, at the commencement of this Act, held in the Public Record Office of Ireland or the State Paper Office,

  (*b*) Departmental records transferred to and accepted for preservation by the National Archives under this Act,

  (*c*) other records or documents (and copies of them) acquired permanently or on loan by the National Archives from public service organisations, institutions or private individuals,

  (*d*) all public records held at the commencement of this section elsewhere than in the Public Record Office of Ireland under an Act repealed by this Act."

Section 2(2) of 1986 states:
"For the purposes of this Act, 'Departmental records' means any of the following—books, maps, plans, drawings, papers, files, photographs, films, microfilms and other micrographic records, sound recordings, pictorial records, magnetic tapes, magnetic discs, optical or video discs, other machine-readable records, other documentary or processed material, made or received, and held in the course of its business, by a Department of State within the meaning of *section 1(2)* or any body which is a committee, commission or tribunal of enquiry appointed from time to time by the Government, a member of the Government or the Attorney General, and includes copies of any such records duly made, but does not include—

  (i) grants, deeds or other instruments of title relating to property for the time being vested in the State, and

  (ii) any part of the permanent collection of a library, museum or gallery."

(4) This Act does not apply to

    (*a*) personal data that in the opinion of the Minister or the Minister for Defence are, or at any time were, kept for the purpose of safeguarding the security of the State,

    (*b*) personal data consisting of information that the person keeping the data is required by law to make available to the public, or

    (*c*) personal data kept by an individual and concerned only with the management of his personal, family or household affairs or kept by an individual only for recreational purposes.

(5)(*a*) A right conferred by this Act shall not prejudice the exercise of a right conferred by the Freedom of Information Act 1997.

    (*b*) The Commissioner and the Information Commissioner shall, in the performance of their functions, co-operate with and provide assistance to each other.

Protection of Privacy of Individuals with regard to Personal Data

Collection, processing, keeping, use and disclosure of personal data

    2.—(1) A data controller shall, as respects personal data kept by him or her, comply with the following provisions:

    (*a*) the data or, as the case may be, the information constituting the data shall have been obtained, and the data shall be processed fairly,

    (*b*) the data shall be accurate and complete and, where necessary, kept up to date,

    (*c*) the data—

        (i)   shall have been obtained only for one or more specified, explicit and legitimate purposes,

        (ii) shall not be further processed in a manner incompatible with that purpose or those purposes,

        (iii) shall be adequate, relevant and not excessive in relation to the purpose or purposes for which they were collected or are further processed, and

        (iv) shall not be kept for longer than is necessary for that purpose or those purposes,

    (*d*) appropriate security measures shall be taken against unauthorised access to, or unauthorised alteration, disclosure or destruction of, the data, in particular where the processing involves the transmission of data over a network, and against all other unlawful forms of processing.

    (2) A data processor shall, as respects personal data processed by him, comply with *paragraph (d)* of *subsection (1)* of this section.

    (3) *Paragraph (a)* of the said *subsection (1)* does not apply to information intended for inclusion in data, or to data, kept for a purpose mentioned in *section 5(1)(a)* of this Act, in any case in which the application of that paragraph to the data would be likely to prejudice any of the matters mentioned in the said *section 5(1)(a)*.

    (4) *Paragraph (b)* of the said *subsection (1)* does not apply to backup data.

    (5)(*a*) Subparagraphs (ii) and (iv) of paragraph (*c*) of the said subsection (1) do not apply to personal data kept for statistical or research or other scientific purposes, and the keeping of which complies with such requirements (if any) as may be prescribed for the purpose of safeguarding the fundamental rights and freedoms of data subjects, and

    (*b*) the data or, as the case may be, the information constituting such data shall not be regarded for the purposes of *paragraph (a)* of the said subsection as having been obtained unfairly by reason only that its use for any such purpose was not disclosed when it was obtained, if the data are not used in such a way that damage or distress is, or is likely to be, caused to any data subject.

    (6) REMOVED

    (7) Where—

    (*a*) personal data are kept for the purpose of direct marketing, and

    (*b*) the data subject concerned requests the data controller in writing—
        (i) not to process the data for that purpose, or
        (ii) to cease processing the data for that purpose, then—
            (I) if the request is under paragraph (b)(i) of this subsection, the data controller—
                (A) shall, where the data are kept only for the purpose aforesaid, as soon as may be and in any event not more than 40 days after the request has been given or sent to him or her, erase the data, and
                (B) shall not, where the data are kept for that purpose and other purposes, process the data for that purpose after the expiration of the period aforesaid,
           (II) if the request is under paragraph (*b*)(ii) of this subsection, as soon as may be and in any event not more than 40 days after the request has been given or sent to the data controller, he or she—
                (A) shall, where the data are kept only for the purpose aforesaid, erase the data, and
                (B) shall, where the data are kept for that purpose and other purposes, cease processing the data for that purpose,
                and
           (III) the data controller shall notify the data subject in writing accordingly and, where appropriate, inform him or her of those other purposes.

(8) Where a data controller anticipates that personal data, including personal data that is required by law to be made available to the public, kept by him or her will be processed for the purposes of direct marketing, the data controller shall inform the persons to whom the data relates that they may object, by means of a request in writing to the data controller and free of charge, to such processing.

  2A.—(1) Personal data shall not be processed by a data controller unless section 2 of this Act (as amended by the *Act of 2003*) is complied with by the data controller and at least one of the following conditions is met:
    (*a*) the data subject has given his or her consent to the processing or, if the data subject, by reason of his or her physical or mental incapacity or age, is or is likely to be unable to appreciate the nature and effect of such consent, it is given by a parent or guardian or a grandparent, uncle, aunt, brother or sister of the data subject and the giving of such consent is not prohibited by law,
    (*b*) the processing is necessary—
        (i) for the performance of a contract to which the data subject is a party,
        (ii) in order to take steps at the request of the data subject prior to entering into a contract,
        (iii) for compliance with a legal obligation to which the data controller is subject other than an obligation imposed by contract, or
        (iv) to prevent—
            (I) injury or other damage to the health of the data subject, or
           (II) serious loss of or damage to property of the data subject,
      or otherwise to protect his or her vital interests where the seeking of the consent of the data subject or another person referred to in paragraph (*a*) of this subsection is likely to result in those interests being damaged,
    (*c*) the processing is necessary—
        (i) for the administration of justice,
        (ii) for the performance of a function conferred on a person by or under an enactment,
        (iii) for the performance of a function of the Government or a Minister of the Government, or
        (iv) for the performance of any other function of a public nature performed in the public interest by a person,

(*d*)   the processing is necessary for the purposes of the legitimate interests pursued by the data controller or by a third party or parties to whom the data are disclosed, except where the processing is unwarranted in any particular case by reason of prejudice to the fundamental rights and freedoms or legitimate interests of the data subject.

(2) The Minister may, after consultation with the Commissioner, by regulations specify particular circumstances in which subsection (1)(*d*) of this section is, or is not, to be taken as satisfied.

2B.—(1) Sensitive personal data shall not be processed by a data controller unless:

(*a*)   sections 2 and 2A (as amended and inserted, respectively, by the *Act of 2003*) are complied with, and

(*b*)   in addition, at least one of the following conditions is met:

(i)   the consent referred to in paragraph (a) of subsection (1) of section 2A (as inserted by the *Act of 2003*) of this Act is explicitly given,

(ii)   the processing is necessary for the purpose of exercising or performing any right or obligation which is conferred or imposed by law on the data controller in connection with employment,

(iii)   the processing is necessary to prevent injury or other damage to the health of the data subject or another person or serious loss in respect of, or damage to, property or otherwise to protect the vital interests of the data subject or of another person in a case where—

(I)   consent to the processing cannot be given by or on behalf of the data subject in accordance with section 2A(1)(a) (inserted by the *Act of 2003*) of this Act, or

(II)   the data controller cannot reasonably be expected to obtain such consent, or the processing is necessary to prevent injury to, or damage to the health of, another person, or serious loss in respect of, or damage to, the property of another person, in a case where such consent has been unreasonably withheld,

(iv)   the processing—

(I)   is carried out in the course of its legitimate activities by any body corporate, or any unincorporated body of persons, that—

(A)   is not established, and whose activities are not carried on, for profit, and

(B)   exists for political, philosophical, religious or trade union purposes,

(II)   is carried out with appropriate safeguards for the fundamental rights and freedoms of data subjects,

(III)   relates only to individuals who either are members of the body or have regular contact with it in connection with its purposes, and

(IV)   does not involve disclosure of the data to a third party without the consent of the data subject,

(v)   the information contained in the data has been made public as a result of steps deliberately taken by the data subject,

(vi)   the processing is necessary—

(I)   for the administration of justice,

(II)   for the performance of a function conferred on a person by or under an enactment, or

(III)   for the performance of a function of the Government or a Minister of the Government,

(vii)   the processing—

(I)   is required for the purpose of obtaining legal advice or for the purposes of, or in connection with, legal proceedings or prospective legal proceedings, or

        (II) is otherwise necessary for the purposes of establishing, exercising or defending legal rights,

  (viii) the processing is necessary for medical purposes and is undertaken by—

        (I) a health professional, or

        (II) a person who in the circumstances owes a duty of confidentiality to the data subject that is equivalent to that which would exist if that person were a health professional,

  (ix) the processing is necessary in order to obtain information for use, subject to and in accordance with the Statistics Act, 1993, only for statistical, compilation and analysis purposes,

  (x) the processing is carried out by political parties, or candidates for election to, or holders of, elective political office, in the course of electoral activities for the purpose of compiling data on people's political opinions and complies with such requirements (if any) as may be prescribed for the purpose of safeguarding the fundamental rights and freedoms of data subjects,

  (xi) the processing is authorised by regulations that are made by the Minister and are made for reasons of substantial public interest,

  (xii) the processing is necessary for the purpose of the assessment, collection or payment of any tax, duty, levy or other moneys owed or payable to the State and the data has been provided by the data subject solely for that purpose,

  (xiii) the processing is necessary for the purposes of determining entitlement to or control of, or any other purpose connected with the administration of any benefit, pension, assistance, allowance, supplement or payment under the Social Welfare (Consolidation) Act, 1993, or any non-statutory scheme administered by the Minister for Social, Community and Family Affairs.

(2) The Minister may by regulations made after consultation with the Commissioner—

  (*a*) exclude the application of subsection (1)(b)(ii) of this section in such cases as may be specified, or

  (*b*) provide that, in such cases as may be specified, the condition in the said subsection (1)(*b*)(ii) is not to be regarded as satisfied unless such further conditions as may be specified are also satisfied.

(3) The Minister may by regulations make such provision as he considers appropriate for the protection of data subjects in relation to the processing of personal data as to—

  (*a*) the commission or alleged commission of any offence by data subjects,

  (*b*) any proceedings for an offence committed or alleged to have been committed by data subjects, the disposal of such proceedings or the sentence of any court in such proceedings,

  (*c*) any act or omission or alleged act or omission of data subjects giving rise to administrative sanctions,

  (*d*) any civil proceedings in a court or other tribunal to which data subjects are parties or any judgment, order or decision of such a tribunal in any such proceedings,

and processing of personal data shall be in compliance with any regulations under this subsection.

(4) In this section—

"health professional" includes a registered medical practitioner, within the meaning of the Medical Practitioners Act, 1978,[8] a registered dentist, within the meaning of the Dentists Act, 1985,[9] or a member of any other class of health worker or social worker standing specified by regulations made by the Minister after consultation with the Minister for Health and

---

[8] *Section 2 of 1978 states*:
  "'registered medical practitioner' means a person whose name is entered in the register;"
[9] Section 2 of 1985 states—
  "'registered dentist' means a person whose name is registered in the register;"

Children and any other Minister of the Government who, having regard to his or her functions, ought, in the opinion of the Minister, to be consulted;

"medical purposes' includes the purposes of preventive medicine, medical diagnosis, medical research, the provision of care and treatment and the management of healthcare services.

    2C.—(1) In determining appropriate security measures for the purposes of section 2(1)(*d*) of this Act, in particular (but without prejudice to the generality of that provision), where the processing involves the transmission of data over a network, a data controller—

        (*a*) may have regard to the state of technological development and the cost of implementing the measures, and

        (*b*) shall ensure that the measures provide a level of security appropriate to—

            (i) the harm that might result from unauthorised or unlawful processing, accidental or unlawful destruction or accidental loss of, or damage to, the data concerned, and

            (ii) the nature of the data concerned.

    (2) A data controller or data processor shall take all reasonable steps to ensure that—

        (*a*) persons employed by him or her, and

        (*b*) other persons at the place of work concerned,

are aware of and comply with the relevant security measures aforesaid.

    (3) Where processing of personal data is carried out by a data processor on behalf of a data controller, the data controller shall—

        (*a*) ensure that the processing is carried out in pursuance of a contract in writing or in another equivalent form between the data controller and the data processor and that the contract provides that the data processor carries out the processing only on and subject to the instructions of the data controller and that the data processor complies with obligations equivalent to those imposed on the data controller by section 2(1)(*d*) of this Act,

        (*b*) ensure that the data processor provides sufficient guarantees in respect of the technical security measures, and organisational measures, governing the processing, and

        (*c*) take reasonable steps to ensure compliance with those measures.

    2D.—(1) Personal data shall not be treated, for the purposes of section 2(1)(*a*) of this Act, as processed fairly unless—

        (*a*) in the case of data obtained from the data subject, the data controller ensures, so far as practicable, that the data subject has, is provided with, or has made readily available to him or her, at least the information specified in subsection (2) of this section,

        (*b*) in any other case, the data controller ensures, so far as practicable, that the data subject has, is provided with, or has made readily available to him or her, at least the information specified in subsection (3) of this section—

            (i) not later than the time when the data controller first processes the data, or

            (ii) if disclosure of the data to a third party is envisaged, not later than the time of such disclosure.

    (2) The information referred to in subsection (1)(*a*) of this section is:

        (*a*) the identity of the data controller,

        (*b*) if he or she has nominated a representative for the purposes of this Act, the identity of the representative,

        (*c*) the purpose or purposes for which the data are intended to be processed, and

        (*d*) any other information which is necessary, having regard to the specific circumstances in which the data are or are to be processed, to enable processing in respect of the data to be fair to the data subject such as information as to the recipients or categories of recipients of the data, as to whether replies to questions asked for the purpose of the collection of the data are obligatory, as to the possible consequences of failure to give such replies and as to the existence of the right of access to and the right to rectify the data concerning him or her.

(3) The information referred to in subsection (1)(*b*) of this section is:

(*a*) the information specified in subsection (2) of this section,

(*b*) the categories of data concerned, and

(*c*) the name of the original data controller.

(4) The said subsection (1)(*b*) does not apply—

(*a*) where, in particular for processing for statistical purposes or for the purposes of historical or scientific research, the provision of the information specified therein proves impossible or would involve a disproportionate effort, or

(*b*) in any case where the processing of the information contained or to be contained in the data by the data controller is necessary for compliance with a legal obligation to which the data controller is subject other than an obligation imposed by contract, if such conditions as may be specified in regulations made by the Minister after consultation with the Commissioner are complied with.

Right to establish existence of personal data

3.—An individual who believes that a person keeps personal data shall, if he so requests the person in writing—

(*a*) be informed by the person whether he keeps any such data, and

(*b*) if he does, be given by the person a description of the data and the purposes for which they are kept, as soon as may be and in any event not more than 21 days after the request has been given or sent to him.

Right of access

4.—(1)(*a*) Subject to the provisions of this Act, an individual shall, if he or she so requests a data controller by notice in writing—

(i) be informed by the data controller whether the data processed by or on behalf of the data controller include personal data relating to the individual,

(ii) if it does, be supplied by the data controller with a description of—

(I) the categories of data being processed by or on behalf of the data controller,

(II) the personal data constituting the data of which that individual is the data subject,

(III) the purpose or purposes of the processing, and

(IV) the recipients or categories of recipients to whom the data are or may be disclosed,

(iii) have communicated to him or her in intelligible form—

(I) the information constituting any personal data of which that individual is the data subject, and

(II) any information known or available to the data controller as to the source of those data unless the communication of that information is contrary to the public interest, and

(iv) where the processing by automatic means of the data of which the individual is the data subject has constituted or is likely to constitute the sole basis for any decision significantly affecting him or her, be informed free of charge by the data controller of the logic involved in the processing, as soon as may be and in any event not more than 40 days after compliance by the individual with the provisions of this section and, where any of the information is expressed in terms that are not intelligible to the average person without explanation, the information shall be accompanied by an explanation of those terms.

(*b*) A request under paragraph (*a*) of this subsection that does not relate to all of its subparagraphs shall, in the absence of any indication to the contrary, be treated as relating to all of them.

(*c*)   (i)   A fee may be payable to the data controller concerned in respect of such a request as aforesaid and the amount thereof shall not exceed such amount as may be prescribed or an amount that in the opinion of the Commissioner is reasonable, having regard to the estimated cost to the data controller of compliance with the request, whichever is the lesser.

     (ii)   A fee paid by an individual to a data controller under *subparagraph (i)* of this paragraph shall be returned to him if his request is not complied with or the data controller rectifies or supplements, or erases part of, the data concerned (and thereby materially modifies the data) or erases all of the data on the application of the individual or in accordance with an enforcement notice or an order of a court.

(2) Where pursuant to provision made in that behalf under this Act there are separate entries in the register in respect of data kept by a data controller for different purposes, subsection (1) of this section shall apply as if it provided for the making of a separate request and the payment of a separate fee in respect of the data to which each entry relates.

(3) An individual making a request under this section shall supply the data controller concerned with such information as he may reasonably require in order to satisfy himself of the identity of the individual and to locate any relevant personal data or information.

(4) Nothing in *subsection (1)* of this section obliges a data controller to disclose to a data subject personal data relating to another individual unless that other individual has consented to the disclosure:

Provided that, where the circumstances are such that it would be reasonable for the data controller to conclude that, if any particulars identifying that other individual were omitted, the data could then be disclosed as aforesaid without his being thereby identified to the data subject, the data controller shall be obliged to disclose the data to the data subject with the omission of those particulars.

(4A)(*a*)Where personal data relating to a data subject consist of an expression of opinion about the data subject by another person, the data may be disclosed to the data subject without obtaining the consent of that person to the disclosure.

(*b*) Paragraph (*a*) of this subsection does not apply –

     (i)   to personal data held by or on behalf of the person in charge of an institution referred to in section 5(1)(*c*) of this Act and consisting of an expression of opinion by another person about the data subject if the data subject is being or was detained in such an institution, or

     (ii)   if the expression of opinion referred to in that paragraph was given in confidence or on the understanding that it would be treated as confidential.

(5) Information supplied pursuant to a request under *subsection (1)* of this section may take account of any amendment of the personal data concerned made since the receipt of the request by the data controller (being an amendment that would have been made irrespective of the receipt of the request) but not of any other amendment.

(6)(*a*) A request by an individual under *subsection (1)* of this section in relation to the results of an examination at which he was a candidate shall be deemed, for the purposes of this section, to be made on—

     (i)   the date of the first publication of the results of the examination, or

     (ii)   the date of the request, whichever is the later; and *paragraph (a)* of the said *subsection (1)* shall be construed and have effect in relation to such a request as if for "40 days" there were substituted "60 days".

(*b*) In this subsection "examination" means any process for determining the knowledge, intelligence, skill or ability of a person by reference to his performance in any test, work or other activity.

(7) A notification of a refusal of a request made by an individual under and in compliance with the preceding provisions of this section shall be in writing and shall include a statement of the reasons for the refusal and an indication that the individual may complain to the Commissioner about the refusal.

(8)(*a*) If and whenever the Minister considers it desirable in the interests of data subjects or in the public interest to do so and by regulations so declares, the application of this section to personal data—

    (i) relating to physical or mental health, or

    (ii) kept for, or obtained in the course of, carrying out social work by a Minister of the Government, a local authority, a health board or a specified voluntary organisation or other body, may be modified by the regulations in such manner, in such circumstances, subject to such safeguards and to such extent as may be specified therein.

  (*b*) Regulations under *paragraph (a)* of this subsection shall be made only after consultation with the Minister for Health and any other Minister of the Government who, having regard to his functions, ought, in the opinion of the Minister, to be consulted and may make different provision in relation to data of different descriptions.

(9) The obligations imposed by subsection (1)(*a*)(iii) (inserted by the *Act of 2003*) of this section shall be complied with by supplying the data subject with a copy of the information concerned in permanent form unless—

  (*a*) the supply of such a copy is not possible or would involve disproportionate effort, or

  (*b*) the data subject agrees otherwise.

(10) Where a data controller has previously complied with a request under subsection (1) of this section, the data controller is not obliged to comply with a subsequent identical or similar request under that subsection by the same individual unless, in the opinion of the data controller, a reasonable interval has elapsed between compliance with the previous request and the making of the current request.

(11) In determining for the purposes of subsection (10) of this section whether the reasonable interval specified in that subsection has elapsed, regard shall be had to the nature of the data, the purpose for which the data are processed and the frequency with which the data are altered.

(12) Subsection (1)(*a*)(iv) of this section is not to be regarded as requiring the provision of information as to the logic involved in the taking of a decision if and to the extent only that such provision would adversely affect trade secrets or intellectual property (in particular any copyright protecting computer software).

(13)(*a*) A person shall not, in connection with—

    (i) the recruitment of another person as an employee,

    (ii) the continued employment of another person, or

    (iii) a contract for the provision of services to him or her by another person, require that other person—

        (I) to make a request under subsection (1) of this section, or

        (II) to supply him or her with data relating to that other person obtained as a result of such a request.

  (*b*) A person who contravenes paragraph (*a*) of this subsection shall be guilty of an offence.

Restriction of right of access

5.—(1) *Section 4* of this Act does not apply to personal data—

  (*a*) kept for the purpose of preventing, detecting or investigating offences, apprehending or prosecuting offenders or assessing or collecting any tax, duty or other moneys owed or payable to the State, a local authority or a health board, in any case in which the application of that section to the data would be likely to prejudice any of the matters aforesaid,

  (*b*) to which, by virtue of *paragraph (a)* of this subsection, the said *section 4* does not apply and which are kept for the purpose of discharging a function conferred by or under any enactment and consisting of information obtained for such a purpose from a person who had it in his possession for any of the purposes mentioned in *paragraph (a)* of this subsection,

(c) in any case in which the application of that section would be likely to prejudice the security of, or the maintenance of good order and discipline in—

   (i) a prison,

   (ii) a place of detention provided under section 2 of the Prison Act, 1970,

   (iii) a military prison or detention barrack within the meaning of the *Defence Act, 1954,*[10] or

   (iv) Saint Patrick's Institution,

(d) kept for the purpose of performing such functions conferred by or under any enactment as may be specified by regulations made by the Minister, being functions that, in the opinion of the Minister, are designed to protect members of the public against financial loss occasioned by—

   (i) dishonesty, incompetence or malpractice on the part of persons concerned in the provision of banking, insurance, investment or other financial services or in the management of companies or similar organisations, or

   (ii) the conduct of persons who have at any time been adjudicated bankrupt, in any case in which the application of that section to the data would be likely to prejudice the proper performance of any of those functions,

(e) in respect of which the application of that section would be contrary to the interests of protecting the international relations of the State,

(f) consisting of an estimate of, or kept for the purpose of estimating, the amount of the liability of the data controller concerned on foot of a claim for the payment of a sum of money, whether in respect of damages or compensation, in any case in which the application of the section would be likely to prejudice the interests of the data controller in relation to the claim,

(g) in respect of which a claim of privilege could be maintained in proceedings in a court in relation to communications between a client and his professional legal advisers or between those advisers,

(gg) kept by the Commissioner or the Information Commissioner for the purposes of his or her functions,

(h) kept only for the purpose of preparing statistics or carrying out research if the data are not used or disclosed (other than to a person to whom a disclosure of such data may be made in the circumstances specified in *section 8* of this Act) for any other purpose and the resulting statistics or the results of the research are not made available in a form that identifies any of the data subjects, or

(i) that are back-up data.

(2) Regulations under *subsections (1)(d)* and *(3)(b)* of this section shall be made only after consultation with any other Minister of the Government who, having regard to his functions, ought, in the opinion of the Minister, to be consulted.

(3)(a) Subject to *paragraph (b)* of this subsection, *section 4* of this Act, as modified by any other provisions thereof, shall apply notwithstanding any provision of or made under any enactment or rule of law that is in force immediately before the passing of this Act and prohibits or restricts the disclosure, or authorises the withholding, of information.

(b) If and whenever the Minister is of opinion that a prohibition, restriction or authorisation referred to in *paragraph (a)* of this subsection in relation to any information ought to prevail in the interests of the data subjects concerned or any other individuals and by regulations so declares, then, while the regulations are in

---

[10] *Section 2(1) of 1954 states:*
"the expression 'detention barrack' means a building or part of a building declared under section 232 to be a detention barrack; ... the expression 'military prison' means a building or part of a building declared under section 232 to be a military prison;"

force, the said *paragraph (a)* shall not apply as respects the provision or rule of law concerned and accordingly *section 4* of this Act, as modified as aforesaid, shall not apply in relation to that information.

Right of rectification or erasure

6.—(1) An individual shall, if he so requests in writing a data controller who keeps personal data relating to him, be entitled to have rectified or, where appropriate, blocked or erased any such data in relation to which there has been a contravention by the data controller of *section 2(1)* of this Act; and the data controller shall comply with the request as soon as may be and in any event not more than 40 days after it has been given or sent to him:

Provided that the data controller shall, as respects data that are inaccurate or not kept up to date, be deemed—

(a) to have complied with the request if he supplements the data with a statement (to the terms of which the individual has assented) relating to the matters dealt with by the data, and

(b) if he supplements the data as aforesaid, not to be in contravention of *paragraph (b)* of the said *section 2(1)*.

(2) Where a data controller complies, or is deemed to have complied, with a request under subsection (1) of this section, he or she shall, as soon as may be and in any event not more than 40 days after the request has been given or sent to him or her, notify—

(a) the individual making the request, and

(b) if such compliance materially modifies the data concerned, any person to whom the data were disclosed during the period of 12 months immediately before the giving or sending of the request unless such notification proves impossible or involves a disproportionate effort, of the notification, blocking, erasure or statement concerned.

6A.—(1) Subject to subsection (3) and unless otherwise provided by any enactment, an individual is entitled at any time, by notice in writing served on a data controller, to request him or her to cease within a reasonable time, or not to begin, processing or processing for a specified purpose or in a specified manner any personal data in respect of which he or she is the data subject if the processing falls within subsection (2) of this section on the ground that, for specified reasons—

(a) the processing of those data or their processing for that purpose or in that manner is causing or likely to cause substantial damage or distress to him or her or to another person, and

(b) the damage or distress is or would be unwarranted.

(2) This subsection applies to processing that is necessary—

(a) for the performance of a task carried out in the public interest or in the exercise of official authority vested in the data controller or in a third party to whom the data are or are to be disclosed, or

(b) for the purposes of the legitimate interests pursued by the data controller to whom the data are or are to be disclosed, unless those interests are overridden by the interests of the data subject in relation to fundamental rights and freedoms and, in particular, his or her right to privacy with respect to the processing of personal data.

(3) Subsection (1) does not apply—

(a) in a case where the data subject has given his or her explicit consent to the processing,

(b) if the processing is necessary—

(i) for the performance of a contract to which the data subject is a party,

(ii) in order to take steps at the request of the data subject prior to his or her entering into a contract,

    (iii) for compliance with any legal obligation to which the data controller or data subject is subject other than one imposed by contract, or

    (iv) to protect the vital interests of the data subject,

  (*c*) to processing carried out by political parties or candidates for election to, or holders of elective political office, in the course of electoral activities, or

  (*d*) in such other cases, if any, as may be specified in regulations made by the Minister after consultation with the Commissioner.

(4) Where a notice under subsection (1) of this section is served on a data controller, he or she shall, as soon as practicable and in any event not later than 20 days after the receipt of the notice, serve a notice on the individual concerned—

  (*a*) stating that he or she has complied or intends to comply with the request concerned, or

  (*b*) stating that he or she is of opinion that the request is unjustified to any extent and the reasons for the opinion and the extent (if any) to which he or she has complied or intends to comply with it.

(5) If the Commissioner is satisfied, on the application to him or her in that behalf of an individual who has served a notice under subsection (1) of this section that appears to the Commissioner to be justified, or to be justified to any extent, that the data controller concerned has failed to comply with the notice or to comply with it to that extent and that not less than 40 days have elapsed since the receipt of the notice by him or her, the Commissioner may, by an enforcement notice served on the data controller, order him or her to take such steps for complying with the request, or for complying with it to that extent, as the Commissioner thinks fit and specifies in the enforcement notice, and that notice shall specify the reasons for the Commissioner being satisfied as aforesaid.

6B.—(1) Subject to subsection (2) of this section, a decision which produces legal effects concerning a data subject or otherwise significantly affects a data subject may not be based solely on processing by automatic means of personal data in respect of which he or she is the data subject and which is intended to evaluate certain personal matters relating to him or her such as, for example (but without prejudice to the generality of the foregoing), his or her performance at work, creditworthiness, reliability or conduct.

(2) Subsection (1) of this section does not apply—

  (*a*) in a case in which a decision referred to in that subsection—

    (i) is made in the course of steps taken—

      (I) for the purpose of considering whether to enter into a contract with the data subject,

      (II) with a view to entering into such a contract, or

      (III) in the course of performing such a contract, or

    (ii) is authorised or required by any enactment and the data subject has been informed of the proposal to make the decision, and

    (iii) either—

      (I) the effect of the decision is to grant a request of the data subject, or

      (II) adequate steps have been taken to safeguard the legitimate interests of the data subject by, for example (but without prejudice to the generality of the foregoing), the making of arrangements to enable him or her to make representations to the data controller in relation to the proposal, or

  (*b*) if the data subject consents to the processing referred to in subsection (1).

Duty of care owed by data controllers and data processors

7.—For the purposes of the law of torts and to the extent that that law does not so provide, a person, being a data controller or a data processor, shall, so far as regards the collection by him of personal data or information intended for inclusion in such data or his dealing with such data, owe a duty of care to the data subject concerned:

Provided that, for the purposes only of this section, a data controller shall be deemed to have complied with the provisions of *section 2(1)(b)* of this Act if and so long as the personal data concerned accurately record data or other information received or obtained by him from the data subject or a third party and include (and, if the data are disclosed, the disclosure is accompanied by)—

(a) an indication that the information constituting the data was received or obtained as aforesaid,

(b) if appropriate, an indication that the data subject has informed the data controller that he regards the information as inaccurate or not kept up to date, and

(c) any statement with which, pursuant to this Act, the data are supplemented.

Disclosure of personal data in certain cases.

8.—Any restrictions in this Act on the processing of personal data do not apply if the processing is—

(a) in the opinion of a member of the Garda Síochána not below the rank of chief superintendent or an officer of the Permanent Defence Force who holds an army rank not below that of colonel and is designated by the Minister for Defence under this paragraph, required for the purpose of safeguarding the security of the State,

(b) required for the purpose of preventing, detecting or investigating offences, apprehending or prosecuting offenders or assessing or collecting any tax, duty or other moneys owed or payable to the State, a local authority or a health board, in any case in which the application of those restrictions would be likely to prejudice any of the matters aforesaid,

(c) required in the interests of protecting the international relations of the State,

(d) required urgently to prevent injury or other damage to the health of a person or serious loss of or damage to property,

(e) required by or under any enactment or by a rule of law or order of a court,

(f) required for the purposes of obtaining legal advice or for the purposes of, or in the course of, legal proceedings in which the person processing is a party or a witness,

(g – formerly h) made at the request or with the consent of the data subject or a person acting on his behalf.

The Data Protection Commissioner

The Commissioner

9.—(1) For the purposes of this Act, there shall be a person (referred to in this Act as the Commissioner) who shall be known as an Coimisinéir Cosanta Sonraí or, in the English language, the Data Protection Commissioner; the Commissioner shall perform the functions conferred on him by this Act.

(1A)(a) The lawfulness of the processing of personal data (including their transmission to the Central Unit of Eurodac established pursuant to the Council Regulation) in accordance with the Council Regulation shall be monitored by the Commissioner.

(b) In paragraph (a) of this subsection, 'the Council Regulation' means Council Regulation (EC) No.2725/2000 of 11 December 2000 concerning the establishment of Eurodac for the comparison of fingerprints for the effective application of the Dublin Convention.

(1B) The Commissioner shall arrange for the dissemination in such form and manner as he or she considers appropriate of—

(a) any Community finding (within the meaning of subsection (2)(b) (inserted by the Act of 2003) of section 11 of this Act),

(b) any decision of the European Commission or the European Council under the procedure provided for in Article 31(2) of the Directive that is made for the purposes of paragraph 3 or 4 of Article 26 of the Directive, and (*c*)   such other information as may appear to him or her to be expedient to give to data controllers in relation to the protection of the rights and freedoms of data subjects in respect of the processing of personal data in countries and territories outside the European Economic Area.

(1C) The Commissioner shall be the supervisory authority in the State for the purposes of the Directive.

(1D) The Commissioner shall also perform any functions in relation to data protection that the Minister may confer on him or her by regulations for the purpose of enabling the Government to give effect to any international obligations of the State.

(2) The provisions of the *Second Schedule* to this Act shall have effect in relation to the Commissioner.

Enforcement of data protection

10.—(1)(*a*) The Commissioner may investigate, or cause to be investigated, whether any of the provisions of this Act have been, are being or are likely to be contravened in relation to an individual either where the individual complains to him of a contravention of any of those provisions or he is otherwise of opinion that there may be such a contravention.

(*b*)   Where a complaint is made to the Commissioner under *paragraph (a)* of this subsection, the Commissioner shall—

(i)   investigate the complaint or cause it to be investigated, unless he is of opinion that it is frivolous or vexatious, and

(ii)   if he or she is unable to arrange, within a reasonable time, for the amicable resolution by the parties concerned of the matter the subject of the complaint, notify in writing the individual who made the complaint of his or her decision in relation to it and that the individual may, if aggrieved by the decision, appeal against it to the Court under section 26 of this Act within 21 days from the receipt by him or her of the notification.

(1A) The Commissioner may carry out or cause to be carried out such investigations as he or she considers appropriate in order to ensure compliance with the provisions of this Act and to identify any contravention thereof.

(2) If the Commissioner is of opinion that a person has contravened or is contravening a provision of this Act (other than a provision the contravention of which is an offence), the Commissioner may, by notice in writing (referred to in this Act as an enforcement notice) served on the person, require him to take such steps as are specified in the notice within such time as may be so specified to comply with the provision concerned.

(3) Without prejudice to the generality of *subsection (2)* of this section, if the Commissioner is of opinion that a data controller has contravened *section 2(1)* of this Act, the relevant enforcement notice may require him—

(*a*)   to block, rectify, erase or destroy any of the data concerned, or

(*b*)   to supplement the data with such statement relating to the matters dealt with by them as the Commissioner may approve of; and as respects data that are inaccurate or not kept up to date, if he supplements them as aforesaid, he shall be deemed not to be in contravention of *paragraph(b)* of the said *section 2(1)*.

(4) An enforcement notice shall—

(*a*)   specify any provision of this Act that, in the opinion of the Commissioner, has been or is being contravened and the reasons for his having formed that opinion, and

(*b*)   subject to *subsection (6)* of this section, state that the person concerned may appeal to the Court under *section 26* of this Act against the requirement specified in the notice within 21 days from the service of the notice on him.

(5) Subject to *subsection (6)* of this section, the time specified in an enforcement notice for compliance with a requirement specified therein shall not be expressed to expire before the end of the period of 21 days specified in *subsection (4)(b)* of this section and, if an appeal is brought against the requirement, the requirement need not be complied with and

subsection (9) of this section shall not apply in relation thereto, pending the determination or withdrawal of the appeal.

(6) If the Commissioner—

    (*a*) by reason of special circumstances, is of opinion that a requirement specified in an enforcement notice should be complied with urgently, and

    (*b*) includes a statement to that effect in the notice,

subsections (4)(b) and *(5)* of this section shall not apply in relation to the notice, but the notice shall contain a statement of the effect of the provisions of *section 26* (other than *subsection (3)*) of this Act and shall not require compliance with the requirement before the end of the period of 7 days beginning on the date on which the notice is served.

(7) On compliance by a data controller with a requirement under *subsection (3)* of this section, he shall, as soon as may be and in any event not more than 40 days after such compliance, notify—

    (*a*) the data subject concerned, and

    (*b*) if such compliance materially modifies the data concerned, any person to whom the data were disclosed during the period beginning 12 months before the date of the service of the enforcement notice concerned and ending immediately before such compliance unless such notification proves impossible or involves a disproportionate effort, of the blocking, rectification, erasure, destruction or statement concerned.

(8) The Commissioner may cancel an enforcement notice and, if he does so, shall notify in writing the person on whom it was served accordingly.

(9) A person who, without reasonable excuse, fails or refuses to comply with a requirement specified in an enforcement notice shall be guilty of an offence.

Restriction on transfer of personal data outside State

11.— (1) The transfer of personal data to a country or territory outside the European Economic Area may not take place unless that country or territory ensures an adequate level of protection for the privacy and the fundamental rights and freedoms of data subjects in relation to the processing of personal data having regard to all the circumstances surrounding the transfer and, in particular, but without prejudice to the generality of the foregoing, to—

    (*a*) the nature of the data,

    (*b*) the purposes for which and the period during which the data are intended to be processed,

    (*c*) the country or territory of origin of the information contained in the data,

    (*d*) the country or territory of final destination of that information,

    (*e*) the law in force in the country or territory referred to in paragraph (*d*),

    (*f*) any relevant codes of conduct or other rules which are enforceable in that country or territory,

    (*g*) any security measures taken in respect of the data in that country or territory, and

    (*h*) the international obligations of that country or territory.

(2)(*a*) Where in any proceedings under this Act a question arises—

      (i) whether the adequate level of protection specified in subsection (1) of this section is ensured by a country or territory outside the European Economic Area to which personal data are to be transferred, and

      (ii) a Community finding has been made in relation to transfers of the kind in question, the question shall be determined in accordance with that finding.

    (*b*) In paragraph (*a*) of this subsection 'Community finding' means a finding of the European Commission made for the purposes of paragraph (4) or (6) of Article 25 of the Directive under the procedure provided for in Article 31(2) of the Directive in relation to whether the adequate level of protection specified in subsection (1) of this section is ensured by a country or territory outside the European Economic Area.

(3) The Commissioner shall inform the Commission and the supervisory authorities of the other Member States of any case where he or she considers that a country or territory outside the European Economic Area does not ensure the adequate level of protection referred to in subsection (1) of this section.

(4)(*a*) This section shall not apply to a transfer of data if—

   (i) the transfer of the data or the information coconstituting the data is required or authorised by or under

    (I) any enactment, or

    (II) any convention or other instrument imposing an international obligation on the State,

  (ii) the data subject has given his or her consent to the transfer,

  (iii) the transfer is necessary—

    (I) for the performance of a contract between the data subject and the data controller, or

    (II) for the taking of steps at the request of the data subject with a view to his or her entering into a contract with the data controller,

  (iv) the transfer is necessary—

    (I) for the conclusion of a contract between the data controller and a person other than the data subject that—

     (A) is entered into at the request of the data subject, and

     (B) is in the interests of the data subject, or

    (II) for the performance of such a contract,

  (v) the transfer is necessary for reasons of substantial public interest,

  (vi) the transfer is necessary for the purpose of obtaining legal advice or for the purpose of or in connection with legal proceedings or prospective legal proceedings or is otherwise necessary for the purposes of establishing or defending legal rights,

  (vii) the transfer is necessary in order to prevent injury or other damage to the health of the data subject or serious loss of or damage to property of the data subject or otherwise to protect his or her vital interests, and informing the data subject of, or seeking his or her consent to, the transfer is likely to damage his or her vital interests,

  (viii) the transfer is of part only of the personal data on a register established by or under an enactment, being—

    (I) a register intended for consultation by the public, or

    (II) a register intended for consultation by persons having a legitimate interest in its subject matter, and, in the case of a register referred to in clause (II) of this subparagraph, the transfer is made, at the request of, or to, a person referred to in that clause and any conditions to which such consultation is subject are complied with by any person to whom the data are or are to be transferred, or

  (ix) the transfer has been authorised by the Commissioner where the data controller adduces adequate safeguards with respect to the privacy and fundamental rights and freedoms of individuals and for the exercise by individuals of their relevant rights under this Act or the transfer is made on terms of a kind approved by the Commissioner as ensuring such safeguards.

 (*b*) The Commissioner shall inform the European Commission and the supervisory authorities of the other states in the European Economic Area of any authorisation or approval under paragraph (*a*)(ix) of this subsection.

 (*c*) The Commissioner shall comply with any decision of the European Commission under the procedure laid down in Article 31.2 of the Directive made for the purposes of paragraph 3 or 4 of Article 26 of the Directive.

(5) The Minister may, after consultation with the Commissioner, by regulations specify—

(*a*) the circumstances in which a transfer of data is to be taken for the purposes of subsection (4)(*a*)(v) of this section to be necessary for reasons of substantial public interest, and

(*b*) the circumstances in which such a transfer which is not required by or under an enactment is not to be so taken.

(6) Where, in relation to a transfer of data to a country or territory outside the European Economic Area, a data controller adduces the safeguards for the data subject concerned referred to in subsection (4)(*a*)(ix) of this section by means of a contract embodying the contractual clauses referred to in paragraph 2 or 4 of Article 26 of the Directive, the data subject shall have the same right—

(*a*) to enforce a clause of the contract conferring rights on him or her or relating to such rights, and

(*b*) to compensation or damages for breach of such a clause, that he or she would have if he or she were a party to the contract.

(7) The Commissioner may, subject to the provisions of this section, prohibit the transfer of personal data from the State to a place outside the State unless such transfer is required or authorised by or under any enactment or required by any convention or other instrument imposing an international obligation on the State.

(8) In determining whether to prohibit a transfer of personal data under this section, the Commissioner shall also consider whether the transfer would be likely to cause damage or distress to any person and have regard to the desirability of facilitating international transfers of data.

(9) A prohibition under subsection (7) of this section shall be effected by the service of a notice (referred to in this Act as a prohibition notice) on the person proposing to transfer the data concerned.

(10) A prohibition notice shall—

(*a*) prohibit the transfer concerned either absolutely or until the person aforesaid has taken such steps as are specified in the notice for protecting the interests of the data subjects concerned,

(*b*) specify the time when it is to take effect,

(*c*) specify the grounds for the prohibition, and

(*d*) subject to subsection (12) of this section, state that the person concerned may appeal to the Court under section 26 of this Act against the prohibition specified in the notice within 21 days from the service of the notice on him or her.

(11) Subject to subsection (12) of this section, the time specified in a prohibition notice for compliance with the prohibition specified therein shall not be expressed to expire before the end of the period of 21 days specified in subsection (10)(*d*) of this section and, if an appeal is brought against the prohibition, the prohibition need not be complied with and subsection (15) of this section shall not apply in relation thereto, pending the determination or withdrawal of the appeal.

(12) If the Commissioner—

(*a*) by reason of special circumstances, is of opinion that a prohibition specified in a prohibition notice should be complied with urgently, and

(*b*) includes a statement to that effect in the notice, subsections (10)(*d*) and (11) of this section shall not apply in relation to the notice but the notice shall contain a statement of the effect of the provisions of section 26 (other than subsection (3)) of this Act and shall not require compliance with the prohibition before the end of the period of 7 days beginning on the date on which the notice is served.

(13) The Commissioner may cancel a prohibition notice and, if he or she does so, shall notify in writing the person on whom it was served accordingly.

(14)(*a*) This section applies, with any necessary modifications, to a transfer of information from the State to a place outside the State for conversion into personal data as it applies to a transfer of personal data from the State to such a place.

(*b*) In paragraph (*a*) of this subsection 'information' means information (not being data) relating to a living individual who can be identified from it.

(15) A person who, without reasonable excuse, fails or refuses to comply with a prohibition specified in a prohibition notice shall be guilty of an offence.

Power to require information

12.—(1) The Commissioner may, by notice in writing (referred to in this Act as an information notice) served on a person, require the person to furnish to him in writing within such time as may be specified in the notice such information in relation to matters specified in the notice as is necessary or expedient for the performance by the Commissioner of his functions.

(2) Subject to *subsection (3)* of this section—

(*a*) an information notice shall state that the person concerned may appeal to the Court under *section 26* of this Act against the requirement specified in the notice within 21 days from the service of the notice on him, and

(*b*) the time specified in the notice for compliance with a requirement specified therein shall not be expressed to expire before the end of the period of 21 days specified in *paragraph (a)* of this subsection and, if an appeal is brought against the requirement, the requirement need not be complied with and *subsection (5)* of this section shall not apply in relation thereto, pending the determination or withdrawal of the appeal.

(3) If the Commissioner—

(*a*) by reason of special circumstances, is of opinion that a requirement specified in an information notice should be complied with urgently, and

(*b*) includes a statement to that effect in the notice, *subsection (2)* of this section shall not apply in relation to the notice, but the notice shall contain a statement of the effect of the provisions of *section 26* (other than *subsection (3)*) of this Act and shall not require compliance with the requirement before the end of the period of 7 days beginning on the date on which the notice is served.

(4)(*a*) No enactment or rule of law prohibiting or restricting the disclosure of information shall preclude a person from furnishing to the Commissioner any information that is necessary or expedient for the performance by the Commissioner of his functions.

(*b*) *Paragraph (a)* of this subsection does not apply to information that in the opinion of the Minister or the Minister for Defence is, or at any time was, kept for the purpose of safeguarding the security of the State or information that is privileged from disclosure in proceedings in any court.

(5) A person who, without reasonable excuse, fails or refuses to comply with a requirement specified in an information notice or who in purported compliance with such a requirement furnishes information to the Commissioner that the person knows to be false or misleading in a material respect shall be guilty of an offence.

12A.—(1) This section applies to any processing that is of a prescribed description, being processing that appears to the Commissioner to be particularly likely—

(*a*) to cause substantial damage or substantial distress to data subjects, or

(*b*) otherwise significantly to prejudice the rights and freedoms of data subjects.

(2) The Commissioner, on receiving—

(*a*) an application under section 17 of this Act by a person to whom section 16 of this Act applies for registration in the register and any prescribed information and any other information that he or she may require, or

(*b*) a request from a data controller in that behalf, shall consider and determine—

(i)   whether any of the processing to which the application or request relates is processing to which this section applies,

(ii) if it does, whether the processing to which this section applies is likely to comply with the provisions of this Act.

(3) Subject to subsection (4) of this section, the Commissioner shall, within the period of 90 days from the day on which he or she receives an application or a request referred to in

subsection (2) of this section, serve a notice on the data controller concerned stating the extent to which, in the opinion of the Commissioner, the proposed processing is likely or unlikely to comply with the provisions of this Act.

(4) Before the end of the period referred to in subsection (3), the Commissioner may, by reason of special circumstances, extend that period once only, by notice in writing served on the data controller concerned, by such further period not exceeding 90 days as the Commissioner may specify in the notice.

(5) If, for the purposes of his or her functions under this section, the Commissioner serves an information notice on the data controller concerned before the end of the period referred to in subsection (3) of this section or that period as extended under subsection (4) of this section—

    (*a*) the period from the date of service of the notice to the date of compliance with the requirement in the notice, or

    (*b*) if the requirement is set aside under section 26 of this Act, the period from the date of such service to the date of such setting aside, shall be added to the period referred to in the said subsection (3) or that period as so extended as aforesaid.

(6) Processing to which this section applies shall not be carried on unless—

    (*a*) the data controller has—

        (i) previously made an application under section 17 of this Act and furnished the information specified in that section to the Commissioner, or

        (ii) made a request under subsection (2) of this section, and

    (*b*) the data controller has complied with any information notice served on him or her in relation to the matter, and

    (*c*)   (i) the period of 90 days from the date of the receipt of the application or request referred to in subsection (3) of this section (or that period as extended under subsections (4) and (5) of this section or either of them) has elapsed without the receipt by the data controller of a notice under the said subsection (3), or

        (ii) the data controller has received a notice under the said subsection (3) stating that the particular processing proposed to be carried on is likely to comply with the provisions of this Act, or

        (iii) the data controller—

            (I) has received a notice under the said subsection (3) stating that, if the requirements specified by the Commissioner (which he or she is hereby authorised to specify) and appended to the notice are complied with by the data controller, the processing proposed to be carried on is likely to comply with the provisions of this Act, and

            (II) has complied with those requirements.

(7) A person who contravenes subsection (6) of this section shall be guilty of an offence.

(8) An appeal against a notice under subsection (3) of this section or a requirement appended to the notice may be made to and heard and determined by the Court under section 26 of this Act and that section shall apply as if such a notice and such a requirement were specified in subsection (1) of the said section 26.

(9) The Minister, after consultation with the Commissioner, may by regulations amend subsections (3), (4) and (6) of this section by substituting for the number of days for the time being specified therein a different number specified in the regulations.

(10) A data controller shall pay to the Commissioner such fee (if any) as may be prescribed in respect of the consideration by the Commissioner, in relation to proposed processing by the data controller, of the matters referred to in paragraphs (i) and (ii) of subsection (2) of this section and different fees may be prescribed in relation to different categories of processing.

(11) In this section a reference to a data controller includes a reference to a data processor.

Codes of practice

13.—(1) The Commissioner shall encourage trade associations and other bodies representing categories of data controllers to prepare codes of practice to be complied with by those categories in dealing with personal data.

(2) The Commissioner shall—

  (*a*) where a code of practice (referred to subsequently in this section as a code) so prepared is submitted to him or her for consideration, consider the code and, after such consultation with such data subjects or persons representing data subjects and with the relevant trade associations or other bodies aforesaid as appears to him or her to be appropriate—

   (i) if he or she is of opinion that the code provides for the data subjects concerned a measure of protection with regard to personal data relating to them that conforms with that provided for by section 2, sections 2A to 2D (inserted by the Act of 2003) and sections 3 and 4 (other than subsection (8)) and 6 of this Act, approve of the code and encourage its dissemination to the data controllers concerned, and

   (ii) in any event notify the association or body concerned of his or her decision to approve or not to approve the code,

  (*b*) where he or she considers it necessary or desirable to do so and after such consultation with any trade associations or other bodies referred to in subsection (1) of this section having an interest in the matter and data subjects or persons representing data subjects as he or she considers appropriate, prepare, and arrange for the dissemination to such persons as he or she considers appropriate of, codes of practice for guidance as to good practice in dealing with personal data, and subsection (3) of this section shall apply to a code of practice prepared under this subsection as it applies to a code,

  (*c*) in such manner and by such means as he or she considers most effective for the purposes of this paragraph, promote the following of good practice by data controllers and, in particular, so perform his or her functions under this Act as to promote compliance with this Act by data controllers,

  (*d*) arrange for the dissemination in such form and manner as he or she considers appropriate of such information as appears to him or her to be expedient to give to the public about the operation of this Act, about the practices in processing of personal data (including compliance with the requirements of this Act) that appear to the Commissioner to be desirable having regard to the interests of data subjects and other persons likely to be affected by such processing and about other matters within the scope of his or her functions under this Act, and may give advice to any person in relation to any of those matters.

(3) Any such code that is so approved of may be laid by the Minister before each House of the Oireachtas and, if each such House passes a resolution approving of it, then—

  (*a*) in so far as it relates to dealing with personal data by the categories of data controllers concerned—

   (i) it shall have the force of law in accordance with its terms, and

   (ii) upon its commencement, references (whether specific or general) in this Act to any of the provisions of the said sections shall be construed (or, if the code is in substitution for a code having the force of law by virtue of this subsection, continue to be construed) as if they were also references to the relevant provisions of the code for the time being having the force of law, and

  (*b*) it shall be deemed to be a statutory instrument to which the *Statutory Instruments Act, 1947,* primarily applies.

(4) This section shall apply in relation to data processors as it applies in relation to categories of data controllers with the modification that the references in this section to the said sections shall be construed as references to *section 2(1)(d)* of this Act and with any other necessary modifications.

(5) The Commissioner shall be paid by a person in relation to whom a service is provided under this section such fee (if any) as may be prescribed and different fees may be prescribed in relation to different such services and different classes of persons.

(6) In proceedings in any court or other tribunal, any provision of a code, or a code of practice, approved under subsection (3) of this section that appears to the court or other tribunal concerned to be relevant to the proceedings may be taken into account in determining the question concerned.

[(2) A code of practice approved under subsection (2) of the said section 13 and in force immediately before the commencement of this section shall continue in force after such commencement as if approved under subsection (2)(inserted by this section) of section 13 of the Principal Act.]

Annual report
14.—(1) The Commissioner shall in each year after the year in which the first Commissioner is appointed prepare a report in relation to his activities under this Act in the preceding year and cause copies of the report to be laid before each House of the Oireachtas.

(2) Notwithstanding *subsection (1)* of this section, if, but for this subsection, the first report under that subsection would relate to a period of less than 6 months, the report shall relate to that period and to the year immediately following that period and shall be prepared as soon as may be after the end of that year.

(3) For the purposes of the law of defamation, a report under subsection (1) shall be absolutely privileged.

Mutual assistance between parties to Convention
15.—(1) The Commissioner is hereby designated for the purposes of Chapter IV (which relates to mutual assistance) of the Convention.

(2) The Minister may make any regulations that he considers necessary or expedient for the purpose of enabling the said Chapter IV to have full effect.

Registration

The register
16.—(1) In this section 'person to whom this section applies' means a data controller and a data processor (other than such (if any) categories of data controller and data processor as may be specified in regulations made by the Minister after consultation with the Commissioner) except in so far as—
    (*a*) they carry out—
        (i) processing whose sole purpose is the keeping in accordance with law of a register that is intended to provide information to the public and is open to consultation either by the public in general or by any person demonstrating a legitimate interest,
        (ii) processing of manual data (other than such categories, if any, of such data as may be prescribed), or
        (iii) any combination of the foregoing categories of processing, or
    (*b*) the data controller is a body that is not established or conducted for profit and is carrying out processing for the purposes of establishing or maintaining membership of or support for the body or providing or administering activities for individuals who are either members of the body or have regular contact with it.

(2) The Commissioner shall establish and maintain a register (referred to in this Act as the register) of persons to whom this section applies and shall make, as appropriate, an entry or entries in the register in respect of each person whose application for registration therein is accepted by the Commissioner.

(3)(*a*) Members of the public may inspect the register free of charge at all reasonable times and may take copies of, or of extracts from, entries in the register.

  (*b*) A member of the public may, on payment to the Commissioner of such fee (if any) as may be prescribed, obtain from the Commissioner a copy (certified by him or by a member of his staff to be a true copy) of, or of an extract from, any entry in the register.

  (*c*) In any proceedings—

    (i) a copy of, or of an extract from, an entry in the register certified by the Commissioner or by a member of his staff to be a true copy shall be evidence of the entry or extract, and

    (ii) a document purporting to be such a copy, and to be certified, as aforesaid shall be deemed to be such a copy and to be so certified unless the contrary is proved.

  (*d*) In any proceedings—

    (i) a certificate signed by the Commissioner or by a member of his staff and stating that there is not an entry in the register in respect of a specified person as a data controller or as a data processor shall be evidence of that fact, and

    (ii) a document purporting to be such a certificate, and to be signed, as aforesaid shall be deemed to be such a certificate and to be so signed unless the contrary is proved.

Applications for registration

17.—(1)(*a*) A person wishing to be registered in the register or to have a registration continued under *section 18* of this Act or to have the particulars in an entry in the register altered shall make an application in writing in that behalf to the Commissioner and shall furnish to him such information as may be prescribed and any other information that he may require.

  (*b*) Where a data controller intends to keep personal data for two or more related purposes, he or she shall make an application for registration in respect of those purposes and, subject to the provisions of this Act, entries shall be made in the register in accordance with any such application,

  (*c*) Where a data controller intends to keep personal data for two or more unrelated purposes, he shall make an application for separate registration in respect of each of those purposes and, subject to the provisions of this Act, entries shall be made in the register in accordance with each such application.

(2) Subject to *subsection (3)* of this section, the Commissioner shall accept an application for registration, made in the prescribed manner and in respect of which such fee as may be prescribed has been paid, from a person to whom *section 16* of this Act applies unless he is of opinion that—

  (*a*) the particulars proposed for inclusion in an entry in the register are insufficient or any other information required by the Commissioner either has not been furnished or is insufficient, or

  (*b*) the person applying for registration is likely to contravene any of the provisions of this Act.

(3) The Commissioner shall not accept such an application for registration as aforesaid from a data controller who keeps sensitive personal data unless he or she is of opinion that appropriate safeguards for the protection of the privacy of the data subjects are being, and will continue to be, provided by him or her.

(4) Where the Commissioner refuses an application for registration, he shall, as soon as may be, notify in writing the person applying for registration of the refusal and the notification shall—

  (*a*) specify the reasons for the refusal, and

  (*b*) state that the person may appeal to the Court under *section 26* of this Act against the refusal within 21 days from the receipt by him of the notification.

(5) If—
  (a) the Commissioner, by reason of special circumstances, is of opinion that a refusal of an application for registration should take effect urgently, and
  (b) the notification of the refusal includes a statement to that effect and a statement of the effect of the provisions of *section 26* (other than *subsection (3)*) of this Act, *paragraph (b)* of *subsection (4)* of this section shall not apply in relation to the notification and *paragraph (b)* of *subsection (6)* of this section shall be construed and have effect as if for the words from and including "21 days" to the end of the paragraph there were substituted "7 days beginning on the date on which the notification was received,".

(6) Subject to *subsection (5)* of this section, a person who has made an application for registration shall—
  (a) until he is notified that it has been accepted or it is withdrawn, or
  (b) if he is notified that the application has been refused, until the end of the period of 21 days within which an appeal may be brought under *section 26* of this Act against the refusal and, if such an appeal is brought, until the determination or withdrawal of the appeal, be treated for the purposes of *section 19* of this Act as if the application had been accepted and the particulars contained in it had been included in an entry in the register on the date on which the application was made.

(7) *Subsections (2)* to *(6)* of this section apply, with any necessary modifications, to an application for continuance of registration and an application for alteration of the particulars in an entry in the register as they apply to an application for registration.

Duration and continuance of registration
  18.—(1) A registration (whether it is the first registration or a registration continued under this section) shall be for the prescribed period and on the expiry thereof the relevant entry shall be removed from the register unless the registration is continued as aforesaid.

(2) The prescribed period (which shall not be less than one year) shall be calculated—
  (a) in the case of a first registration from the date on which the relevant entry was made in the register, and
  (b) in the case of a registration which has been continued under this section, from the day following the expiration of the latest prescribed period.

(3) The Commissioner shall, subject to the provisions of this Act, continue a registration, whether it has previously been continued under this section or not.

(4) Notwithstanding the foregoing provisions of this section, the Commissioner may at any time, at the request of the person to whom an entry relates, remove it from the register.

Effect of registration
  19.—(1) A data controller to whom *section 16* of this Act applies shall not keep personal data unless there is for the time being an entry in the register in respect of him.

(2) A data controller in respect of whom there is an entry in the register shall not—
  (a) keep personal data of any description other than that specified in the entry,
  (b) keep or use personal data for a purpose other than the purpose or purposes described in the entry,
  (c) if the source from which such data, and any information intended for inclusion in such data, are obtained is required to be described in the entry, obtain such data or information from a source that is not so described,
  (d) disclose such data to a person who is not described in the entry (other than a person to whom a disclosure of such data may be made in the circumstances specified in *section 8* of this Act),
  (e) directly or indirectly transfer such data to a place outside the State other than one named or described in the entry.

(3) An employee or agent (not being a data processor) of a data controller mentioned in *subsection (2)* of this section shall, as respects personal data kept or, as the case may be, to

be kept by the data controller, be subject to the same restrictions in relation to the use, source, disclosure or transfer of the data as those to which the data controller is subject under that subsection.

(4) A data processor to whom *section 16* applies shall not process personal data unless there is for the time being an entry in the register in respect of him.

(5) If and whenever a person in respect of whom there is an entry in the register changes his address, he shall thereupon notify the Commissioner of the change.

(6) A person who contravenes *subsection (1), (4)* or *(5)*, or knowingly contravenes any other provision, of this section shall be guilty of an offence.

Regulations for registration

20.—(1) The following matters, and such other matters (if any) as may be necessary or expedient for the purpose of enabling *sections 16* to *19* of this Act to have full effect, may be prescribed:

(a) the procedure to be followed in relation to applications by persons for registration, continuance of registration or alteration of the particulars in an entry in the register or for withdrawal of such applications,

(b) the information required to be furnished to the Commissioner by such persons, and

(c) the particulars to be included in entries in the register, and different provision may be made in relation to the matters aforesaid as respects different categories of persons.

(2) A person who in purported compliance with a requirement prescribed under this section furnishes information to the Commissioner that the person knows to be false or misleading in a material respect shall be guilty of an offence.

Miscellaneous

Unauthorised disclosure by data processor

21.—(1) Personal data processed by a data processor shall not be disclosed by him, or by an employee or agent of his, without the prior authority of the data controller on behalf of whom the data are processed.

(2) A person who knowingly contravenes *subsection (1)* of this section shall be guilty of an offence.

Disclosure of personal data obtained without authority

22.—(1) A person who—

(a) obtains access to personal data, or obtains any information constituting such data, without the prior authority of the data controller or data processor by whom the data are kept, and

(b) discloses the data or information to another person, shall be guilty of an offence.

(2) *Subsection (1)* of this section does not apply to a person who is an employee or agent of the data controller or data processor concerned.

22A.—(1) Personal data that are processed only for journalistic, artistic or literary purposes shall be exempt from compliance with any provision of this Act specified in subsection (2) of this section if—

(a) the processing is undertaken solely with a view to the publication of any journalistic, literary or artistic material,

(b) the data controller reasonably believes that, having regard in particular to the special importance of the public interest in freedom of expression, such publication would be in the public interest, and

(c) the data controller reasonably believes that, in all the circumstances, compliance with that provision would be incompatible with journalistic, artistic or literary purposes.

(2) The provisions referred to in subsection (1) of this section are—

    (*a*) section 2 (as amended by the *Act of 2003*), other than subsection (1)(d),

    (*b*) sections 2A, 2B, 2C and 2E (which sections were inserted by the *Act of 2003*),

    (*c*) section 3,

    (*d*) sections 4 and 6 (which sections were amended by the *Act of 2003*), and

    (*e*) sections 6A and 6B (which sections were inserted by the *Act of 2003*).

(3) In considering for the purposes of subsection (1)(*b*) of this section whether publication of the material concerned would be in the public interest, regard may be had to any code of practice approved under subsections (1) or (2) of section 13 (as amended by the *Act of 2003*) of this Act.

(4) In this section 'publication', in relation to journalistic, artistic or literary material, means the act of making the material available to the public or any section of the public in any form or by any means.

Provisions in relation to certain non-residents and to data kept or processed outside State

23.— Repealed

Powers of authorised officer. Subsections (3), (4) & (5) repealed

24.—(1) In this section "authorised officer" means a person authorised in writing by the Commissioner to exercise, for the purposes of this Act, the powers conferred by this section.

(2) An authorised officer may, for the purpose of obtaining any information that is necessary or expedient for the performance by the Commissioner of his functions, on production of the officer's authorisation, if so required—

    (*a*) at all reasonable times enter premises that he reasonably believes to be occupied by a data controller or a data processor, inspect the premises and any data therein (other than data consisting of information specified in *section 12(4)(b)* of this Act) and inspect, examine, operate and test any data equipment therein,

    (*b*) require any person on the premises, being a data controller, a data processor or an employee of either of them, to disclose to the officer any such data and produce to him any data material (other than data material consisting of information so specified) that is in that person's power or control and to give to him such information as he may reasonably require in regard to such data and material,

    (*c*) either on the premises or elsewhere, inspect and copy or extract information from such data, or inspect and copy or take extracts from such material, and

    (*d*) require any person mentioned in *paragraph (b)* of this subsection to give to the officer such information as he may reasonably require in regard to the procedures employed for complying with the provisions of this Act, the sources from which such data are obtained, the purposes for which they are kept, the persons to whom they are disclosed and the data equipment in the premises

(6) A person who obstructs or impedes an authorised officer in the exercise of a power, or, without reasonable excuse, does not comply with a requirement, under this section or who in purported compliance with such a requirement gives information to an authorised officer that he knows to be false or misleading in a material respect shall be guilty of an offence.

Service of notices

25.—Any notice authorised by this Act to be served on a person by the Commissioner may be served—

    (*a*) if the person is an individual—

        (i) by delivering it to him, or

        (ii) by sending it to him by post addressed to him at his usual or last-known place of residence or business, or

        (iii) by leaving it for him at that place,

(*b*)   if the person is a body corporate or an unincorporated body of persons, by sending it to the body by post to, or addressing it to and leaving it at, in the case of a company, its registered office (within the meaning of the *Companies Act, 1963*)[11] and, in any other case, its principal place of business.

Appeals to Circuit Court
26.—(1) An appeal may be made to and heard and determined by the Court against—
(*a*)   a requirement specified in an enforcement notice or an information notice,
(*b*)   a prohibition specified in a prohibition notice,
(*c*)   a refusal by the Commissioner under section 17 of this Act, notified by him under that section, and
(*d*)   a decision of the Commissioner in relation to a complaint under *section 10(1)(a)* of this Act, and such an appeal shall be brought within 21 days from the service on the person concerned of the relevant notice or, as the case may be, the receipt by such person of the notification of the relevant refusal or decision.

(2) The jurisdiction conferred on the Court by this Act shall be exercised by the judge for the time being assigned to the circuit where the appellant ordinarily resides or carries on any profession, business or occupation or, at the option of the appellant, by a judge of the Court for the time being assigned to the Dublin circuit.

(3)(*a*) Subject to *paragraph (b)* of this subsection, a decision of the Court under this section shall be final.
(*b*)   An appeal may be brought to the High Court on a point of law against such a decision; and references in this Act to the determination of an appeal shall be construed as including references to the determination of any such appeal to the High Court and of any appeal from the decision of that Court.

(4) Where—
(*a*)   a person appeals to the Court pursuant to *paragraph (a), (b)* or *(c)* of *subsection (1)* of this section,
(*b*)   the appeal is brought within the period specified in the notice or notification mentioned in paragraph (c) of this subsection, and
(*c*)   the Commissioner has included a statement in the relevant notice or notification to the effect that by reason of special circumstances he is of opinion that the requirement or prohibition specified in the notice should be complied with, or the refusal specified in the notification should take effect, urgently, then, notwithstanding any provision of this Act, if the Court, on application to it in that behalf, so determines, non-compliance by the person with a requirement or prohibition specified in the notice, or, as the case may be, a contravention by him of *section 19* of this Act, during the period ending with the determination or withdrawal of the appeal or during such other period as may be determined as aforesaid shall not constitute an offence.

---

[11] *Section 113 of 1963 states*:
    "(1) A company shall, as from the day on which it begins to carry on business or as from the fourteenth day after the date of its incorporation, whichever is the earlier, have a registered office in the State to which all communications and notices may be addressed.
    (2) Notice of the situation of the registered office, and of any change therein, shall be given within 14 days after the date of the incorporation of the company or of the change, as the case may be, to the registrar of companies, who shall record the same. The inclusion in the annual return of a company of a statement as to the address of its registered office shall not be taken to satisfy the obligation imposed by this subsection.
    (3) If default is made in complying with this section, the company and every officer of the company who is in default shall be liable to a fine not exceeding £100.
    (4) Proceedings in relation to an offence under this section may be brought and prosecuted by the registrar of companies."

Evidence in proceedings

27.—(1) In any proceedings—

    (*a*) a certificate signed by the Minister or the Minister for Defence and stating that in his opinion personal data are, or at any time were, kept for the purpose of safeguarding the security of the State shall be evidence of that opinion,

    (*b*) a certificate—

        (i) signed by a member of the Garda Síochána not below the rank of chief superintendent or an officer of the Permanent Defence Force who holds an army rank not below that of colonel and is designated by the Minister for Defence under *section 8 (a)* of this Act, and

        (ii) stating that in the opinion of the member or, as the case may be, the officer a disclosure of personal data is required for the purpose aforesaid, shall be evidence of that opinion, and

    (*c*) a document purporting to be a certificate under *paragraph (a)* or *(b)* of this subsection and to be signed by a person specified in the said *paragraph (a)* or *(b)*, as appropriate, shall be deemed to be such a certificate and to be so signed unless the contrary is proved.

(2) Information supplied by a person in compliance with a request under *section 3* or *4 (1)* of this Act, a requirement under this Act or a direction of a court in proceedings under this Act shall not be admissible in evidence against him or his spouse in proceedings for an offence under this Act.

Hearing of proceedings

28.—The whole or any part of any proceedings under this Act may, at the discretion of the court, be heard otherwise than in public.

Offences by directors, etc. of bodies corporate

29.—(1) Where an offence under this Act has been committed by a body corporate and is proved to have been committed with the consent or connivance of or to be attributable to any neglect on the part of a person, being a director, manager, secretary or other officer of that body corporate, or a person who was purporting to act in any such capacity, that person, as well as the body corporate, shall be guilty of that offence and be liable to be proceeded against and punished accordingly.

(2) Where the affairs of a body corporate are managed by its members, *subsection (1)* of this section shall apply in relation to the acts and defaults of a member in connection with his functions of management as if he were a director or manager of the body corporate.

Prosecution of summary offences by Commissioner

30.—(1) Summary proceedings for an offence under this Act may be brought and prosecuted by the Commissioner.

(2) Notwithstanding section 10(4) of the Petty Sessions (Ireland) Act, 1851, summary proceedings for an offence under this Act may be instituted within one year from the date of the offence.

Penalties

31.—(1) A person guilty of an offence under this Act shall be liable—

    (*a*) on summary conviction, to a fine not exceeding €3,000, or

    (*b*) on conviction on indictment, to a fine not exceeding €100,000.

(2) Where a person is convicted of an offence under this Act, the court may order any data material which appears to the court to be connected with the commission of the offence to be forfeited or destroyed and any relevant data to be erased.

(3) The court shall not make an order under *subsection (2)* of this section in relation to data material or data where it considers that some person other than the person convicted of the offence concerned may be the owner of, or otherwise interested in, the data unless such

steps as are reasonably practicable have been taken for notifying that person and giving him an opportunity to show cause why the order should not be made.

(4) *Section 13* of the *Criminal Procedure Act, 1967,*[12] shall apply in relation to an offence under this Act that is not being prosecuted summarily as if, in lieu of the penalties provided for in subsection (3)(*a*) of that section, there were specified therein the fine provided for in *subsection (1)(a)* of this section and the reference in subsection (2)(*a*) of the said section 13 to the penalties provided for by subsection (3) shall be construed and have effect accordingly.

Laying of regulations before Houses of Oireachtas

32.—Every regulation made under this Act (other than *section 2*) shall be laid before each House of the Oireachtas as soon as may be after it is made and, if a resolution annulling the regulation is passed by either such House within the next 21 days on which that House has sat after the regulation is laid before it, the regulation shall be annulled accordingly, but without prejudice to the validity of anything previously done thereunder.

Fees

33.—(1) Fees under this Act shall be paid into or disposed of for the benefit of the Exchequer in accordance with the directions of the Minister for Finance.

(2) The Public Offices Fees Act, 1879, shall not apply in respect of any fees under this Act.

Expenses of Minister

34.—The expenses incurred by the Minister in the administration of this Act shall, to such extent as may be sanctioned by the Minister for Finance, be paid out of moneys provided by the Oireachtas.

---

[12] *Section 13 of the 1967 Act states*:

"(1) This section applies to all indictable offences except the following—an offence under the Treason Act, 1939, murder, attempt to murder, conspiracy to murder, piracy or a grave breach such as is referred to in section 3(1)(i) of the Geneva Conventions Act, 1962, including an offence by an accessory before or after the fact.

(2) If at any time the District Court ascertains that a person charged with an offence to which this section applies wishes to plead guilty and the Court is satisfied that he understands the nature of the offence and the facts alleged, the Court may—

(*a*) with the consent of the Attorney General, deal with the offence summarily, in which case the accused shall be liable to the penalties provided for by subsection (3), or

(*b*) if the accused signs a plea of guilty, send him forward for sentence with that plea to a court to which, if he had pleaded not guilty, he could lawfully have been sent forward for trial.

(3)(*a*) On conviction by the District Court for an offence dealt with summarily under subsection (2)(*a*), the accused shall be liable to a fine not exceeding £100 or, at the discretion of the Court, to imprisonment for a term not exceeding twelve months, or to both such fine and imprisonment.

(*b*) In the case, however, of an offence under section 11 of the Wireless Telegraphy Act, 1926, the District Court shall not impose a fine exceeding £10 or a term of imprisonment exceeding one month.

(4)(*a*) Where a person is sent forward for sentence under this section he may withdraw his written plea and plead not guilty to the charge.

(*b*) In that event, the court shall enter a plea of not guilty, which shall have the same operation and effect in all respects as an order of a justice of the District Court sending the accused forward for trial to that court on that charge, and the Attorney General shall cause to be served on him any documents required to be supplied to the accused and not already served.

(5) This section shall not affect the jurisdiction of the Court under section 2 of the Criminal Justice Act, 1951."

Short title and commencement

35.—(1) This Act may be cited as the *Data Protection Act 1988*

(2) This Act shall come into operation on such day or days as, by order or orders made by the Minister under this section, may be fixed therefore either generally or with reference to any particular purpose or provision and different days may be so fixed for different purposes and different provisions.

36. — (1) This Act may be cited as the Data Protection (Amendment) Act 2003.

(2) This Act and the Principal Act may be cited together as the Data Protection Acts 1988 and 2003, and shall be construed together as one.

(3) Subject to the subsequent provisions of this section, this Act shall come into operation on such day or days as, by order or orders made by the Minister under this section, may be fixed thereof either generally or with reference to any particular purpose or provision and different days may be so fixed for different purposes and different provisions including the application of section 22(1) to different provisions specified therein.

(4) This Act in so far as it –

   (*a*)   amends section 2 of the Principal Act and applies it to manual data, and

   (*b*)   inserts sections 2A and 2B into that Act, comes into operation on 24 October 2007 in respect of manual data held in relevant filing systems on the passing of this Act

(5) Notwithstanding subsection (4), a data controller shall, if so requested in writing by a data subject when making a request under section 4 of the Principal Act –

   (*a*)   rectify, erase, block or destroy any data relating to him or her which are incomplete or inaccurate, or

   (*b*)   cease holding manual data relating to him or her in a way incompatible with the legitimate purposes pursued by the data controller.

1988/25 CONVENTION FOR THE PROTECTION OF INDIVIDUALS WITH REGARD TO AUTOMATIC PROCESSING OF PERSONAL DATA DONE AT STRASBOURG ON THE 28TH DAY OF JANUARY, 1981

PREAMBLE

The member States of the Council of Europe, signatory hereto,

Considering that the aim of the Council of Europe is to achieve greater unity between its members, based in particular on respect for the rule of law, as well as human rights and fundamental freedoms;

Considering that it is desirable to extend the safeguards for everyone's rights and fundamental freedoms, and in particular the right to the respect for privacy, taking account of the increasing flow across frontiers of personal data undergoing automatic processing; Reaffirming at the same time their commitment to freedom of information regardless of frontiers;

Recognising that it is necessary to reconcile the fundamental values of the respect for privacy and the free flow of information between peoples,

Have agreed as follows:

CHAPTER I – GENERAL PROVISIONS

ARTICLE 1

Object and purpose

The purpose of this convention is to secure in the territory of each Party for every individual, whatever his nationality or residence, respect for his rights and fundamental freedoms, and in particular his right to privacy, with regard to automatic processing of personal data relating to him ("data protection").

ARTICLE 2

Definitions

For the purposes of this convention:

a. "personal data" means any information relating to an identified or identifiable individual ("data subject");

b. "automated data file" means any set of data undergoing automatic processing;

c. "automatic processing includes the following operations if carried out in whole or in part by automated means: storage of data, carrying out of logical and/or arithmetical operations on those data, their alteration, erasure, retrieval or dissemination;

d. "controller of the file" means the natural or legal person, public authority, agency or any other body who is competent according to the national law to decide what should be the purpose of the automated data file, which categories of personal data should be stored and which operations should be applied to them.

ARTICLE 3

Scope

1. The Parties undertake to apply this convention to automated personal data files and automatic processing of personal data in the public and private sectors.

2. Any State may, at the time of signature or when depositing its instrument of ratification, acceptance, approval or accession, or at any later time, give notice by a declaration addressed to the Secretary General of the Council of Europe:

a. that it will not apply this convention to certain categories of automated personal data files, a list of which will be deposited. In this list it shall not include, however, categories of automated data files subject under its domestic law to data protection provisions. Consequently, it shall amend this list by a new declaration whenever additional categories of automated personal data files are subjected to data protection provisions under its domestic law;

b. that it will also apply this convention to information relating to groups of persons, associations, foundations, companies, corporations and any other bodies consisting directly or indirectly of individuals, whether or not such bodies possess legal personality;

c. that it will also apply this convention to personal data files which are not processed automatically.

3. Any State which has extended the scope of this convention by any of the declarations provided for in sub-paragraph 2.*b* or *c* above may give notice in the said declaration that such extensions shall apply only to certain categories of personal data files, a list of which will be deposited.

4. Any Party which has excluded certain categories of automated personal data files by a declaration provided for in sub-paragraph 2.*a* above may not claim the application of this convention to such categories by a Party which has not excluded them.

5. Likewise, a Party which has not made one or other of the extensions provided for in sub-paragraphs 2.*b* or *c* above may not claim the application of this convention on these points with respect to a Party which has made such extensions.

6. The declarations provided for in paragraph 2 above shall take effect from the moment of the entry into force of the convention with regard to the State which has made them if they have been made at the time of signature or deposit of its instrument of ratification, acceptance, approval or accession, or three months after their receipt by the Secretary General of the Council of Europe if they have been made at any later time. These declarations may be withdrawn, in whole or in part, by a notification addressed to the Secretary General of the Council of Europe. Such withdrawals shall take effect three months after the date of receipt of such notification.

CHAPTER II – BASIC PRINCIPLES FOR DATA PROTECTION

ARTICLE 4

Duties of the Parties

1. Each Party shall take the necessary measures in its domestic law to give effect to the basic principles for data protection set out in this chapter.

2. These measures shall be taken at the latest at the time of entry into force of this convention in respect of that Party.

ARTICLE 5

Quality of data

Personal data undergoing automatic processing shall be:
   a. obtained and processed fairly and lawfully;
   b. stored for specified and legitimate purposes and not used in a way incompatible with those purposes;
   c. adequate, relevant and not excessive in relation to the purposes for which they are stored;
   d. accurate and, where necessary, kept up to date;
   e. preserved in a form which permits identification of the data subjects for no longer than is required for the purpose for which those data are stored.

ARTICLE 6

Special categories of data

Personal data revealing racial origin, political opinions or religious or other beliefs, as well as personal data concerning health or sexual life, may not be processed automatically unless domestic law provides appropriate safeguards. The same shall apply to personal data relating to criminal convictions.

ARTICLE 7

Data security

Appropriate security measures shall be taken for the protection of personal data stored in automated data files against accidental or unauthorised destruction or accidental loss as well as against unauthorised access, alteration or dissemination.

ARTICLE 8

Additional safeguards for the data subject

Any person shall be enabled:

a. to establish the existence of an automated personal data file, its main purposes, as well as the identity and habitual residence or principal place of business of the controller of the file;

b. to obtain at reasonable intervals and without excessive delay or expense confirmation of whether personal data relating to him are stored in the automated data file as well as communication to him of such data in an intelligible form;

c. to obtain, as the case may be, rectification or erasure of such data if these have been processed contrary to the provisions of domestic law giving effect to the basic principles set out in Articles 5 and 6 of this convention;

d. to have a remedy if a request for confirmation or, as the case may be, communication, rectification or erasure as referred to in paragraphs b and c of this article is not complied with.

ARTICLE 9

Exceptions and restrictions

1. No exception to the provisions of Articles 5, 6 and 8 of this convention shall be allowed except within the limits defined in this article.

2. Derogation from the provisions of Articles 5, 6 and 8 of this convention shall be allowed when such derogation is provided for by the law of the Party and constitutes a necessary measure in a democratic society in the interests of:

a. protecting State security, public safety, the monetary interests of the State or the suppression of criminal offences;

b. protecting the data subject or the rights and freedoms of others.

3. Restrictions on the exercise of the rights specified in Article 8, paragraphs *b, c* and *d*, may be provided by law with respect to automated personal data files used for statistics or for scientific research purposes when there is obviously no risk of an infringement of the privacy of the data subjects.

ARTICLE 10

Sanctions and remedies

Each Party undertakes to establish appropriate sanctions and remedies for violations of provisions of domestic law giving effect to the basic principles for data protection set out in this chapter.

ARTICLE 11

Extended protection

None of the provisions of this chapter shall be interpreted as limiting or otherwise affecting the possibility for a Party to grant data subjects a wider measure of protection than that stipulated in this convention.

CHAPTER III – TRANSBORDER DATA FLOWS

ARTICLE 12

Transborder flows of personal data and domestic law

1. The following provisions shall apply to the transfer across national borders, by whatever medium, of personal data undergoing automatic processing or collected with a view to their being automatically processed.

2. A Party shall not, for the sole purpose of the protection of privacy, prohibit or subject to special authorisation transborder flows of personal data going to the territory of another Party.

3. Nevertheless, each Party shall be entitled to derogate from the provisions of paragraph 2:
   a. insofar as its legislation includes specific regulations for certain categories of personal data or of automated personal data files, because of the nature of those data or those files, except where the regulations of the other Party provide an equivalent protection;
   b. when the transfer is made from its territory to the territory of a non-Contracting State through the intermediary of the territory of another Party, in order to avoid such transfers resulting in circumvention of the legislation of the Party referred to at the beginning of this paragraph.

CHAPTER IV – MUTUAL ASSISTANCE

ARTICLE 13

Co-operation between Parties

1. The Parties agree to render each other mutual assistance in order to implement this convention.

2. For that purpose:
   a. each Party shall designate one or more authorities, the name and address of each of which it shall communicate to the Secretary General of the Council of Europe;
   b. each Party which has designated more than one authority shall specify in its communication referred to in the previous sub-paragraph the competence of each authority.

3. An authority designated by a Party shall at the request of an authority designated by another Party:
   a. furnish information on its law and administrative practice in the field of data protection;
   b. take, in conformity with its domestic law and for the sole purpose of protection of privacy, all appropriate measures for furnishing factual information relating to specific automatic processing carried out in its territory, with the exception however of the personal data being processed.

ARTICLE 14

Assistance to data subjects resident abroad

1. Each Party shall assist any person resident abroad to exercise the rights conferred by its domestic law giving effect to the principles set out in Article 8 of this convention.
2. When such a person resides in the territory of another Party he shall be given the option of submitting his request through the intermediary of the authority designated by that Party.

3. The request for assistance shall contain all the necessary particulars, relating *inter alia* to:
    a. the name, address and any other relevant particulars identifying the person making the request;
    b. the automated personal data file to which the request pertains, or its controller;
    c. the purpose of the request.

ARTICLE 15

Safeguards concerning assistance rendered by designated authorities

1. An authority designated by a Party which has received information from an authority designated by another Party either accompanying a request for assistance or in reply to its own request for assistance shall not use that information for purposes other than those specified in the request for assistance.

2. Each Party shall see to it that the persons belonging to or acting on behalf of the designated authority shall be bound by appropriate obligations of secrecy or confidentiality with regard to that information.

3. In no case may a designated authority be allowed to make under Article 14, paragraph 2, a request for assistance on behalf of a data subject resident abroad, of its own accord and without the express consent of the person concerned.

ARTICLE 16

Refusal of requests for assistance

A designated authority to which a request for assistance is addressed under Articles 13 or 14 of this convention may not refuse to comply with it unless:

    a. the request is not compatible with the powers in the field of data protection of the authorities responsible for replying;
    b. the request does not comply with the provisions of this convention;
    c. compliance with the request would be incompatible with the sovereignty, security or public policy (*ordre public*) of the Party by which it was designated, or with the rights and fundamental freedoms of persons under the jurisdiction of that Party.

ARTICLE 17

Costs and procedures of assistance

1. Mutual assistance which the Parties render each other under Article 13 and assistance they render to data subjects abroad under Article 14 shall not give rise to the payment of any costs or fees other than those incurred for experts and interpreters. The latter costs or fees shall be borne by the Party which has designated the authority making the request for assistance.

2. The data subject may not be charged costs or fees in connection with the steps taken on his behalf in the territory of another Party other than those lawfully payable by residents of that Party.

3. Other details concerning the assistance relating in particular to the forms and procedures and the languages to be used, shall be established directly between the Parties concerned.

CHAPTER V – CONSULTATIVE COMMITTEE

ARTICLE 18

Composition of the committee

1. A Consultative Committee shall be set up after the entry into force of this convention.

2. Each Party shall appoint a representative to the committee and a deputy representative. Any member State of the Council of Europe which is not a Party to the convention shall have the right to be represented on the committee by an observer.

3. The Consultative Committee may, by unanimous decision, invite any non-member State of the Council of Europe which is not a Party to the convention to be represented by an observer at a given meeting.

ARTICLE 19

Functions of the committee

The Consultative Committee:
    a. may make proposals with a view to facilitating or improving the application of the convention;
    b. may make proposals for amendment of this convention in accordance with Article 21;
    c. shall formulate its opinion on any proposal for amendment of this convention which is referred to it in accordance with Article 21, paragraph 3;
    d. may, at the request of a Party, express an opinion on any question concerning the application of this convention.

ARTICLE 20

Procedure

1. The Consultative Committee shall be convened by the Secretary General of the Council of Europe. Its first meeting shall be held within twelve months of the entry into force of this convention. It shall subsequently meet at least once every two years and in any case when one-third of the representatives of the Parties request its convocation.

2. A majority of representatives of the Parties shall constitute a quorum for a meeting of the Consultative Committee.

3. After each of its meetings, the Consultative Committee shall submit to the Committee of Ministers of the Council of Europe a report on its work and on the functioning of the convention.

4. Subject to the provisions of this convention, the Consultative Committee shall draw up its own Rules of Procedure.

CHAPTER VI – AMENDMENTS

ARTICLE 21

Amendments

1. Amendments to this convention may be proposed by a Party, the Committee of Ministers of the Council of Europe or the Consultative Committee.

2. Any proposal for amendment shall be communicated by the Secretary General of the Council of Europe to the member States of the Council of Europe and to every non-member State which has acceded to or has been invited to accede to this convention in accordance with the provisions of Article 23.

3. Moreover, any amendment proposed by a Party or the Committee of Ministers shall be communicated to the Consultative Committee, which shall submit to the Committee of Ministers its opinion on that proposed amendment.

4. The Committee of Ministers shall consider the proposed amendment and any opinion submitted by the Consultative Committee and may approve the amendment.

5. The text of any amendment approved by the Committee of Ministers in accordance with paragraph 4 of this article shall be forwarded to the Parties for acceptance.

6. Any amendment approved in accordance with paragraph 4 of this article shall come into force on the thirtieth day after all Parties have informed the Secretary General of their acceptance thereof.

CHAPTER VII – FINAL CLAUSES

ARTICLE 22

Entry into force

1. This convention shall be open for signature by the member States of the Council of Europe. It is subject to ratification, acceptance or approval. Instruments of ratification, acceptance or approval shall be deposited with the Secretary General of the Council of Europe.

2. This convention shall enter into force on the first day of the month following the expiration of a period of three months after the date on which five member States of the Council of Europe have expressed their consent to be bound by the convention in accordance with the provisions of the preceding paragraph.

3. In respect of any member State which subsequently expresses its consent to be bound by it, the convention shall enter into force on the first day of the month following the expiration of a period of three months after the date of the deposit of the instrument of ratification, acceptance or approval.

ARTICLE 23

Accession by non-member States

1. After the entry into force of this convention, the Committee of Ministers of the Council of Europe may invite any State not a member of the Council of Europe to accede to this convention by a decision taken by the majority provided for in Article 20.*d* of the Statute of the Council of Europe and by the unanimous vote of the representatives of the Contracting States entitled to sit on the committee.

2. In respect of any acceding State, the convention shall enter into force on the first day of the month following the expiration of a period of three months after the date of deposit of the instrument of accession with the Secretary General of the Council of Europe.

ARTICLE 24

Territorial clause

1. Any State may at the time of signature or when depositing its instrument of ratification, acceptance, approval or accession, specify the territory or territories to which this convention shall apply.

2. Any State may at any later date, by a declaration addressed to the Secretary General of the Council of Europe, extend the application of this convention to any other territory specified in the declaration. In respect of such territory the convention shall enter into force on the first day of the month following the expiration of a period of three months after the date of receipt of such declaration by the Secretary General.

3. Any declaration made under the two preceding paragraphs may, in respect of any territory specified in such declaration, be withdrawn by a notification addressed to the Secretary General. The withdrawal shall become effective on the first day of the month following the expiration of a period of six months after the date of receipt of such notification by the Secretary General.

ARTICLE 25

Reservations

No reservation may be made in respect of the provisions of this convention.

ARTICLE 26

Denunciation

1. Any Party may at any time denounce this convention by means of a notification addressed to the Secretary General of the Council of Europe.

2. Such denunciation shall become effective on the first day of the month following the expiration of a period of six months after the date of receipt of the notification by the Secretary General.

ARTICLE 27

Notifications

The Secretary General of the Council of Europe shall notify the member States of the Council and any State which has acceded to this convention of:
    a. any signature;
    b. the deposit of any instrument of ratification, acceptance, approval or accession;
    c. any date of entry into force of this convention in accordance with Articles 22, 23 and 24;
    d. any other act, notification or communication relating to this convention.

In witness whereof the undersigned, being duly authorised thereto, have signed this Convention.

Done at Strasbourg, the 28th day of January 1981, in English and in French, both texts being equally authoritative, in a single copy which shall remain deposited in the archives of the Council of Europe. The Secretary General of the Council of Europe shall transmit certified copies to each member State of the Council of Europe and to any State invited to accede to this Convention.

THE DATA PROTECTION COMMISSIONER

1. The Commissioner shall be a body corporate and shall be independent in the performance of his functions.

2. (1) The Commissioner shall be appointed by the Government and, subject to the provisions of this Schedule, shall hold office upon such terms and conditions as the Government may determine.
    (2) The Commissioner—
        (*a*) may at any time resign his office as Commissioner by letter addressed to the Secretary to the Government and the resignation shall take effect on and from the date of receipt of the letter,
        (*b*) may at any time be removed from office by the Government if, in the opinion of the Government, he has become incapable through ill-health of effectively performing his functions or has committed stated misbehaviour, and
        (*c*) shall, in any case, vacate the office of Commissioner on reaching the age of 65 years.

3. The term of office of a person appointed to be the Commissioner shall be such term not exceeding 5 years as the Government may determine at the time of his appointment and, subject to the provisions of this Schedule, he shall be eligible for re-appointment to the office.

4. (1) Where the Commissioner is—
        (*a*) nominated as a member of Seanad Éireann,
        (*b*) elected as a member of either House of the Oireachtas, the European Parliament or a local authority, or
        (*c*) regarded pursuant to *section 15* (inserted by the *European Assembly Elections Act, 1984*) of the *European Assembly Elections Act, 1977*, as having been elected to such Parliament to fill a vacancy, he shall thereupon cease to be the Commissioner.
    (2) A person who is for the time being—
        (i)   entitled under the standing orders of either House of the Oireachtas to sit therein,
        (ii) a member of the European Parliament, or
        (iii) entitled under the standing orders of a local authority to sit therein, shall, while he is so entitled or is such a member, be disqualified for holding the office of Commissioner.

5. The Commissioner shall not hold any other office or employment in respect of which emoluments are payable.

6. There shall be paid to the Commissioner, out of moneys provided by the Oireachtas, such remuneration and allowances for expenses as the Minister, with the consent of the Minister for Finance, may from time to time determine.

7.   (*a*) The Minister shall, with the consent of the Minister for Finance, make and carry out, in accordance with its terms, a scheme or schemes for the granting of pensions, gratuities or other allowances on retirement or death to or in respect of persons who have held the office of Commissioner.
    (*b*) The Minister may, with the consent of the Minister for Finance, at any time make and carry out, in accordance with its terms, a scheme or schemes amending or revoking a scheme under this paragraph.
    (*c*) A scheme under this paragraph shall be laid before each House of the Oireachtas as soon as may be after it is made and, if a resolution annulling the scheme is

passed by either such House within the next 21 days on which that House has sat after the scheme is laid before it, the scheme shall be annulled accordingly, but without prejudice to the validity of anything previously done thereunder.

8. (1) The Minister may appoint to be members of the staff of the Commissioner such number of persons as may be determined from time to time by the Minister, with the consent of the Minister for Finance.

(2) Members of the staff of the Commissioner shall be civil servants.

(3) The functions of the Commissioner under this Act may be performed during his temporary absence by such member of the staff of the Commissioner as he may designate

(4) The Minister may delegate to the Commissioner the powers exercisable by him under the *Civil Service Commissioners Act, 1956*, and the Civil Service Regulation Acts, 1956 and 1958, as the appropriate authority in relation to members of the staff of the Commissioner and, if he does so, then so long as the delegation remains in force—

> (*a*) those powers shall, in lieu of being exercisable by the Minister, be exercisable by the Commissioner, and
>
> (*b*) the Commissioner shall, in lieu of the Minister, be for the purposes of this Act the appropriate authority in relation to members of the staff of the Commissioner.

9. (1) The Commissioner shall keep in such form as may be approved of by the Minister, with the consent of the Minister for Finance, all proper and usual accounts of all moneys received or expended by him and all such special accounts (if any) as the Minister, with the consent of the Minister for Finance, may direct.

(2) Accounts kept in pursuance of this paragraph in respect of each year shall be submitted by the Commissioner in the following year on a date (not later than a date specified by the Minister) to the Comptroller and Auditor General for audit and, as soon as may be after the audit, a copy of those accounts, or of such extracts from those accounts as the Minister may specify, together with the report of the Comptroller and Auditor General on the accounts, shall be presented by the Commissioner to the Minister who shall cause copies of the documents presented to him to be laid before each House of the Oireachtas.

10.(1) A person who holds or held the office of Commissioner or who is or was a member of the staff of the Commissioner shall not disclose to a person other than the Commissioner or such a member any information that is obtained by him or her in his capacity as Commissioner or as such a member that could reasonably be regarded as confidential without the consent of the person to whom it relates.

(2) A person who contravenes subparagraph (1) of this paragraph shall be guilty of an offence.

(THIRD SCHEDULE) – REPEALED UNDER 2003 ACT

PUBLIC AUTHORITIES AND OTHER BODIES AND PERSONS

257309_1

INDEX